The Great Books Reading & Discussion Program

SECOND SERIES · VOLUME TWO

The Great Books Foundation

A Nonprofit Educational Corporation

Designed by Don Walkoe Design, Chicago

Handmade marbled paper, photographed on cover,
courtesy of Andrews, Nelson, Whitehead.

•

Published and distributed by

The Great Books Foundation
A Nonprofit Educational Corporation
40 East Huron Street
Chicago, Illinois 60611

Acknowledgments

"The Crito" by Plato from *Socrates and Legal Obligation*, translated by R. E. Allen. Copyright 1980 by the University of Minnesota. Reprinted by permission of the publisher, University of Minnesota Press.

"The Virtues" from *Ethics* in Volume 5 of *The Middle Works, 1899–1924* by John Dewey, edited by Jo Ann Boydston. Reprinted by permission of the publisher, Center for Dewey Studies, Southern Illinois University at Carbondale.

"Iphigeneia at Aulis" by Euripides, translated by W. S. Merwin and George E. Dimock, Jr. from *The Greek Tragedy in New Translations*, edited by William Arrowsmith. Copyright 1978 by W. S. Merwin and George E. Dimock, Jr. Reprinted by permission of the publisher, Oxford University Press, Inc.

"Notes from the Underground" from *Great Short Works of Fyodor Dostoevsky*, translated by David Magarshack. Published 1968 by Harper & Row, Publishers, Inc. Reprinted by permission of Mrs. Elsie D. Magarshack.

"Billy Budd, Sailor" from *Billy Budd, Sailor (An Inside Narrative)* by Herman Melville, edited by Harrison Hayford and Merton M. Sealts, Jr. Copyright 1962 by The University of Chicago. Reprinted by permission of the publisher, The University of Chicago Press.

"The Knight of Faith" from *Fear and Trembling; Repetition* by Søren Kierkegaard, translated and edited by Howard V. Hong and Edna H. Hong. Copyright 1983 by Howard V. Hong. Reprinted by permission of the publisher, Princeton University Press.

"The Persian Wars" from *Herodotus: The Histories*, Books VII and VIII, translated by Aubrey de Sélincourt. Copyright 1954 by the Estate of Aubrey de Sélincourt. Reprinted by permission of the publisher, Penguin Books, Ltd.

A source note appears, together with biographical information about the author, opposite the opening page of each work in this series. Footnotes by the author are not bracketed; footnotes by GBF or a translator are [bracketed].

CONTENTS

*

THOMAS HOBBES was born in Westport, England, in 1588 to a clergyman who abandoned the family and left young Hobbes to the care of an uncle. After his early education in church and private schools was completed, Hobbes entered Oxford when he was fifteen. He graduated in 1608 and attached himself to the family of Lord William Cavendish as a tutor, remaining close with the family for many years. As a tutor, Hobbes was able to pursue classical studies—his translation of Thucydides was published in 1629—and to travel to Europe for extended periods, meeting Galileo, Descartes, and other thinkers. Scientific theories affected the development of Hobbes as a political philosopher. In 1629 he "fell in love" with geometry as a means to "truth," and Galileo's law of inertia fascinated him. The turmoil of the English civil wars and events leading up to them also spurred Hobbes on in his work, which includes *Human Nature* (1650), *The Elements of Law, Moral and Politick* (1650), and *Leviathan* (1651). Hobbes also wrote an autobiography in Latin verse and translated Homer's *Iliad*. He died in 1679.

From *Hobbes: Selections,* edited by Frederick J. E. Woodbridge. Publisher: Charles Scribner's Sons, 1958. Portions of Chapters XIII, XIV, XV, XVII, and XVIII.

Origin of Government

OF THE NATURAL CONDITION OF MANKIND AS CONCERNING THEIR FELICITY AND MISERY

Nature has made men so equal, in the faculties of the body, and mind; as that though there be found one man sometimes manifestly stronger in body, or of quicker mind than another; yet when all is reckoned together, the difference between man, and man, is not so considerable, as that one man can thereupon claim to himself any benefit, to which another may not pretend, as well as he. For as to the strength of body, the weakest has strength enough to kill the strongest, either by secret machination, or by confederacy with others, that are in the same danger with himself.

And as to the faculties of the mind, setting aside the arts grounded upon words, and especially that skill of proceeding upon general, and infallible rules, called science; which very few have, and but in few things; as being not a native faculty, born with us; nor attained, as prudence, while we look after somewhat else, I find yet a greater equality amongst men, than that of strength. For prudence is but experience; which equal time, equally bestows on all men, in those things they equally apply themselves unto. That which may perhaps make such equality incredible, is but a vain conceit of one's own wisdom, which almost all men think they have in a greater degree, than the vulgar; that is, than all men but themselves, and a few others, whom by fame, or for concurring with themselves, they approve. For such is the nature of men, that howsoever they may acknowledge many others to be more witty, or more eloquent, or more learned; yet they will hardly believe there be many so wise as themselves; for they see their own wit at hand, and other men's at a distance. But this proves rather that men are in that point equal, than unequal. For there is not ordinarily a greater sign of the equal distribution of anything, than that every man is contented with his share.

From this equality of ability, arises equality of hope in the attaining of our ends. And therefore if any two men desire the same thing, which nevertheless they cannot both enjoy, they become enemies; and in the way to their end, which is principally their own conservation, and sometimes their delectation only, endeavour to destroy, or subdue one another. And from hence it comes to pass, that where an invader has no more to fear than another man's single power; if one plant, sow, build, or possess a convenient seat, others may probably be expected to come prepared with forces united, to dispossess, and deprive him, not only of the fruit of his labour, but also of his life, or liberty. And the invader again is in the like danger of another.

And from this diffidence[1] of one another, there is no way for any man to secure himself, so reasonable, as anticipation; that is, by force, or wiles, to master the persons of all men he can, so long, till he see no other power great enough to endanger him: and this is no more than his own conservation requires, and is generally allowed. Also because there be some, that taking pleasure in contemplating their own power in the acts of conquest, which they pursue farther than their security requires; if others, that otherwise would be glad to be at ease within modest bounds, should not by invasion increase their power, they would not be able, long time, by standing only on their defence, to subsist. And by consequence, such augmentation of dominion

---

[1] [Distrust.]

over men being necessary to a man's conservation, it ought to be allowed him.

Again, men have no pleasure, but on the contrary a great deal of grief, in keeping company, where there is no power able to over-awe them all. For every man looks that his companion should value him, at the same rate he sets upon himself: and upon all signs of contempt, or undervaluing, naturally endeavours, as far as he dares (which amongst them that have no common power to keep them in quiet, is far enough to make them destroy each other), to extort a greater value from his contemners, by damage; and from others, by the example.

So that in the nature of man, we find three principal causes of quarrel. First, competition; secondly, diffidence; thirdly, glory.

The first makes men invade for gain; the second, for safety; and the third, for reputation. The first use violence, to make themselves masters of other men's persons, wives, children, and cattle; the second, to defend them; the third, for trifles, as a word, a smile, a different opinion, and any other sign of undervalue, either direct in their persons, or by reflection in their kindred, their friends, their nation, their profession, or their name.

Hereby it is manifest, that during the time men live without a common power to keep them all in awe, they are in that condition which is called war; and such a war, as is of every man, against every man. For WAR consists not in battle only, or the act of fighting; but in a tract of time, wherein the will to contend by battle is sufficiently known: and therefore the notion of *time* is to be considered in the nature of war; as it is in the nature of weather. For as the nature of foul weather lies not in a shower or two of rain; but in an inclination thereto of many days together: so the nature of war consists not in actual fighting; but in the known disposition thereto, during all the time there is no assurance to the contrary. All other time is PEACE.

Whatsoever therefore is consequent to a time of war, where every man is enemy to every man; the same is consequent to the time wherein men live without other security, than what their own strength, and their own invention shall furnish them withal. In such condition, there is no place for industry; because the fruit thereof is uncertain: and consequently no culture of the earth; no navigation, nor use of the commodities that may be imported by sea; no commodious building; no instruments of moving, and removing, such things as require much force; no knowledge of the face of the earth; no account of time; no arts; no letters; no society; and which is worst of all, continual fear, and danger of violent death; and the life of man, solitary, poor, nasty, brutish, and short.

It may seem strange to some man, that has not well weighed these things; that nature should thus dissociate, and render men apt to invade, and destroy one another: and he may therefore, not trusting to this inference, made from the passions, desire perhaps to have the same confirmed by experience. Let him therefore consider with himself, when taking a journey, he arms himself, and seeks to go well accompanied; when going to sleep, he locks his doors; when even in his house he locks his chests; and this when he knows there be laws, and public officers, armed, to revenge all injuries shall be done him; what opinion he has of his fellow-subjects, when he rides armed; of his fellow citizens, when he locks his doors; and of his children, and servants, when he locks his chests. Does he not there as much accuse mankind by his actions, as I do by my words? But neither of us accuse man's nature in it. The desires, the other passions of man, are in themselves no sin. No more are the actions, that proceed from those passions, till they know a law that forbids them: which till laws be made they cannot know: nor can any law be made, till they have agreed upon the person that shall make it.

It may peradventure be thought, there was never such a time, nor condition of war as this; and I believe it was never generally so, over all the world: but there are many places, where they live so now. For the savage people in many places of America, except the government of small families, the concord whereof depends on the natural lust, have no government at all; and live at this day in that brutish manner, as I said before. Howsoever, it may be perceived what manner of life there would be, where there were no common power to fear, by the manner of life, which men that have formerly lived under a peaceful government, use to degenerate into, in a civil war.

But though there had never been any time, wherein particular men were in a condition of war one against another; yet in all times, kings, and persons of sovereign authority, because of their independency, are in continual jealousies, and in the state and posture of gladiators; having their weapons pointing, and their eyes fixed on one another: that is, their forts, garrisons, and guns upon the frontiers of their kingdoms; and continual spies upon their neighbours; which is a posture of war. But because they uphold thereby, the industry of their subjects; there does not follow from it, that misery, which accompanies the liberty of particular men.

To this war of every man, against every man, this also is consequent; that nothing can be unjust. The notions of right and wrong, justice and injustice have there no place. Where there is no common power, there is no law: where no law, no injustice. Force, and fraud, are in war the two cardinal virtues. Justice, and injustice, are none of the faculties neither of the body, nor mind. If they were, they might be in a man that were alone in the world, as well as his senses, and passions. They are qualities that relate to men in society, not in solitude. It is consequent also to the same condition, that there be no propriety,[2] no dominion, no *mine* and *thine* distinct; but only that to be every man's, that he can get: and for so long, as he can

---

[2] [Private ownership; possessorship; privately owned possessions; property.]

keep it. And thus much for the ill condition, which man by mere nature is actually placed in; though with a possibility to come out of it, consisting partly in the passions, partly in his reason.

The passions that incline men to peace are fear of death; desire of such things as are necessary to commodious living; and a hope by their industry to obtain them. And reason suggests convenient articles of peace, upon which men may be drawn to agreement. These articles, are they, which otherwise are called the Laws of Nature: whereof I shall speak more particularly. . . .

OF THE FIRST AND SECOND NATURAL LAWS AND OF CONTRACTS

The RIGHT OF NATURE, which writers commonly call *jus naturale,* is the liberty each man has to use his own power, as he will himself, for the preservation of his own nature; that is to say, of his own life; and consequently, of doing anything, which in his own judgment, and reason, he shall conceive to be the aptest means thereunto.

By LIBERTY, is understood, according to the proper signification of the word, the absence of external impediments: which impediments may often take away part of a man's power to do what he would; but cannot hinder him from using the power left him, according as his judgment, and reason, shall dictate to him.

A LAW OF NATURE, *lex naturalis,* is a precept or general rule, found out by reason, by which a man is forbidden to do that which is destructive of his life, or takes away the means of preserving the same; and to omit that by which he thinks it may be best preserved. For though they that speak of this subject, use to confound *jus,* and *lex, right* and *law:* yet they ought to be distinguished; because RIGHT consists in liberty to do, or to forbear: whereas LAW determines and binds to one of them: so that law, and right, differ as much as obligation, and liberty; which in one and the same matter are inconsistent.

And because the condition of man . . . is a condition of war of everyone against everyone; in which case everyone is governed by his own reason; and there is nothing he can make use of, that may not be a help unto him, in preserving his life against his enemies; it follows, that in such a condition, every man has a right to everything; even to one another's body. And therefore, as long as this natural right of every man to everything endures, there can be no security to any man, how strong or wise soever he be, of living out the time, which nature ordinarily allows men to live. And consequently it is a precept, or general rule of reason, *that every man ought to endeavour peace, as far as he has hope of obtaining it; and when he cannot obtain it, that he may seek, and use, all helps, and advantages of war.* The first branch of which rule contains the first, and fundamental, law of nature; which is, *to seek peace, and follow it.* The second, the sum of the right of nature; which is, *by all means we can, to defend ourselves.*

From this fundamental law of nature, by which men are commanded to endeavour peace, is derived this second law; *that a man be willing, when others are so too, as far-forth, as for peace, and defence of himself he shall think it necessary, to lay down this right to all things; and be contented with so much liberty against other men, as he would allow other men against himself.* For as long as every man holds this right, of doing anything he likes; so long are all men in the condition of war. But if other men will not lay down their right, as well as he; then there is no reason for any one, to divest himself of his: for that were to expose himself to prey, which no man is bound to, rather than to dispose himself to peace. This is that law of the Gospel; *whatsoever you require that others should do to you, that do ye to them.* And that law of all men, *quod tibi fieri non vis, alteri ne feceris.*[3]

To *lay down* a man's *right* to anything, is to *divest* himself of the *liberty,* of hindering another of the benefit of his own right to the same. For he that renounces, or passes away his right, gives not to any other man a right which he had not before; because there is nothing to which every man had not right by nature: but only stands out of his way, that he may enjoy his own original right, without hindrance from him; not without hindrance from another. So that the effect which redounds to one man, by another man's defect of right, is but so much diminution of impediments to the use of his own right original.

Right is laid aside, either by simply renouncing it; or by transferring it to another. By *simply* RENOUNCING, when he cares not to whom the benefit thereof redounds. By TRANSFERRING; when he intends the benefit thereof to some certain person, or persons. And when a man has in either manner abandoned, or granted away his right; then he is said to be OBLIGED, or BOUND, not to hinder those to whom such right is granted, or abandoned, from the benefit of it: and that he *ought,* and it is his DUTY, not to make void that voluntary act of his own: and that such hindrance is INJUSTICE, and INJURY, as being *sine jure;* the right being before renounced, or transferred. So that *injury,* or *injustice,* in the controversies of the world, is somewhat like to that, which in the disputations of scholars is called *absurdity.* For as it is there called an absurdity, to contradict what one maintained in the beginning: so in the world, it is called injustice, and injury, voluntarily to undo that which from the beginning he had voluntarily done. The way by which a man either simply renounces, or transfers his right, is a declaration, or signification, by some voluntary and sufficient

---

[3] [Do not do to another what you would not have done to you.]

sign, or signs, that he does so renounce, or transfer; or has so renounced, or transferred the same, to him that accepts it. And these signs are either words only, or actions only; or, as it happens most often, both words, and actions. And the same are the BONDS, by which men are bound, and obliged: bonds that have their strength, not from their own nature, for nothing is more easily broken than a man's word, but from fear of some evil consequence upon the rupture.

Whensoever a man transfers his right, or renounces it; it is either in consideration of some right reciprocally transferred to himself; or for some other good he hopes for thereby. For it is a voluntary act: and of the voluntary acts of every man, the object is some *good to himself*. And therefore there be some rights which no man can be understood by any words, or other signs, to have abandoned, or transferred. As first a man cannot lay down the right of resisting them, that assault him by force, to take away his life; because he cannot be understood to aim thereby, at any good to himself. The same may be said of wounds, and chains, and imprisonment; both because there is no benefit consequent to such patience; as there is to the patience of suffering another to be wounded, or imprisoned: as also because a man cannot tell, when he sees men proceed against him by violence, whether they intend his death or not. And lastly the motive, and end for which this renouncing, and transferring of right is introduced, is nothing else but the security of a man's person, in his life, and in the means of so preserving life, as not to be weary of it. And therefore if a man by words, or other signs, seems to despoil himself of the end, for which those signs were intended; he is not to be understood as if he meant it, or that it was his will; but that he was ignorant of how such words and actions were to be interpreted.

The mutual transferring of right, is that which men call CONTRACT. . . .

Again, one of the contractors may deliver the thing contracted for on his part, and leave the other to perform his part at some determinate time after, and in the mean time be trusted; and then the contract on his part is called PACT, or COVENANT: or both parts may contract now, to perform hereafter: in which cases, he that is to perform in time to come, being trusted, his performance is called *keeping of promise,* or faith; and the failing of performance, if it be voluntary, *violation of faith.* . . .

If a covenant be made, wherein neither of the parties perform presently, but trust one another; in the condition of mere nature, which is a condition of war of every man against every man, upon any reasonable suspicion, it is void: but if there be a common power set over them both, with right and force sufficient to compel performance, it is not void. For he that performs first, has no assurance the other will perform after; because the bonds of words are too weak to bridle men's ambition, avarice, anger, and other passions, without the fear of some coercive power; which in the condition of mere nature, where all men are equal, and judges of the justness of their own fears, cannot possibly be supposed. And therefore he which performs first, does but betray himself to his enemy; contrary to the right, he can never abandon, of defending his life, and means of living.

But in a civil estate,[4] where there is a power set up to constrain those that would otherwise violate their faith, that fear is no more reasonable; and for that cause, he which by the covenant is to perform first, is obliged so to do. . . .

The force of words, being, as I have formerly noted, too weak to hold men to the performance of their covenants; there are in man's nature but two imaginable helps to strengthen it. And those are either a fear of the consequence of breaking their word; or a glory, or pride in appearing not to need to break it. This latter is a generosity too rarely found to be presumed on, especially in the pursuers of wealth, command, or sensual pleasure; which are the greatest part of mankind. The passion to be

---

[4] [Civil state; community under government.]

reckoned upon is fear; whereof there be two very general objects: one, the power of spirits invisible; the other, the power of those men they shall therein offend. Of these two, though the former be the greater power, yet the fear of the latter is commonly the greater fear. The fear of the former is in every man, his own religion: which has place in the nature of man before civil society. The latter has not so; at least not place enough, to keep men to their promises; because in the condition of mere nature, the inequality of power is not discerned, but by the event of battle. So that before the time of civil society, or in the interruption thereof by war, there is nothing can strengthen a covenant of peace agreed on, against the temptations of avarice, ambition, lust, or other strong desire, but the fear of that invisible power, which they every one worship as God; and fear as a revenger of their perfidy. . . .

OF OTHER LAWS OF NATURE

From that law of nature, by which we are obliged to transfer to another, such rights, as being retained, hinder the peace of mankind, there follows a third; which is this, *that men perform their covenants made:* without which, covenants are in vain, and but empty words; and the right of all men to all things remaining, we are still in the condition of war.

And in this law of nature, consists the fountain and original of JUSTICE. For where no covenant has preceded, there has no right been transferred, and every man has right to everything; and consequently, no action can be unjust. But when a covenant is made, then to break it is *unjust:* and the definition of INJUSTICE is no other than *the not performance of covenant.* And whatsoever is not unjust, is *just.*

But because covenants of mutual trust, where there is a fear of not performance on either part, as has been said in the former chapter, are invalid; though the original of justice be the making of covenants; yet injustice actually there can be none, till the cause of such fear be taken away; which while men are in the natural condition of war, cannot be done. Therefore before the names of just, and unjust, can have place, there must be some coercive power to compel men equally to the performance of their covenants, by the terror of some punishment, greater than the benefit they expect by the breach of their covenant; and to make good that propriety, which by mutual contract men acquire, in recompense of the universal right they abandon: and such power there is none before the erection of a commonwealth.[5] And this is also to be gathered out of the ordinary definition of justice in the Schools: for they say that *justice is the constant will of giving to every man his own.* And therefore where there is no *own,* there is no propriety, there is no injustice; and where there is no coercive power erected, that is, where there is no commonwealth, there is no propriety; all men having right to all things: therefore where there is no commonwealth, there nothing is unjust. So that the nature of justice consists in keeping of valid covenants: but the validity of covenants begins not but with the constitution of a civil power, sufficient to compel men to keep them: and then it is also that propriety begins.

The fool has said in his heart, there is no such thing as justice; and sometimes also with his tongue; seriously alleging that every man's conservation, and contentment, being committed to his own care, there could be no reason, why every man might not do what he thought conduced thereunto: and therefore also to make, or not make; keep, or not keep covenants, was not against reason, when it conduced to one's benefit. . . . From such reasoning as this, successful wickedness has obtained the name of virtue: and some that in all other things have disallowed the violation of faith; yet have allowed it, when it is for the getting of a kingdom. And the heathen that believed that Saturn was

---

[5] [A state; a community under government.]

deposed by his son Jupiter, believed nevertheless the same Jupiter to be the avenger of injustice: . . . a man will be very prone to infer; that when the heir apparent of a kingdom, shall kill him that is in possession, though his father; you may call it injustice, or by what other name you will; yet it can never be against reason, seeing all the voluntary actions of men tend to the benefit of themselves; and those actions are most reasonable that conduce most to their ends. This specious reasoning is nevertheless false. . . .

For the manifestation whereof, we are to consider; first, that when a man does a thing, which notwithstanding anything can be foreseen, and reckoned on, tends to his own destruction, howsoever some accident which he could not expect arriving may turn it to his benefit; yet such events do not make it reasonably or wisely done. Secondly, that in a condition of war, wherein every man to every man, for want of a common power to keep them all in awe, is an enemy, there is no man who can hope by his own strength, or wit, to defend himself from destruction, without the help of confederates; where everyone expects the same defence by the confederation, that anyone else does: and therefore he which declares he thinks it reason to deceive those that help him, can in reason expect no other means of safety, than what can be had from his own single power. He therefore that breaks his covenant, and consequently declares that he thinks he may with reason do so, cannot be received into any society that unite themselves for peace and defence, but by the error of them that receive him; nor when he is received, be retained in it, without seeing the danger of their error; which errors a man cannot reasonably reckon upon as the means of his security: and therefore if he be left, or cast out of society, he perishes; and if he lives in society, it is by the errors of other men, which he could not foresee, nor reckon upon; and consequently against the reason of his preservation; and so, as all men that contribute not to his destruction, forbear him only out of ignorance of what is good for themselves. . . .

And for the other instance of attaining sovereignty by rebellion; it is manifest, that though the event follow, yet because it cannot reasonably be expected, but rather the contrary; and because by gaining it so, others are taught to gain the same in like manner, the attempt thereof is against reason. Justice therefore, that is to say, keeping of covenant, is a rule of reason, by which we are forbidden to do anything destructive to our life; and consequently a law of nature. . . .

As justice depends on antecedent covenant; so does GRATITUDE depend on antecedent grace; that is to say, antecedent free gift: and is the fourth law of nature; which may be conceived in this form, *that a man which receives benefit from another of mere grace, endeavour that he which gives it, have no reasonable cause to repent him of his good will.* For no man gives, but with intention of good to himself; because gift is voluntary; and of all voluntary acts, the object is to every man his own good; of which if men see they shall be frustrated, there will be no beginning of benevolence, or trust; nor consequently of mutual help; nor of reconciliation of one man to another; and therefore they are to remain still in the condition of *war;* which is contrary to the first and fundamental law of nature, which commands men to *seek peace.* The breach of this law, is called *ingratitude;* and has the same relation to grace, that injustice has to obligation by covenant.

A fifth law of nature is COMPLAISANCE; that is to say, *that every man strive to accommodate himself to the rest.* For the understanding whereof, we may consider, that there is in men's aptness to society, a diversity of nature, rising from their diversity of affections; not unlike to that we see in stones brought together for building of an edifice. For as that stone which by the asperity, and irregularity of figure, takes more room from others, than itself fills; and for the hardness, cannot be easily made plain, and thereby hinders the building, is by the builders cast away as unprofitable, and troublesome: so also, a man that by asperity of nature will strive to retain those things which to himself are superfluous, and to others necessary; and for the stubbornness of his passions, cannot be corrected, is to be left, or cast out of society, as cumbersome thereunto. For seeing every man, not only by right, but also by necessity of nature, is supposed to endeavour all he can, to obtain that which is necessary for his conservation; he that shall oppose himself against it, for things superfluous, is guilty of the war that thereupon is to follow; and therefore does that which is contrary to the fundamental law of nature, which commands *to seek peace.* The observers of this law may be called SOCIABLE: the Latins call them *commodi;* the contrary, *stubborn, insociable, froward, intractable.*

A sixth law of nature is this, *that upon caution of the future time, a man ought to pardon the offences past of them that repenting, desire it.* For PARDON is nothing but granting of peace; which though granted to them that persevere in their hostility, be not peace, but fear; yet not granted to them that give caution of the future time, is sign of an aversion to peace; and therefore contrary to the law of nature.

A seventh is, *that in revenges,* that is, retribution of evil for evil, *men look not at the greatness of the evil past, but the greatness of the good to follow.* Whereby we are forbidden to inflict punishment with any other design, than for correction of the offender, or direction of others. For this law is consequent to the next before it, that commands pardon, upon security of the future time. Besides, revenge without respect to the example, and profit to come, is a triumph, or glorying in the hurt of another, tending to no end; for the end is always somewhat to come; and glorying to no end, is vain-glory, and contrary to reason, and to hurt without reason, tends to the introduction of war; which is against the law of nature; and is commonly styled by the name of *cruelty.*

And because all signs of hatred, or contempt, provoke to fight; insomuch as most men choose rather to hazard their life, than not to be revenged; we may in the eighth place, for a law of nature, set down this precept, *that no man by deed, word, countenance, or gesture, declare hatred, or contempt of another*. The breach of which law is commonly called *contumely*.

The question who is the better man, has no place in the condition of mere nature; where, as has been shown before, all men are equal. The inequality that now is, has been introduced by the laws civil. I know that Aristotle in the first book of his *Politics,* for a foundation of his doctrine, makes men by nature, some more worthy to command, meaning the wiser sort, such as he thought himself to be for his philosophy; others to serve, meaning those that had strong bodies, but were not philosophers as he; as if master and servant were not introduced by consent of men, but by difference of wit: which is not only against reason; but also against experience. For there are very few so foolish that had not rather govern themselves, than be governed by others: nor when the wise in their own conceit, contend by force with them who distrust their own wisdom, do they always, or often, or almost at any time, get the victory. If nature therefore have made men equal, that equality is to be acknowledged: or if nature have made men unequal; yet because men that think themselves equal, will not enter into conditions of peace, but upon equal terms, such equality must be admitted. And therefore for the ninth law of nature, I put this, *that every man acknowledge another for his equal by nature*. The breach of this precept is *pride*.

On this law, depends another, *that at the entrance into conditions of peace, no man require to reserve to himself any right which he is not content should be reserved to everyone of the rest*. As it is necessary for all men that seek peace to lay down certain rights of nature; that is to say, not to have liberty to do all they list: so is it necessary for man's life to retain some; as right to govern their own bodies; enjoy air, water, motion, ways to go from place to place; and all things else, without which a man cannot live, or not live well. If in this case, at the making of peace, men require for themselves that which they would not have to be granted to others, they do contrary to the precedent law, that commands the acknowledgment of natural equality, and therefore also against the law of nature. The observers of this law are those we call *modest,* and the breakers *arrogant* men. The Greeks call the violation of this law *pleonexia;* that is, a desire of more than their share.

Also, if *a man be trusted to judge between man and man,* it is a precept of the law of nature, *that he deal equally between them.* For without that, the controversies of men cannot be determined but by war. He therefore that is partial in judgment, does what in him lies, to deter men from the use of judges, and arbitrators; and consequently, against the fundamental law of nature, is the cause of war.

The observance of this law, from the equal distribution to each man, of that which in reason belongs to him, is called EQUITY, and, as I have said before, distributive justice: the violation, *acception of persons, prosopolepsia.*

And from this follows another law, *that such things as cannot be divided, be enjoyed in common, if it can be; and if the quantity of the thing permit, without stint; otherwise proportionably to the number of them that have right.* For otherwise the distribution is unequal, and contrary to equity.

But some things there be, that can neither be divided, nor enjoyed in common. Then, the law of nature, which prescribes equity, requires, *that the entire right; or else, making the use alternate, the first possession, be determined by lot.* For equal distribution, is of the law of nature; and other means of equal distribution cannot be imagined.

Of *lots* there be two sorts, *arbitrary,* and *natural.* Arbitrary, is that which is agreed on by the competitors: natural, is either *primogeniture,* which the Greek calls *kleronomia,* which signifies, *given by lot;* or *first seizure.*

And therefore those things which cannot be enjoyed in common, nor divided, ought to be adjudged to the first possessor; and in some cases to the first born, as acquired by lot.

It is also a law of nature, *that all men that mediate peace, be allowed safe conduct.* For the law that commands peace, as the *end,* commands intercession, as the *means;* and to intercession the means is safe conduct.

And because, though men be never so willing to observe these laws, there may nevertheless arise questions concerning a man's action; first, whether it were done, or not done; secondly, if done, whether against the law, or not against the law; the former whereof is called a question *of fact;* the latter a question *of right:* therefore unless the parties to the question, covenant mutually to stand to the sentence of another, they are as far from peace as ever. This other to whose sentence they submit is called an ARBITRATOR. And therefore it is of the law of nature, *that they that are at controversy, submit their right to the judgment of an arbitrator.*

And seeing every man is presumed to do all things in order to his own benefit, no man is a fit arbitrator in his own cause; and if he were never so fit; yet equity allowing to each party equal benefit, if one be admitted to be judge, the other is to be admitted also; and so the controversy, that is, the cause of war, remains, against the law of nature.

For the same reason no man in any cause ought to be received for arbitrator, to whom greater profit, or honour, or pleasure apparently arises out of the victory of one party, than of the other: for he has taken, though an unavoidable bribe, yet a bribe; and no man can be obliged to trust him. And thus also the controversy, and the condition of war remains, contrary to the law of nature.

And in a controversy of *fact,* the judge being to give no more credit to one, than to the other, if there be no other arguments, must give credit to a third; or to a third and fourth; or more:

for else the question is undecided, and left to force, contrary to the law of nature.

These are the laws of nature, dictating peace, for a means of the conservation of men in multitudes; and which only concern the doctrine of civil society. There be other things tending to the destruction of particular men; as drunkenness, and all other parts of intemperance; which may therefore also be reckoned amongst those things which the law of nature has forbidden; but are not necessary to be mentioned, nor are pertinent enough to this place.

And though this may seem too subtle a deduction of the laws of nature, to be taken notice of by all men; whereof the most part are too busy in getting food, and the rest too negligent to understand; yet to leave all men inexcusable, they have been contracted into one easy sum, intelligible even to the meanest capacity; and that is, *Do not that to another, which thou wouldest not have done to thyself;* which shows him that he has no more to do in learning the laws of nature, but, when weighing the actions of other men with his own, they seem too heavy to put them into the other part of the balance, and his own into their place, that his own passions, and self-love, may add nothing to the weight; and then there is none of these laws of nature that will not appear unto him very reasonable.

The laws of nature oblige *in foro interno;* that is to say, they bind to a desire they should take place: but *in foro externo;* that is, to the putting them in act, not always. For he that should be modest, and tractable, and perform all he promises, in such time, and place, where no man else should do so, should but make himself a prey to others, and procure his own certain ruin, contrary to the ground of all laws of nature, which tend to nature's preservation. And again, he that having sufficient security, that others shall observe the same laws towards him, observes them not himself, seeks not peace, but war; and consequently the destruction of his nature by violence. . . .

The laws of nature are immutable and eternal; for injustice, ingratitude, arrogance, pride, iniquity, acception of persons, and the rest, can never be made lawful. For it can never be that war shall preserve life, and peace destroy it.

The same laws, because they oblige only to a desire, and endeavour, I mean an unfeigned and constant endeavour, are easy to be observed. For in that they require nothing but endeavour, he that endeavours their performance, fulfills them; and he that fulfills the law, is just.

And the science of them is the true and only moral philosophy. For moral philosophy is nothing else but the science of what is *good* and *evil,* in the conversation and society of mankind. *Good* and *evil* are names that signify our appetites, and aversions; which in different tempers, customs, and doctrines of men are different: and divers men differ not only in their judgment on the senses of what is pleasant, and unpleasant, to the taste, smell, hearing, touch, and sight; but also of what is conformable, or disagreeable, to reason, in the actions of common life. Nay, the same man, in divers times, differs from himself; and one time praises, that is, calls good, what another time he dispraises, and calls evil: from whence arise disputes, controversies, and at last war. And therefore so long as a man is in the condition of mere nature, which is a condition of war, as private appetite is the measure of good, and evil: and consequently all men agree on this, that peace is good, and therefore also the way, or means of peace, which, as I have shown before, are *justice, gratitude, modesty, equity, mercy,* and the rest of the laws of nature, are good; that is to say, *moral virtues,* and their contrary *vices,* evil. Now the science of virtue and vice is moral philosophy; and therefore the true doctrine of the laws of nature is the true moral philosophy. But the writers of moral philosophy, though they acknowledge the same virtues and vices; yet not seeing wherein consisted their goodness; nor that they come to be praised, as the means of peaceable, sociable, and comfortable living, place them in a mediocrity of passions: and if not the cause, but the degree of daring, made fortitude; or not the cause, but the quantity of a gift, made liberality.

These dictates of reason, men used to call by the name of laws, but improperly: for they are but conclusions, or theorems, concerning what conduces to the conservation and defence of themselves; whereas law, properly, is the word of him, that by right has command over others. But yet if we consider the same theorems, as delivered in the word of God, that by right commands all things; then are they properly called laws.

* * *

OF THE CAUSES, GENERATION, AND DEFINITION OF A COMMONWEALTH

The final cause, end, or design of men who naturally love liberty and dominion over others, in the introduction of that restraint upon themselves, in which we see them live in commonwealths, is the foresight of their own preservation, and of a more contented life thereby; that is to say, of getting themselves out from that miserable condition of war, which is necessarily consequent, as has been shown, to the natural passions of men, when there is no visible power to keep them in awe, and tie them by fear of punishment to the performance of their covenants, and observation of those laws of nature set down. . . .

For the laws of nature, as *justice, equity, modesty, mercy,* and, in sum, *doing to others, as we would be done to,* of themselves, without the terror of some power to cause them to be observed, are contrary to our natural passions that carry us to partiality, pride, revenge, and the like. And covenants, without the sword, are but words, and of no strength to secure a man at all. Therefore notwithstanding the laws of nature (which everyone has then kept, when he has the will to keep them, when he can do it safely) if there be no power erected, or not great enough for our security; every man will, and may lawfully rely on his own strength and art, for caution against all other men. . . .

So now do cities and kingdoms which are but greater families, for their own security enlarge their dominions, upon all pretences of danger, and fear of invasion, or assistance that may be given to invaders, and endeavour as much as they can, to subdue, or weaken their neighbours, by open force and secret arts, for want of other caution, justly; and are remembered for it in after ages with honour.

Nor is it the joining together of a small number of men that gives them this security; because in small numbers, small additions on the one side or the other, make the advantage of strength so great, as is sufficient to carry the victory; and therefore gives encouragement to an invasion. The multitude sufficient to confide in for our security is not determined by any certain number, but by comparison with the enemy we fear; and is then sufficient, when the odds of the enemy is not of so visible and conspicuous moment, to determine the event of war, as to move him to attempt.

And be there never so great a multitude; yet if their actions be directed according to their particular judgments, and particular appetites, they can expect thereby no defence, nor protection, neither against a common enemy, nor against the injuries of one another. For being distracted in opinions concerning the best use and application of their strength, they do not help but hinder one another; and reduce their strength by mutual opposition to nothing: whereby they are easily not only subdued by a very few that agree together; but also when there is no common enemy, they make war upon each other, for their particular interests. For if we could suppose a great multitude of men to consent in the observation of justice, and other laws of nature, without a common power to keep them all in awe; we might as well suppose all mankind to do the same; and then there neither would be, nor need to be any civil government, or commonwealth at all; because there would be peace without subjection.

Nor is it enough for the security, which men desire should last all the time of their life, that they be governed, and directed by one judgment, for a limited time; as in one battle, or one war. For though they obtain a victory by their unanimous endeavour against a foreign enemy; yet afterwards, when either they have no common enemy, or he that by one part is held for an enemy, is by another part held for a friend, they must need by the difference of their interests to dissolve, and fall again into a war amongst themselves. . . .

The only way to erect such a common power as may be able to defend them from the invasion of foreigners, and the injuries of one another, and thereby to secure them in such sort as that by their own industry, and by the fruits of the earth, they may nourish themselves and live contentedly; is to confer all their power and strength upon one man, or upon one assembly of men, that may reduce all their wills, by plurality of voices, unto one will: which is as much as to say, to appoint one man, or assembly of men, to bear their person;[6] and everyone to own, and acknowledge himself to be author of whatsoever he that so bears their person, shall act, or cause to be acted, in those things which concern the common peace and safety; and therein to submit their wills, everyone to his will, and their judgments, to his judgment. This is more than consent, or concord; it is a real unity of them all, in one and the same person, made by covenant of every man with every man, in such manner, as if every man should say to every man, *I authorize and give up my right of governing myself, to this man, or to this assembly of men, on this condition, that thou give up thy right to him, and authorize all his actions in like manner.* This done, the multitude so united

---

[6] [to represent them.]

in one person, is called a COMMONWEALTH. . . . This is the generation of that great LEVIATHAN, or rather, to speak more reverently, of that *mortal god,* to which we owe under the *immortal God,* our peace and defence. For by this authority, given him by every particular man in the commonwealth, he has the use of so much power and strength conferred on him, that by terror thereof, he is enabled to form the wills of them all, to peace at home, and mutual aid against their enemies abroad. And in him consists the essence of the commonwealth; which, to define it, is *one person, of whose acts a great multitude, by mutual covenants one with another, have made themselves everyone the author, to the end he may use the strength and means of them all, as he shall think expedient, for their peace and common defence.*

And he . . . is called SOVEREIGN, and said to have *sovereign power;* and everyone besides, his SUBJECT.

The attaining to this sovereign power is by two ways. One by natural force; as when a man makes his children, to submit themselves, and their children to his government, as being able to destroy them if they refuse; or by war subdues his enemies to his will, giving them their lives on that condition. The other is when men agree amongst themselves to submit to some man, or assembly of men, voluntarily, on confidence to be protected by him against all others. This latter may be called a political commonwealth, or commonwealth by *institution;* and the former, a commonwealth by *acquisition.* And first, I shall speak of a commonwealth by institution.

OF THE RIGHTS OF SOVEREIGNS
BY INSTITUTION

A *commonwealth* is said to be *instituted* when a *multitude* of men do agree, and *covenant, everyone, with everyone,* that to whatsoever *man,* or *assembly of men,* shall be given by the major part, the *right* to *present* the person of them all, that is to say, to be their *representative;* everyone, as well he that *voted for it,* as he that *voted against it,* shall *authorize* all the actions and judgments, of that man, or assembly of men, in the same manner, as if they were his own, to the end, to live peaceably amongst themselves, and be protected against other men.

From this institution of a commonwealth are derived all the *rights,* and *faculties* of him, or them, on whom the sovereign power is conferred by the consent of the people assembled.

First, because they covenant, it is to be understood they are not obliged by former covenant to anything repugnant hereunto. And consequently they that have already instituted a commonwealth, being thereby bound by covenant to own the actions and judgments of one, cannot lawfully make a new covenant, amongst themselves, to be obedient to any other, in anything whatsoever, without his permission. And therefore, they that are subjects to a monarch cannot without his leave cast off monarchy, and return to the confusion of a disunited multitude; nor transfer their person from him that bears it, to another man, or other assembly of men: for they are bound every man to every man, to own, and be reputed author of all, that he that already is their sovereign, shall do: . . . and they have also every man given the sovereignty to him that bears their person; and therefore if they depose him, they take from him that which is his own, and so again it is injustice. Besides, if he that attempts to depose his sovereign be killed, or punished by him for such attempt, he is author of his own punishment, as being . . . author of all his sovereign shall do: and because it is injustice for a man to do anything for which he may be punished by his own authority, he is also upon that title, unjust. And whereas some men have pretended for their disobedience to their sovereign, a new covenant, made not with men, but with God; this also is unjust: for there is no covenant with God, but by mediation of somebody that represents God's person; which none does but God's lieutenant, who has the sovereignty under God. But this pretence of covenant with God is so evident a lie, even in the pretenders' own consciences, that it is not only an act of an unjust, but also of a vile, and unmanly disposition.

Secondly, because the right of bearing the person of them all is given to him they make sovereign, by covenant only of one to another, and not of him to any of them; there can happen no breach of covenant on the part of the sovereign; and consequently none of his subjects, by any pretence of forfeiture, can be freed from his subjection. . . . Besides, if any one, or more of them, pretend a breach of the covenant made by the sovereign at his institution; and others, or one other of his subjects, or himself alone, pretend there was no such breach, there is in this case no judge to decide the controversy; it returns therefore to the sword again; and every man recovers the right of protecting himself by his own strength, contrary to the design they had in the institution. It is therefore in vain to grant sovereignty by way of precedent covenant. The opinion that any monarch receives his power by covenant, that is to say, on condition, proceeds from want of understanding this easy truth, that covenants being but words and breath, have no force to oblige, contain, constrain, or protect any man, but what it has from the public sword; that is, from the untied hands of that man, or assembly of men that has the sovereignty, and whose actions are avouched by them all, and performed by the strength of them all, in him united. But when an assembly of men is made sovereign; then no man imagines any such covenant to have passed in the institution; for no man is so dull as to say, for example, the people of Rome made a covenant with the Romans, to hold the sovereignty on such or such conditions; which not performed, the Romans might lawfully depose the Roman people. That men see not the reason to be alike in a monarchy, and in a popular government, proceeds from the ambition of some, that are kinder to the government of an assembly, whereof they may hope to participate, than of monarchy, which they despair to enjoy.

Thirdly, because the major part has by consenting voices declared a sovereign; he that dissented must now consent with the rest; that is, be contented to avow all the actions he shall do, or else justly be destroyed by the rest. For if he voluntarily entered into the congregation of them that were assembled, he sufficiently declared thereby his will, and therefore tacitly covenanted, to stand to what the major part should ordain: and therefore if he . . . make protestation against any of their decrees, he does contrary to his covenant, and therefore unjustly. And whether . . . his consent be asked, or not, he must either submit to their decrees, or be left in the condition of war he was in before; wherein he might without injustice be destroyed by any man whatsoever.

Fourthly, because every subject is by this institution author of all the actions and judgments of the sovereign instituted; it follows that whatsoever he does, it can be no injury to any of his subjects; nor ought he to be by any of them accused of injustice. For . . . by this institution of a commonwealth, every particular man is author of all the sovereign does: and consequently he that complains of injury from his sovereign, complains of that whereof he himself is author; and therefore ought not to accuse any man but himself; no, nor himself of injury; because to do injury to one's self is impossible. It is true that they that have sovereign power may commit iniquity; but not injustice. . . .

Fifthly, and consequently to that which was said last, no man that has sovereign power can justly be put to death, or otherwise in any manner by his subjects punished. For seeing every subject is author of the actions of his sovereign; he punishes another for the actions committed by himself.

And because the end of this institution, is the peace and defence of them all; and whosoever has right to the end, has right to the means; it belongs of right, to whatsoever man, or assembly that has the sovereignty, to be judge both of the means of peace and defence, and also of the hindrances and disturbances of the same; and to do whatsoever he shall think necessary to be done, both beforehand, for the preserving of peace and security, by prevention of discord at home, and hostility from abroad; and, when peace and security are lost, for the recovery of the same. And therefore,

Sixthly, it is annexed to the sovereignty, to be judge of what opinions and doctrines are averse, and what conducing to peace; and consequently, on what occasions, how far, and what men are to be trusted withal, in speaking to multitudes of people; and who shall examine the doctrines of all books before they be published. For the actions of men proceed from their opinions; and in the well-governing of opinions, consists the well-governing of men's actions, in order to their peace, and concord. And though in matter of doctrine, nothing ought to be regarded but the truth; yet this is not repugnant to regulating the same by peace. For doctrine repugnant to peace, can no more be true than peace and concord can be against the law of nature. It is untrue that in a commonwealth, whereby the negligence, or unskilfulness of governors, and teachers, false doctrines are by time generally received; the contrary truths may be generally offensive. Yet the most sudden, and rough bustling in of a new truth that can be, does never break the peace, but only sometimes awakes the war. For those men that are so remissly governed that they dare take up arms to defend, or introduce an opinion, are still in war; and their condition not peace, but only a cessation of arms for fear of one another. . . . It belongs therefore to him that has the sovereign power, to be judge, or constitute all judges of opinions and doctrines, as a thing necessary to peace; thereby to prevent discord and civil war.

Seventhly, is annexed to the sovereignty, the whole power of prescribing the rules, whereby every man may know what goods he may enjoy, and what actions he may do, without being molested by any of his fellow-subjects; and this is it men call *propriety.*[7] For before constitution of sovereign power, as has already been shown, all men had right to all things; which necessarily causes war: and therefore this propriety, being necessary to peace, and depending on sovereign power, is the act of that power, in order to the public peace. These rules of propriety, or *meum* and *tuum,*[8] and of *good, evil, lawful,* and *unlawful* in the actions of subjects, are the civil laws; that is to say, the laws of each commonwealth in particular. . . .

Eighthly, is annexed to the sovereignty, the right of judicature; that is to say, of hearing and deciding all controversies. . . . For without the decision of controversies, there is no protection of one subject against the injuries of another; the laws concerning *meum* and *tuum* are in vain; and to every man remains, from the natural and necessary appetite of his own conservation, the right of protecting himself by his private strength, which is the condition of war, and contrary to the end for which every commonwealth is instituted.

Ninthly, is annexed to the sovereignty, the right of making war and peace with other nations and commonwealths; that is to say, of judging when it is for the public good, and how great forces are to be assembled, armed, and paid for that end; and to levy money upon the subjects, to defray the expenses thereof. For the power by which the people are to be defended consists in their armies; and the strength of an army, in the union of their strength under one command; which command the sovereign instituted, therefore has; because the command of the *militia,* without other institution, makes him that has it sovereign. And therefore whosoever is made general of an army, he that has the sovereign power is always generalissimo.

Tenthly, is annexed to the sovereignty, the choosing of all counsellors, ministers, magistrates, and officers, both in peace,

---

[7] [Private ownership; possessorship; also, the laws governing private ownership.]
[8] ["Mine" and "yours."]

and war. For seeing the sovereign is charged with the end, which is the common peace and defence, he is understood to have power to use such means, as he shall think most fit for his discharge.

Eleventhly, to the sovereign is committed the power of rewarding with riches, or honour, and of punishing with corporal or pecuniary punishment, or with ignominy, every subject according to the law he has formerly made; or if there be no law made, according as he shall judge most to conduce to the encouraging of men to serve the commonwealth, or deterring of them from doing disservice to the same.

Lastly, considering what value men are naturally apt to set upon themselves; what respect they look for from others; and how little they value other men; from whence continually arise amongst them, emulation, quarrels, factions, and at last war; . . . it is necessary that there be laws of honour, and a public rate of the worth of such men as have deserved, or are able to deserve well of the commonwealth; and that there be force in the hands of some or other, to put those laws in execution. But it has already been shown that not only the whole *militia,* or forces of the commonwealth; but also the judicature of all controversies, is annexed to the sovereignty. To the sovereign therefore it belongs also to give titles of honour; and to appoint what order of place, and dignity, each man shall hold; and what signs of respect, in public or private meetings, they shall give to one another.

These are the rights, which make the essence of sovereignty; and which are the marks whereby a man may discern in what man, or assembly of men, the sovereign power is placed, and resides. For these are incommunicable, and inseparable. The power to coin money; to dispose of the estate and persons of infant heirs; to have preemption in markets; and all other statute prerogatives, may be transferred by the sovereign; and yet the power to protect his subjects be retained. But if he transfer the *militia,* he retains the judicature in vain, for want of execution of the laws: or if he grant away the power of raising money; the *militia* is in vain; or if he give away the government of doctrines, men will be frighted into rebellion with the fear of spirits. And so if we consider any one of the said rights, we shall presently see that the holding of all the rest will produce no effect, in the conservation of peace and justice, the end for which all commonwealths are instituted. And this division is it, whereof it is said, *a kingdom divided in itself cannot stand. . . .* If there had not first been an opinion received of the greatest part of England, that these powers were divided between the King, and the Lords, and the House of Commons, the people had never been divided and fallen into this civil war; first between those that disagreed in politics; and after between the dissenters about the liberty of religion; which have so instructed men in this point of sovereign right, that there be few now in England that do not see that these rights are inseparable, and will be so generally acknowledged at the next return of peace; and so continue, till their miseries are forgotten; and no longer, except the vulgar be better taught than they have hitherto been.

And because they are essential and inseparable rights, it follows necessarily that in whatsoever words any of them seem to be granted away, yet if the sovereign power itself be not in direct terms renounced, and the name of sovereign no more given by the grantees to him that grants them, the grant is void: for when he has granted all he can, if we grant back the sovereignty, all is restored, as inseparably annexed thereunto. . . .

And as the power, so also the honour of the sovereign ought to be greater than that of any, or all the subjects. For in the sovereignty is the fountain of honour. The dignities of lord, earl, duke, and prince are his creatures. As in the presence of the master, the servants are equal, and without any honour at all; so are the subjects, in the presence of the sovereign. And though they shine some more, some less, when they are out of his sight;

yet in his presence, they shine no more than the stars in the presence of the sun.

But a man may here object that the condition of subjects is very miserable; as being obnoxious to the lusts, and other irregular passions of him, or them that have so unlimited a power in their hands. And commonly they that live under a monarch, think it the fault of monarchy; and they that live under the government of democracy, or other sovereign assembly, attribute all the inconvenience to that form of commonwealth; whereas the power in all forms, if they be perfect enough to protect them, is the same: not considering that the state of man can never be without some incommodity or other; and that the greatest that in any form of government can possibly happen to the people in general, is scarce sensible in respect of the miseries, and horrible calamities, that accompany a civil war, or that dissolute condition of masterless men, without subjection to laws, and a coercive power to tie their hands from rapine and revenge: nor considering that the greatest pressure of sovereign governors proceeds not from any delight or profit they can expect in the damage or weakening of their subjects, in whose vigour consists their own strength and glory; but in the restiveness of themselves, that unwillingly contributing to their own defence, make it necessary for their governors to draw from them what they can in time of peace, that they may have . . . sudden need to resist, or take advantage on their enemies. For all men are by nature provided of notable multiplying glasses, that is, their passions and self-love, through which every little payment appears a great grievance; but are destitute of those prospective glasses, namely moral and civil science, to see afar off the miseries that hang over them, and cannot without such payments be avoided.

HERMAN MELVILLE, a merchant's son, was born in New York City in 1819. His father died in 1832, and for years the family endured hard times. Melville had little formal education to speak of. He worked in a bank and on a farm, reluctantly taught school, and studied surveying before finally joining the crew of the "Acushnet," a whaling ship bound for the South Seas, in 1841. During the voyage, Melville reportedly jumped ship and was held captive by cannibals for four months on an island in the Pacific. This adventure and others inspired Melville's first novel, *Typee: A Peep at Polynesian Life* (1846), written after he returned from the sea in 1844. The popularity of *Typee* encouraged Melville to write nine other novels, some acclaimed but others almost totally disregarded. Melville's early success faded. He continued writing, but had to earn a livelihood by other means, conducting lecture tours and working as a customs inspector for nineteen years. He died in 1891, obscure and embittered.

From *Billy Budd, Sailor (An Inside Narrative)*, edited by Harrison Hayford and Merton M. Sealts, Jr. Publisher: The University of Chicago Press, 1962.

Billy Budd, Sailor

(AN INSIDE NARRATIVE)

1

In the time before steamships, or then more frequently than now, a stroller along the docks of any considerable seaport would occasionally have his attention arrested by a group of bronzed mariners, man-of-war's men or merchant sailors in holiday attire, ashore on liberty. In certain instances they would flank, or like a bodyguard quite surround, some superior figure of their own class, moving along with them like Aldebaran among the lesser lights of his constellation. That signal object was the "Handsome Sailor" of the less prosaic time alike of the military and merchant navies. With no perceptible trace of the vainglorious about him, rather with the offhand unaffectedness of natural regality, he seemed to accept the spontaneous homage of his shipmates.

A somewhat remarkable instance recurs to me. In Liverpool, now half a century ago, I saw under the shadow of the great dingy street-wall of Prince's Dock (an obstruction long since removed) a common sailor so intensely black that he must needs have been a native African of the unadulterate blood of Ham —a symmetric figure much above the average height. The two ends of a gay silk handkerchief thrown loose about the neck danced upon the displayed ebony of his chest, in his ears were big hoops of gold, and a Highland bonnet with a tartan band set off his shapely head. It was a hot noon in July; and his face, lustrous with perspiration, beamed with barbaric good humor. In jovial sallies right and left, his white teeth flashing into view, he rollicked along, the center of a company of his shipmates. These were made up of such an assortment of tribes and complexions as would have well fitted them to be marched up by Anacharsis Cloots before the bar of the first French Assembly as Representatives of the Human Race. At each spontaneous tribute rendered by the wayfarers to this black pagod of a fellow—the tribute of a pause and stare, and less frequently an exclamation—the motley retinue showed that they took that sort of pride in the evoker of it which the Assyrian priests doubtless showed for their grand sculptured Bull when the faithful prostrated themselves.

To return. If in some cases a bit of a nautical Murat in setting forth his person ashore, the Handsome Sailor of the period in question evinced nothing of the dandified Billy-be-Damn, an amusing character all but extinct now, but occasionally to be encountered, and in a form yet more amusing than the original, at the tiller of the boats on the tempestuous Erie Canal or, more likely, vaporing in the groggeries along the towpath. Invariably a proficient in his perilous calling, he was also more or less of a mighty boxer or wrestler. It was strength and beauty. Tales of his prowess were recited. Ashore he was the champion; afloat the spokesman; on every suitable occasion always foremost. Close-reefing topsails in a gale, there he was, astride the weather yardarm-end, foot in the Flemish horse as stirrup, both hands tugging at the earring as at a bridle, in very much the attitude of young Alexander curbing the fiery Bucephalus. A superb figure, tossed up as by the horns of Taurus against the thunderous sky, cheerily hallooing to the strenuous file along the spar.

The moral nature was seldom out of keeping with the physical make. Indeed, except as toned by the former, the comeliness and power, always attractive in masculine conjunction, hardly could have drawn the sort of honest homage the Handsome Sailor in some examples received from his less gifted associates.

center of interest

heavenly

Such a cynosure, at least in aspect, and something such too
in nature, though with important variations made apparent as
the story proceeds, was welkin-eyed Billy Budd—or Baby Budd,
as more familiarly, under circumstances hereafter to be given,
he at last came to be called—aged twenty-one, a foretopman of
the British fleet toward the close of the last decade of the eigh-
teenth century. It was not very long prior to the time of the
narration that follows that he had entered the King's service,
having been impressed on the Narrow Seas from a homeward-
bound English merchantman into a seventy-four outward bound,
H.M.S. *Bellipotent;* which ship, as was not unusual in those
hurried days, having been obliged to put to sea short of her
proper complement of men. Plump upon Billy at first sight in
the gangway the boarding officer, Lieutenant Ratcliffe, pounced,
even before the merchantman's crew was formally mustered on
the quarter-deck for his deliberate inspection. And him only he
elected. For whether it was because the other men when ranged
before him showed to ill advantage after Billy, or whether he
had some scruples in view of the merchantman's being rather
short-handed, however it might be, the officer contented himself
with his first spontaneous choice. To the surprise of the ship's
company, though much to the lieutenant's satisfaction, Billy
made no demur. But, indeed, any demur would have been as
idle as the protest of a goldfinch popped into a cage.

Noting this uncomplaining acquiescence, all but cheerful, one
might say, the shipmaster turned a surprised glance of silent
reproach at the sailor. The shipmaster was one of those worthy
mortals found in every vocation, even the humbler ones—the
sort of person whom everybody agrees in calling "a respectable
man." And—nor so strange to report as it may appear to be—
though a ploughman of the troubled waters, lifelong contending
with the intractable elements, there was nothing this honest soul
at heart loved better than simple peace and quiet. For the rest,
he was fifty or thereabouts, a little inclined to corpulence, a

prepossessing face, unwhiskered, and of an agreeable color—a rather full face, humanely intelligent in expression. On a fair day with a fair wind and all going well, a certain musical chime in his voice seemed to be the veritable unobstructed outcome of the innermost man. He had much prudence, much conscientiousness, and there were occasions when these virtues were the cause of overmuch disquietude in him. On a passage, so long as his craft was in any proximity to land, no sleep for Captain Graveling. He took to heart those serious responsibilities not so heavily borne by some shipmasters.

Now while Billy Budd was down in the forecastle getting his kit together, the *Bellipotent*'s lieutenant, burly and bluff, nowise disconcerted by Captain Graveling's omitting to proffer the customary hospitalities on an occasion so unwelcome to him, an omission simply caused by preoccupation of thought, unceremoniously invited himself into the cabin, and also to a flask from the spirit locker, a receptacle which his experienced eye instantly discovered. In fact he was one of those sea dogs in whom all the hardship and peril of naval life in the great prolonged wars of his time never impaired the natural instinct for sensuous enjoyment. His duty he always faithfully did; but duty is sometimes a dry obligation, and he was for irrigating its aridity, whensoever possible, with a fertilizing decoction of strong waters. For the cabin's proprietor there was nothing left but to play the part of the enforced host with whatever grace and alacrity were practicable. As necessary adjuncts to the flask, he silently placed tumbler and water jug before the irrepressible guest. But excusing himself from partaking just then, he dismally watched the unembarrassed officer deliberately diluting his grog a little, then tossing it off in three swallows, pushing the empty tumbler away, yet not so far as to be beyond easy reach, at the same time settling himself in his seat and smacking his lips with high satisfaction, looking straight at the host.

These proceedings over, the master broke the silence; and there lurked a rueful reproach in the tone of his voice: "Lieutenant, you are going to take my best man from me, the jewel of 'em."

"Yes, I know," rejoined the other, immediately drawing back the tumbler preliminary to a replenishing. "Yes, I know. Sorry."

"Beg pardon, but you don't understand, Lieutenant. See here, now. Before I shipped that young fellow, my forecastle was a rat-pit of quarrels. It was black times, I tell you, aboard the *Rights* here. I was worried to that degree my pipe had no comfort for me. But Billy came; and it was like a Catholic priest striking peace in an Irish shindy. Not that he preached to them or said or did anything in particular; but a virtue went out of him, sugaring the sour ones. They took to him like hornets to treacle; all but the buffer of the gang, the big shaggy chap with the fire-red whiskers. He indeed, out of envy, perhaps, of the new-comer, and thinking such a 'sweet and pleasant fellow,' as he mockingly designated him to the others, could hardly have the spirit of a gamecock, must needs bestir himself in trying to get up an ugly row with him. Billy forebore with him and reasoned with him in a pleasant way—he is something like myself, Lieutenant, to whom aught like a quarrel is hateful—but nothing served. So, in the second dogwatch one day, the Red Whiskers in presence of the others, under pretense of showing Billy just whence a sirloin steak was cut—for the fellow had once been a butcher—insultingly gave him a dig under the ribs. Quick as lightning Billy let fly his arm. I dare say he never meant to do quite as much as he did, but anyhow he gave the burly fool a terrible drubbing. It took about half a minute, I should think. And, lord bless you, the lubber was astonished at the celerity. And will you believe it, Lieutenant, the Red Whiskers now really loves Billy—loves him, or is the biggest hypocrite that ever I heard of. But they all love him. Some of 'em do his washing, darn his old trousers for him; the carpenter is at odd times making a pretty little chest of drawers for him. Anybody will do anything for Billy Budd; and it's the happy family here.

But now, Lieutenant, if that young fellow goes—I know how it will be aboard the *Rights*. Not again very soon shall I, coming up from dinner, lean over the capstan smoking a quiet pipe—no, not very soon again, I think. Ay, Lieutenant, you are going to take away the jewel of 'em; you are going to take away my peacemaker!" And with that the good soul had really some ado in checking a rising sob.

"Well," said the lieutenant, who had listened with amused interest to all this and now was waxing merry with his tipple; "well, blessed are the peacemakers, especially the fighting peacemakers. And such are the seventy-four beauties some of which you see poking their noses out of the portholes of yonder warship lying to for me," pointing through the cabin window at the *Bellipotent*. "But courage! Don't look so downhearted, man. Why, I pledge you in advance the royal approbation. Rest assured that His Majesty will be delighted to know that in a time when his hardtack is not sought for by sailors with such avidity as should be, a time also when some shipmasters privily resent the borrowing from them a tar or two for the service; His Majesty, I say, will be delighted to learn that *one* shipmaster at least cheerfully surrenders to the King the flower of his flock, a sailor who with equal loyalty makes no dissent.—But where's my beauty? Ah," looking through the cabin's open door, "here he comes; and, by Jove, lugging along his chest—Apollo with his portmanteau!—My man," stepping out to him, "you can't take that big box aboard a warship. The boxes there are mostly shot boxes. Put your duds in a bag, lad. Boot and saddle for the cavalryman, bag and hammock for the man-of-war's man."

The transfer from chest to bag was made. And, after seeing his man into the cutter and then following him down, the lieutenant pushed off from the *Rights-of-Man*. That was the merchant ship's name, though by her master and crew abbreviated in sailor fashion into the *Rights*. The hardheaded Dundee owner was a staunch admirer of Thomas Paine, whose book in rejoinder to Burke's arraignment of the French Revolution had then been published for some time and had gone everywhere. In christening his vessel after the title of Paine's volume the man of Dundee was something like his contemporary shipowner, Stephen Girard of Philadelphia, whose sympathies, alike with his native land and its liberal philosophers, he evinced by naming his ships after Voltaire, Diderot, and so forth.

But now, when the boat swept under the merchantman's stern, and officer and oarsmen were noting—some bitterly and others with a grin—the name emblazoned there; just then it was that the new recruit jumped up from the bow where the coxswain had directed him to sit, and waving hat to his silent shipmates sorrowfully looking over at him from the taffrail, bade the lads a genial good-bye. Then, making a salutation as to the ship herself, "And good-bye to you too, old *Rights-of-Man*."

"Down, sir!" roared the lieutenant, instantly assuming all the rigor of his rank, though with difficulty repressing a smile.

To be sure, Billy's action was a terrible breach of naval decorum. But in that decorum he had never been instructed; in consideration of which the lieutenant would hardly have been so energetic in reproof but for the concluding farewell to the ship. This he rather took as meant to convey a covert sally on the new recruit's part, a sly slur at impressment in general, and that of himself in especial. And yet, more likely, if satire it was in effect, it was hardly so by intention, for Billy, though happily endowed with the gaiety of high health, youth, and a free heart, was yet by no means of a satirical turn. The will to it and the sinister dexterity were alike wanting. To deal in double meanings and insinuations of any sort was quite foreign to his nature.

As to his enforced enlistment, that he seemed to take pretty much as he was wont to take any vicissitude of weather. Like the animals, though no philosopher, he was, without knowing it, practically a fatalist. And it may be that he rather liked this adventurous turn in his affairs, which promised an opening into novel scenes and martial excitements.

Aboard the *Bellipotent* our merchant sailor was forthwith rated as an able seaman and assigned to the starboard watch of the foretop. He was soon at home in the service, not at all disliked for his unpretentious good looks and a sort of genial happy-go-lucky air. No merrier man in his mess: in marked contrast to certain other individuals included like himself among the impressed portion of the ship's company; for these when not actively employed were sometimes, and more particularly in the last dogwatch when the drawing near of twilight induced revery, apt to fall into a saddish mood which in some partook of sullenness. But they were not so young as our foretopman, and no few of them must have known a hearth of some sort, others may have had wives and children left, too probably, in uncertain circumstances, and hardly any but must have had acknowledged kith and kin, while for Billy, as will shortly be seen, his entire family was practically invested in himself.

2

Though our new-made foretopman was well received in the top and on the gun decks, hardly here was he that cynosure he had previously been among those minor ship's companies of the merchant marine, with which companies only had he hitherto consorted.

He was young; and despite his all but fully developed frame, in aspect looked even younger than he really was, owing to a lingering adolescent expression in the as yet smooth face all but feminine in purity of natural complexion but where, thanks to his seagoing, the lily was quite suppressed and the rose had some ado visibly to flush through the tan.

To one essentially such a novice in the complexities of factitious life, the abrupt transition from his former and simpler sphere to the ampler and more knowing world of a great warship; this might well have abashed him had there been any conceit or vanity in his composition. Among her miscellaneous multitude, the *Bellipotent* mustered several individuals who however inferior in grade were of no common natural stamp, sailors more signally susceptive of that air which continuous martial discipline and repeated presence in battle can in some degree impart even to the average man. As the Handsome Sailor, Billy Budd's position aboard the seventy-four was something analogous to that of a rustic beauty transplanted from the provinces and brought into competition with the highborn dames of the court. But this change of circumstances he scarce noted. As little did he observe that something about him provoked an ambiguous smile in one or two harder faces among the bluejackets. Nor less unaware was he of the peculiar favorable effect his person and demeanor had upon the more intelligent gentlemen of the quarter-deck. Nor could this well have been otherwise. Cast in a mold peculiar to the finest physical examples of those Englishmen in whom the Saxon strain would seem not at all to partake of any Norman or other admixture, he showed in face that humane look of reposeful good nature which the Greek sculptor in some instances gave to his heroic strong man, Hercules. But this again was subtly modified by another and pervasive quality. The ear, small and shapely, the arch of the foot, the curve in mouth and nostril, even the indurated hand dyed to the orange-tawny of the toucan's bill, a hand telling alike of the halyards and tar bucket; but, above all, something in the mobile expression, and every chance attitude and movement, something suggestive of a mother eminently favored by Love and the Graces; all this strangely indicated a lineage in direct contradiction to his lot. The mysteriousness here became less mysterious through a matter of fact elicited when Billy at the capstan was being formally mustered into the service. Asked by the officer, a small, brisk little gentleman as it chanced, among other questions, his place of birth, he replied, "Please, sir, I don't know."

"Don't know where you were born? Who was your father?"

"God knows, sir."

Struck by the straightforward simplicity of these replies, the officer next asked, "Do you know anything about your beginning?"

"No, sir. But I have heard that I was found in a pretty silk-lined basket hanging one morning from the knocker of a good man's door in Bristol."

"*Found,* say you? Well," throwing back his head and looking up and down the new recruit; "well, it turns out to have been a pretty good find. Hope they'll find some more like you, my man; the fleet sadly needs them."

Yes, Billy Budd was a foundling, a presumable by-blow, and, evidently, no ignoble one. Noble descent was as evident in him as in a blood horse.

For the rest, with little or no sharpness of faculty or any trace of the wisdom of the serpent, nor yet quite a dove, he possessed that kind and degree of intelligence going along with the unconventional rectitude of a sound human creature, one to whom not yet has been proffered the questionable apple of knowledge. He was illiterate; he could not read, but he could sing, and like the illiterate nightingale was sometimes the composer of his own song.

Of self-consciousness he seemed to have little or none, or about as much as we may reasonably impute to a dog of Saint Bernard's breed.

Habitually living with the elements and knowing little more of the land than as a beach, or, rather, that portion of the terraqueous globe providentially set apart for dance-houses, doxies, and tapsters, in short what sailors call a "fiddler's green," his simple nature remained unsophisticated by those moral obliquities which are not in every case incompatible with that manufacturable thing known as respectability. But are sailors, frequenters of fiddlers' greens, without vices? No; but less often than with landsmen do their vices, so called, partake of crookedness of heart, seeming less to proceed from viciousness than exuberance of vitality after long constraint: frank manifestations in accordance with natural law. By his original constitution aided by the co-operating influences of his lot, Billy in many respects was little more than a sort of upright barbarian, much such perhaps as Adam presumably might have been ere the urbane Serpent wriggled himself into his company.

And here be it submitted that apparently going to corroborate the doctrine of man's Fall, a doctrine now popularly ignored, it is observable that where certain virtues pristine and unadulterate peculiarly characterize anybody in the external uniform of civilization, they will upon scrutiny seem not to be derived from custom or convention, but rather to be out of keeping with these, as if indeed exceptionally transmitted from a period prior to Cain's city and citified man. The character marked by such qualities has to an unvitiated taste an untampered-with flavor like that of berries, while the man thoroughly civilized, even in a fair specimen of the breed, has to the same moral palate a questionable smack as of a compounded wine. To any stray inheritor of these primitive qualities found, like Caspar Hauser, wandering dazed in any Christian capital of our time, the good-natured poet's famous invocation, near two thousand years ago, of the good rustic out of his latitude in the Rome of the Caesars, still appropriately holds:

> Honest and poor, faithful in word and thought,
> What hath thee, Fabian, to the city brought?

Though our Handsome Sailor had as much of masculine beauty as one can expect anywhere to see; nevertheless, like the beautiful woman in one of Hawthorne's minor tales, there was just one thing amiss in him. No visible blemish indeed, as with the lady; no, but an occasional liability to a vocal defect. Though in the hour of elemental uproar or peril he was everything that a sailor should be, yet under sudden provocation of strong heart-feeling his voice, otherwise singularly musical, as if expressive of the harmony within, was apt to develop an organic hesitancy, in fact more or less of a stutter or even worse. In this particular Billy was a striking instance that the arch interferer, the envious marplot of Eden, still has more or less to do with every human consignment to this planet of Earth. In every case, one way or another he is sure to slip in his little card, as much as to remind us—I too have a hand here.

The avowal of such an imperfection in the Handsome Sailor should be evidence not alone that he is not presented as a conventional hero, but also that the story in which he is the main figure is no romance.

3   Nore Mutiny

At the time of Billy Budd's arbitrary enlistment into the *Bellipotent* that ship was on her way to join the Mediterranean fleet. No long time elapsed before the junction was effected. As one of that fleet the seventy-four participated in its movements, though at times on account of her superior sailing qualities, in the absence of frigates, dispatched on separate duty as a scout and at times on less temporary service. But with all this the story has little concernment, restricted as it is to the inner life of one particular ship and the career of an individual sailor.

It was the summer of 1797. In the April of that year had occurred the commotion at Spithead followed in May by a second and yet more serious outbreak in the fleet at the Nore. The latter is known, and without exaggeration in the epithet, as "the Great Mutiny." It was indeed a demonstration more menacing to England than the contemporary manifestoes and conquering and proselyting armies of the French Directory. To the British Empire the Nore Mutiny was what a strike in the fire brigade would be to London threatened by general arson. In a crisis when the kingdom might well have anticipated the famous signal that some years later published along the naval line of battle what it was that upon occasion England expected of Englishmen; *that* was the time when at the mastheads of the three-deckers and seventy-fours moored in her own roadstead—a fleet the right arm of a Power then all but the sole free conservative one of the Old World—the bluejackets, to be numbered by thousands, ran up with huzzas the British colors with the union and cross wiped out; by that cancellation transmuting the flag of founded law and freedom defined, into the enemy's red meteor of unbridled and unbounded revolt. Reasonable discontent growing out of practical grievances in the fleet had been ignited into irrational combustion as by live cinders blown across the Channel from France in flames.

The event converted into irony for a time those spirited strains of Dibdin—as a song-writer no mean auxiliary to the English government at that European conjuncture—strains celebrating, among other things, the patriotic devotion of the British tar: "And as for my life, 'tis the King's!"

Such an episode in the Island's grand naval story her naval historians naturally abridge; one of them (William James) candidly acknowledging that fain would he pass it over did not "impartiality forbid fastidiousness." And yet his mention is less a narration than a reference, having to do hardly at all with details. Nor are these readily to be found in the libraries. Like some other events in every age befalling states everywhere, including America, the Great Mutiny was of such character that national pride along with views of policy would fain shade it off into the historical background. Such events cannot be ignored, but there is a considerate way of historically treating them. If a well-constituted individual refrains from blazoning aught amiss or calamitous in his family, a nation in the like circumstance may without reproach be equally discreet.

Though after parleyings between government and the ringleaders, and concessions by the former as to some glaring abuses, the first uprising—that at Spithead—with difficulty was put down, or matters for the time pacified; yet at the Nore the unforeseen renewal of insurrection on a yet larger scale, and emphasized in the conferences that ensued by demands deemed by the authorities not only inadmissible but aggressively insolent, indicated—if the Red Flag did not sufficiently do so—what was the spirit animating the men. Final suppression, however, there was; but only made possible perhaps by the unswerving loyalty of the marine corps and a voluntary resumption of loyalty among influential sections of the crews.

To some extent the Nore Mutiny may be regarded as analogous to the distempering irruption of contagious fever in a frame constitutionally sound, and which anon throws it off.

At all events, of these thousands of mutineers were some of the tars who not so very long afterwards—whether wholly prompted thereto by patriotism, or pugnacious instinct, or by both—helped to win a coronet for Nelson at the Nile, and the naval crown of crowns for him at Trafalgar. To the mutineers, those battles and especially Trafalgar were a plenary absolution and a grand one. For all that goes to make up scenic naval display and heroic magnificence in arms, those battles, especially Trafalgar, stand unmatched in human annals.

4   *Admiral Nelson*

In this matter of writing, resolve as one may to keep to the main road, some bypaths have an enticement not readily to be withstood. I am going to err into such a bypath. If the reader will keep me company I shall be glad. At the least, we can promise ourselves that pleasure which is wickedly said to be in sinning, for a literary sin the divergence will be.

Very likely it is no new remark that the inventions of our time have at last brought about a change in sea warfare in degree corresponding to the revolution in all warfare effected by the original introduction from China into Europe of gunpowder. The first European firearm, a clumsy contrivance, was, as is well known, scouted by no few of the knights as a base implement, good enough peradventure for weavers too craven to stand up crossing steel with steel in frank fight. But as ashore knightly valor, though shorn of its blazonry, did not cease with the knights, neither on the seas—though nowadays in encounters there a certain kind of displayed gallantry be fallen out of date as hardly applicable under changed circumstances—did the nobler qualities of such naval magnates as Don John of Austria, Doria, Van Tromp, Jean Bart, the long line of British admirals, and the American Decaturs of 1812 become obsolete with their wooden walls.

Nevertheless, to anybody who can hold the Present at its worth without being inappreciative of the Past, it may be forgiven, if to such an one the solitary old hulk at Portsmouth, Nelson's *Victory,* seems to float there, not alone as the decaying monument of a fame incorruptible, but also as a poetic reproach, softened by its picturesqueness, to the *Monitors* and yet mightier hulls of the European ironclads. And this not altogether because such craft are unsightly, unavoidably lacking the symmetry and grand lines of the old battleships, but equally for other reasons.

There are some, perhaps, who while not altogether inaccessible to that poetic reproach just alluded to, may yet on behalf of the new order be disposed to parry it; and this to the extent of iconoclasm, if need be. For example, prompted by the sight of the star inserted in the *Victory*'s quarter-deck designating the spot where the Great Sailor fell, these martial utilitarians may suggest considerations implying that Nelson's ornate publication of his person in battle was not only unnecessary, but not military, nay, savored of foolhardiness and vanity. They may add, too, that at Trafalgar it was in effect nothing less than a challenge to death; and death came; and that but for his bravado the victorious admiral might possibly have survived the battle, and so, instead of having his sagacious dying injunctions overruled by his immediate successor in command, he himself when the contest was decided might have brought his shattered fleet to anchor, a proceeding which might have averted the deplorable loss of life by shipwreck in the elemental tempest that followed the martial one.

Well, should we set aside the more than disputable point whether for various reasons it was possible to anchor the fleet, then plausibly enough the Benthamites of war may urge the above. But the *might-have-been* is but boggy ground to build on. And, certainly, in foresight as to the larger issue of an encounter, and anxious preparations for it—buoying the deadly way and mapping it out, as at Copenhagen—few commanders have been so painstakingly circumspect as this same reckless declarer of his person in fight.

duty

Personal prudence, even when dictated by quite other than selfish considerations, surely is no special virtue in a military man; while an excessive love of glory, impassioning a less burning impulse, the honest sense of duty, is the first. If the name *Wellington* is not so much of a trumpet to the blood as the simpler name *Nelson,* the reason for this may perhaps be inferred from the above. Alfred in his funeral ode on the victor of Waterloo ventures not to call him the greatest soldier of all time, though in the same ode he invokes Nelson as "the greatest sailor since our world began."

At Trafalgar Nelson on the brink of opening the fight sat down and wrote his last brief will and testament. If under the presentiment of the most magnificent of all victories to be crowned by his own glorious death, a sort of priestly motive led him to dress his person in the jewelled vouchers of his own shining deeds; if thus to have adorned himself for the altar and the sacrifice were indeed vainglory, then affectation and fustian is each more heroic line in the great epics and dramas, since in such lines the poet but embodies in verse those exaltations of sentiment that a nature like Nelson, the opportunity being given, vitalizes into acts.

pretentious speech

5

Yes, the outbreak at the Nore was put down. But not every grievance was redressed. If the contractors, for example, were no longer permitted to ply some practices peculiar to their tribe everywhere, such as providing shoddy cloth, rations not sound or false in the measure; not the less impressment, for one thing, went on. By custom sanctioned for centuries, and judicially maintained by a Lord Chancellor as late as Mansfield, that mode of manning the fleet, a mode now fallen into a sort of abeyance but never formally renounced, it was not practicable to give up in those years. Its abrogation would have crippled the indispensable fleet, one wholly under canvas, no steam power, its innumerable sails and thousands of cannon, everything in short, worked by muscle alone; a fleet the more insatiate in demand for men, because then multiplying its ships of all grades against contingencies present and to come of the convulsed Continent.

Discontent foreran the Two Mutinies, and more or less it lurkingly survived them. Hence it was not unreasonable to apprehend some return of trouble sporadic or general. One instance of such apprehensions: In the same year with this story, Nelson, then Rear Admiral Sir Horatio, being with the fleet off the Spanish coast, was directed by the admiral in command to shift his pennant from the *Captain* to the *Theseus;* and for this reason: that the latter ship having newly arrived on the station from home, where it had taken part in the Great Mutiny, danger was apprehended from the temper of the men; and it was thought that an officer like Nelson was the one, not indeed to terrorize the crew into base subjection, but to win them, by force of his mere presence and heroic personality, back to an allegiance if not as enthusiastic as his own yet as true.

So it was that for a time, on more than one quarter-deck, anxiety did exist. At sea, precautionary vigilance was strained against relapse. At short notice an engagement might come on. When it did, the lieutenants assigned to batteries felt it incumbent on them, in some instances, to stand with drawn swords behind the men working the guns.

6

But on board the seventy-four in which Billy now swung his hammock, very little in the manner of the men and nothing obvious in the demeanor of the officers would have suggested to an ordinary observer that the Great Mutiny was a recent event. In their general bearing and conduct the commissioned officers of a warship naturally take their tone from the commander, that is if he have that ascendancy of character that ought to be his.

Captain the Honorable Edward Fairfax Vere, to give his full title, was a bachelor of forty or thereabouts, a sailor of distinction even in a time prolific of renowned seamen. Though allied to the higher nobility, his advancement had not been altogether owing to influences connected with that circumstance. He had seen much service, been in various engagements, always acquitting himself as an officer mindful of the welfare of his men, but never tolerating an infraction of discipline; thoroughly versed in the science of his profession, and intrepid to the verge of temerity, though never injudiciously so. For his gallantry in the West Indian waters as flag lieutenant under Rodney in that admiral's crowning victory over De Grasse, he was made a post captain.

Ashore, in the garb of a civilian, scarce anyone would have taken him for a sailor, more especially that he never garnished unprofessional talk with nautical terms, and grave in his bearing, evinced little appreciation of mere humor. It was not out of keeping with these traits that on a passage when nothing demanded his paramount action, he was the most undemonstrative of men. Any landsman observing this gentleman not conspicuous by his stature and wearing no pronounced insignia, emerging from his cabin to the open deck, and noting the silent deference

of the officers retiring to leeward, might have taken him for the
King's guest, a civilian aboard the King's ship, some highly
honorable discreet envoy on his way to an important post. But
in fact this unobtrusiveness of demeanor may have proceeded
from a certain unaffected modesty of manhood sometimes accompanying a resolute nature, a modesty evinced at all times
not calling for pronounced action, which shown in any rank of
life suggests a virtue aristocratic in kind. As with some others
engaged in various departments of the world's more heroic ac-
tivities, Captain Vere though practical enough upon occasion
would at times betray a certain dreaminess of mood. Standing
alone on the weather side of the quarter-deck, one hand holding
by the rigging, he would absently gaze off at the blank sea. At
the presentation to him then of some minor matter interrupting
the current of his thoughts, he would show more or less iras-
cibility; but instantly he would control it.

In the navy he was popularly known by the appellation "Starry
Vere." How such a designation happened to fall upon one who
whatever his sterling qualities was without any brilliant ones,
was in this wise: A favorite kinsman, Lord Denton, a freehearted
fellow, had been the first to meet and congratulate him upon
his return to England from his West Indian cruise; and but the
day previous turning over a copy of Andrew Marvell's poems
had lighted, not for the first time, however, upon the lines
entitled "Appleton House," the name of one of the seats of
their common ancestor, a hero in the German wars of the sev-
enteenth century, in which poem occur the lines:

> This 'tis to have been from the first
> In a domestic heaven nursed,
> Under the discipline severe
> Of Fairfax and the starry Vere.

And so, upon embracing his cousin fresh from Rodney's great
victory wherein he had played so gallant a part, brimming over

with just family pride in the sailor of their house, he exuberantly exclaimed, "Give ye joy, Ed; give ye joy, my starry Vere!" This got currency, and the novel prefix serving in familiar parlance readily to distinguish the *Bellipotent*'s captain from another Vere his senior, a distant relative, an officer of like rank in the navy, it remained permanently attached to the surname.

7

In view of the part that the commander of the *Bellipotent* plays in scenes shortly to follow, it may be well to fill out that sketch of him outlined in the previous chapter.

Aside from his qualities as a sea officer Captain Vere was an exceptional character. Unlike no few of England's renowned sailors, long and arduous service with signal devotion to it had not resulted in absorbing and *salting* the entire man. He had a marked leaning toward everything intellectual. He loved books, never going to sea without a newly replenished library, compact but of the best. The isolated leisure, in some cases so wearisome, falling at intervals to commanders even during a war cruise, never was tedious to Captain Vere. With nothing of that literary taste which less heeds the thing conveyed than the vehicle, his bias was toward those books to which every serious mind of superior order occupying any active post of authority in the world naturally inclines: books treating of actual men and events no matter of what era—history, biography, and unconventional writers like Montaigne, who, free from cant and convention, honestly and in the spirit of common sense philosophize upon realities. In this line of reading he found confirmation of his own more reserved thoughts—confirmation which he had vainly sought in social converse, so that as touching most fundamental topics, there had got to be established in him some positive convictions which he forefelt would abide in him essentially unmodified so long as his intelligent part remained unimpaired. In view of the troubled period in which his lot was cast, this was well for him. His settled convictions were as a dike against those invading waters of novel opinion social, political, and otherwise, which carried away as in a torrent no few minds in those days, minds by nature not inferior to his own. While other members of that aristocracy to which by birth he belonged were incensed at the innovators mainly because their theories were inimical to the privileged classes, Captain Vere disinterestedly opposed them not alone because they seemed to him insusceptible of embodiment in lasting institutions, but at war with the peace of the world and the true welfare of mankind.

With minds less stored than his and less earnest, some officers of his rank, with whom at times he would necessarily consort, found him lacking in the companionable quality, a dry and bookish gentleman, as they deemed. Upon any chance withdrawal from their company one would be apt to say to another something like this: "Vere is a noble fellow, Starry Vere. 'Spite the gazettes, Sir Horatio" (meaning him who became Lord Nelson) "is at bottom scarce a better seaman or fighter. But between you and me now, don't you think there is a queer streak of the pedantic running through him? Yes, like the King's yarn in a coil of navy rope?"

Some apparent ground there was for this sort of confidential criticism; since not only did the captain's discourse never fall into the jocosely familiar, but in illustrating of any point touching the stirring personages and events of the time he would be as apt to cite some historic character or incident of antiquity as he would be to cite from the moderns. He seemed unmindful of the circumstance that to his bluff company such remote allusions, however pertinent they might really be, were altogether alien to men whose reading was mainly confined to the journals. But considerateness in such matters is not easy to natures constituted like Captain Vere's. Their honesty prescribes to them directness, sometimes far-reaching like that of a migratory fowl that in its flight never heeds when it crosses a frontier.

8   *Claggert*

The lieutenants and other commissioned gentlemen forming Captain Vere's staff it is not necessary here to particularize, nor needs it to make any mention of any of the warrant officers. But among the petty officers was one who, having much to do with the story, may as well be forthwith introduced. His portrait I essay, but shall never hit it. This was John Claggart, the master-at-arms. But that sea title may to landsmen seem somewhat equivocal. Originally, doubtless, that petty officer's function was the instruction of the men in the use of arms, sword or cutlass. But very long ago, owing to the advance in gunnery making hand-to-hand encounters less frequent and giving to niter and sulphur the pre-eminence over steel, that function ceased; the master-at-arms of a great warship becoming a sort of chief of police charged among other matters with the duty of preserving order on the populous lower gun decks.

Claggart was a man about five-and-thirty, somewhat spare and tall, yet of no ill figure upon the whole. His hand was too small and shapely to have been accustomed to hard toil. The face was a notable one, the features all except the chin cleanly cut as those on a Greek medallion; yet the chin, beardless as Tecumseh's, had something of strange protuberant broadness in its make that recalled the prints of the Reverend Dr. Titus Oates, the historic deponent with the clerical drawl in the time of Charles II and the fraud of the alleged Popish Plot. It served Claggart in his office that his eye could cast a tutoring glance. His brow was of the sort phrenologically associated with more than average intellect; silken jet curls partly clustering over it, making a foil to the pallor below, a pallor tinged with a faint shade of amber akin to the hue of time-tinted marbles of old. This complexion, singularly contrasting with the red or deeply bronzed visages of the sailors, and in part the result of his official seclusion from the sunlight, though it was not exactly displeasing, nevertheless seemed to hint of something defective or abnormal in the constitution and blood. But his general aspect and manner were so suggestive of an education and career incongruous with his naval function that when not actively engaged in it he looked like a man of high quality, social and moral, who for reasons of his own was keeping incog. Nothing was known of his former life. It might be that he was an Englishman; and yet there lurked a bit of accent in his speech suggesting that possibly he was not such by birth, but through naturalization in early childhood. Among certain grizzled sea gossips of the gun decks and forecastle went a rumor perdue that the master-at-arms was a *chevalier* who had volunteered into the King's navy by way of compounding for some mysterious swindle whereof he had been arraigned at the King's Bench. The fact that nobody could substantiate this report was, of course, nothing against its secret currency. Such a rumor once started on the gun decks in reference to almost anyone below the rank of a commissioned officer would, during the period assigned to this narrative, have seemed not altogether wanting in credibility to the tarry old wiseacres of a man-of-war crew. And indeed a man of Claggart's accomplishments, without prior nautical experience entering the navy at mature life, as he did, and necessarily allotted at the start to the lowest grade in it; a man too who never made allusion to his previous life ashore; these were circumstances which in the dearth of exact knowledge as to his true antecedents opened to the invidious a vague field for unfavorable surmise.

But the sailors' dogwatch gossip concerning him derived a vague plausibility from the fact that now for some period the British navy could so little afford to be squeamish in the matter of keeping up the muster rolls, that not only were press gangs notoriously abroad both afloat and ashore, but there was little or no secret about another matter, namely, that the London police were at liberty to capture any able-bodied suspect, any questionable fellow at large, and summarily ship him to the dockyard or fleet. Furthermore, even among voluntary enlistments there were instances where the motive thereto partook neither of patriotic impulse nor yet of a random desire to experience a bit of sea life and martial adventure. Insolvent debtors of minor grade, together with the promiscuous lame ducks of morality, found in the navy a convenient and secure refuge, secure because, once enlisted aboard a King's ship, they were as much in sanctuary as the transgressor of the Middle Ages harboring himself under the shadow of the altar. Such sanctioned irregularities, which for obvious reasons the government would hardly think to parade at the time and which consequently, and as affecting the least influential class of mankind, have all but dropped into oblivion, lend color to something for the truth whereof I do not vouch, and hence have some scruple in stating; something I remember having seen in print though the book I cannot recall; but the same thing was personally communicated to me now more than forty years ago by an old pensioner in a cocked hat with whom I had a most interesting talk on the terrace at Greenwich, a Baltimore Negro, a Trafalgar man. It was to this effect: In the case of a warship short of hands whose speedy sailing was imperative, the deficient quota, in lack of any other way of making it good, would be eked out by drafts culled direct from the jails. For reasons previously suggested it would not perhaps be easy at the present day directly to prove or disprove the allegation. But allowed as a verity, how significant would it be of England's straits at the time confronted by those wars which like a flight of harpies rose shrieking from the din and dust of the fallen Bastille. That era appears measurably clear to us who look back at it, and but read of it. But to the grandfathers of us graybeards, the more thoughtful of them, the genius of it presented an aspect like that of Camoëns' Spirit of the Cape, an eclipsing menace mysterious and prodigious. Not America was exempt from apprehension. At the height of Napoleon's unexampled conquests, there were Americans who had fought at Bunker Hill who looked forward to the possibility that the Atlantic might prove no barrier against the ultimate schemes of this French portentous upstart from the revolutionary chaos who seemed in act of fulfilling judgment prefigured in the Apocalypse.

But the less credence was to be given to the gun-deck talk touching Claggart, seeing that no man holding his office in a man-of-war can ever hope to be popular with the crew. Besides, in derogatory comments upon anyone against whom they have a grudge, or for any reason or no reason mislike, sailors are much like landsmen: they are apt to exaggerate or romance it.

About as much was really known to the *Bellipotent*'s tars of the master-at-arms' career before entering the service as an astronomer knows about a comet's travels prior to its first observable appearance in the sky. The verdict of the sea quidnuncs *nosy ones* has been cited only by way of showing what sort of moral impression the man made upon rude uncultivated natures whose conceptions of human wickedness were necessarily of the narrowest, limited to ideas of vulgar rascality—a thief among the swinging hammocks during a night watch, or the man-brokers and land-sharks of the seaports.

It was no gossip, however, but fact that though, as before hinted, Claggart upon his entrance into the navy was, as a novice, assigned to the least honorable section of a man-of-war's crew, embracing the drudgery, he did not long remain there. The superior capacity he immediately evinced, his constitutional sobriety, an ingratiating deference to superiors, together with a peculiar ferreting genius manifested on a singular occasion; all this, capped by a certain austere patriotism, abruptly advanced him to the position of master-at-arms.

Of this maritime chief of police the ship's corporals, so called, were the immediate subordinates, and compliant ones; and this, as is to be noted in some business departments ashore, almost to a degree inconsistent with entire moral volition. His place put various converging wires of underground influence under the chief's control, capable when astutely worked through his understrappers of operating to the mysterious discomfort, if nothing worse, of any of the sea commonalty.

9

Life in the foretop well agreed with Billy Budd. There, when not actually engaged on the yards yet higher aloft, the topmen, who as such had been picked out for youth and activity, constituted an aerial club lounging at ease against the smaller stun'sails rolled up into cushions, spinning yarns like the lazy gods, and frequently amused with what was going on in the busy world of the decks below. No wonder then that a young fellow of Billy's disposition was well content in such society. Giving no cause of offense to anybody, he was always alert at a call. So in the merchant service it had been with him. But now such a punctiliousness in duty was shown that his topmates would sometimes good-naturedly laugh at him for it. This heightened alacrity had its cause, namely, the impression made upon him by the first formal gangway-punishment he had ever witnessed, which befell the day following his impressment. It had been incurred by a little fellow, young, a novice afterguardsman absent from his assigned post when the ship was being put about; a dereliction resulting in a rather serious hitch to that maneuver, one demanding instantaneous promptitude in letting go and making fast. When Billy saw the culprit's naked back under the scourge, gridironed with red welts and worse, when he marked the dire expression in the liberated man's face as with his woolen shirt flung over him by the executioner he rushed forward from the spot to bury himself in the crowd, Billy was horrified. He resolved that never through remissness would he make himself liable to such a visitation or do or omit aught that might merit even verbal reproof. What then was his surprise and concern when ultimately he found himself getting into petty trouble occasionally about such matters as the stowage of his bag or something amiss in his hammock, matters under the police oversight of the ship's corporals of the lower decks, and which brought down on him a vague threat from one of them.

So heedful in all things as he was, how could this be? He could not understand it, and it more than vexed him. When he spoke to his young topmates about it they were either lightly incredulous or found something comical in his unconcealed anxiety. "Is it your bag, Billy?" said one. "Well, sew yourself up in it, bully boy, and then you'll be sure to know if anybody meddles with it."

Now there was a veteran aboard who because his years began to disqualify him for more active work had been recently assigned duty as mainmastman in his watch, looking to the gear belayed at the rail roundabout that great spar near the deck. At off-times the foretopman had picked up some acquaintance with him, and now in his trouble it occurred to him that he might be the sort of person to go to for wise counsel. He was an old Dansker long anglicized in the service, of few words, many wrinkles, and some honorable scars. His wizened face, time-tinted and weather-stained to the complexion of an antique parchment, was here and there peppered blue by the chance explosion of a gun cartridge in action.

He was an *Agamemnon* man, some two years prior to the time of this story having served under Nelson when still captain in that ship immortal in naval memory, which dismantled and in part broken up to her bare ribs is seen a grand skeleton in Haden's etching. As one of a boarding party from the *Agamemnon* he had received a cut slantwise along one temple and cheek leaving a long pale scar like a streak of dawn's light falling athwart the dark visage. It was on account of that scar and the affair in which it was known that he had received it, as well as from his blue-peppered complexion, that the Dansker went

wisdom

among the *Bellipotent*'s crew by the name of "Board-Her-in-
the-Smoke."

Now the first time that his small weasel eyes happened to
light on Billy Budd, a certain grim internal merriment set all
his ancient wrinkles into antic play. Was it that his eccentric
unsentimental old sapience, primitive in its kind, saw or thought
it saw something which in contrast with the warship's environ-
ment looked oddly incongruous in the Handsome Sailor? But
after slyly studying him at intervals, the old Merlin's equivocal
merriment was modified; for now when the twain would meet,
it would start in his face a quizzing sort of look, but it would
be but momentary and sometimes replaced by an expression of
speculative query as to what might eventually befall a nature
like that, dropped into a world not without some mantraps and
against whose subtleties simple courage lacking experience and
address, and without any touch of defensive ugliness, is of little
avail; and where such innocence as man is capable of does yet
in a moral emergency not always sharpen the faculties or en-
lighten the will.

bear

However it was, the Dansker in his ascetic way rather took
to Billy. Nor was this only because of a certain philosophic
interest in such a character. There was another cause. While the
old man's eccentricities, sometimes bordering on the ursine,
repelled the juniors, Billy, undeterred thereby, revering him as
a salt hero, would make advances, never passing the old *Agamemnon* man without a salutation marked by that respect which
is seldom lost on the aged, however crabbed at times or whatever
their station in life.

not understood

There was a vein of dry humor, or what not, in the mastman;
and, whether in freak of patriarchal irony touching Billy's youth
and athletic frame, or for some other and more recondite reason,
from the first in addressing him he always substituted *Baby* for
Billy, the Dansker in fact being the originator of the name by
which the foretopman eventually became known aboard ship.

Well then, in his mysterious little difficulty going in quest of the wrinkled one, Billy found him off duty in a dogwatch ruminating by himself, seated on a shot box of the upper gun deck, now and then surveying with a somewhat cynical regard certain of the more swaggering promenaders there. Billy recounted his trouble, again wondering how it all happened. The salt seer attentively listened, accompanying the foretopman's recital with queer twitchings of his wrinkles and problematical little sparkles of his small ferret eyes. Making an end of his story, the foretopman asked, "And now, Dansker, do tell me what you think of it."

The old man, shoving up the front of his tarpaulin and deliberately rubbing the long slant scar at the point where it entered the thin hair, laconically said, "Baby Budd, *Jemmy Legs*" (meaning the master-at-arms) "is down on you." *heavenly*

"*Jemmy Legs!*" ejaculated Billy, his welkin eyes expanding. "What for? Why, he calls me 'the sweet and pleasant young fellow,' they tell me."

"Does he so?" grinned the grizzled one; then said, "Ay, Baby lad, a sweet voice has Jemmy Legs."

"No, not always. But to me he has. I seldom pass him but there comes a pleasant word."

"And that's because he's down upon you, Baby Budd."

Such reiteration, along with the manner of it, incomprehensible to a novice, disturbed Billy almost as much as the mystery for which he had sought explanation. Something less unpleasingly oracular he tried to extract; but the old sea Chiron, thinking perhaps that for the nonce he had sufficiently instructed his young Achilles, pursed his lips, gathered all his wrinkles together, and would commit himself to nothing further. *Present*

Years, and those experiences which befall certain shrewder men subordinated lifelong to the will of superiors, all this had developed in the Dansker the pithy guarded cynicism that was his leading characteristic.

10

The next day an incident served to confirm Billy Budd in his incredulity as to the Dansker's strange summing up of the case submitted. The ship at noon, going large before the wind, was rolling on her course, and he below at dinner and engaged in some sportful talk with the members of his mess, chanced in a sudden lurch to spill the entire contents of his soup pan upon the new-scrubbed deck. Claggart, the master-at-arms, official rattan in hand, happened to be passing along the battery in a bay of which the mess was lodged, and the greasy liquid streamed just across his path. Stepping over it, he was proceeding on his way without comment, since the matter was nothing to take notice of under the circumstances, when he happened to observe who it was that had done the spilling. His countenance changed. Pausing, he was about to ejaculate something hasty at the sailor, but checked himself, and pointing down to the streaming soup, playfully tapped him from behind with his rattan, saying in a low musical voice peculiar to him at times, "Handsomely done, my lad! And handsome is as handsome did it, too!" And with that passed on. Not noted by Billy, as not coming within his view, was the involuntary smile, or rather grimace, that accompanied Claggart's equivocal words. Aridly it drew down the thin corners of his shapely mouth. But everybody taking his remark as meant for humorous, and at which therefore as coming from a superior they were bound to laugh "with counterfeited glee," acted accordingly; and Billy, tickled, it may be, by the allusion to his being the Handsome Sailor, merrily joined in; then addressing his messmates exclaimed, "There now, who says that Jemmy Legs is down on me!"

"And who said he was, Beauty?" demanded one Donald with some surprise. Whereat the foretopman looked a little foolish, recalling that it was only one person, Board-Her-in-the-Smoke, who had suggested what to him was the smoky idea that this master-at-arms was in any peculiar way hostile to him. Meantime that functionary, resuming his path, must have momentarily worn some expression less guarded than that of the bitter smile, usurping the face from the heart—some distorting expression perhaps, for a drummer-boy heedlessly frolicking along from the opposite direction and chancing to come into light collision with his person was strangely disconcerted by his aspect. Nor was the impression lessened when the official, impetuously giving him a sharp cut with the rattan, vehemently exclaimed, "Look where you go!"

11

What was the matter with the master-at-arms? And, be the matter what it might, how could it have direct relation to Billy Budd, with whom prior to the affair of the spilled soup he had never come into any special contact official or otherwise? What indeed could the trouble have to do with one so little inclined to give offense as the merchant-ship's "peacemaker," even him who in Claggart's own phrase was "the sweet and pleasant young fellow"? Yes, why should Jemmy Legs, to borrow the Dansker's expression, be "down" on the Handsome Sailor? But, at heart and not for nothing, as the late chance encounter may indicate to the discerning, down on him, secretly down on him, he assuredly was.

Now to invent something touching the more private career of Claggart, something involving Billy Budd, of which something the latter should be wholly ignorant, some romantic incident implying that Claggart's knowledge of the young bluejacket began at some period anterior to catching sight of him on board the seventy-four—all this, not so difficult to do, might avail in a way more or less interesting to account for whatever of enigma may appear to lurk in the case. But in fact there was nothing of the sort. And yet the cause necessarily to be assumed as the sole one assignable is in its very realism as much charged with that prime element of Radcliffian romance, the mysterious, as any that the ingenuity of the author of *The Mysteries of Udolpho* could devise. For what can more partake of the mysterious than an antipathy spontaneous and profound such as is evoked in certain exceptional mortals by the mere aspect of some other mortal, however harmless he may be, if not called forth by this very harmlessness itself?

Now there can exist no irritating juxtaposition of dissimilar personalities comparable to that which is possible aboard a great warship fully manned and at sea. There, every day among all ranks, almost every man comes into more or less of contact with almost every other man. Wholly there to avoid even the sight of an aggravating object one must needs give it Jonah's toss or jump overboard himself. Imagine how all this might eventually operate on some peculiar human creature the direct reverse of a saint!

But for the adequate comprehending of Claggart by a normal nature these hints are insufficient. To pass from a normal nature to him one must cross "the deadly space between." And this is best done by indirection.

Long ago an honest scholar, my senior, said to me in reference to one who like himself is now no more, a man so unimpeachably respectable that against him nothing was ever openly said though among the few something was whispered, "Yes, X——is a nut not to be cracked by the tap of a lady's fan. You are aware that I am the adherent of no organized religion, much less of any philosophy built into a system. Well, for all that, I think that to try and get into X——, enter his labyrinth and get out again, without a clue derived from some source other than what is known as 'knowledge of the world'—that were hardly possible, at least for me."

"Why," said I, "X——, however singular a study to some, is yet human, and knowledge of the world assuredly implies the knowledge of human nature, and in most of its varieties."

"Yes, but a superficial knowledge of it, serving ordinary purposes. But for anything deeper, I am not certain whether to know the world and to know human nature be not two distinct branches of knowledge, which while they may coexist in the same heart, yet either may exist with little or nothing of the other. Nay, in an average man of the world, his constant rubbing with it blunts that finer spiritual insight indispensable to the understanding of the essential in certain exceptional characters, whether evil ones or good. In a matter of some importance I have seen a girl wind an old lawyer about her little finger. Nor was it the dotage of senile love. Nothing of the sort. But he knew law better than he knew the girl's heart. Coke and Blackstone hardly shed so much light into obscure spiritual places as the Hebrew prophets. And who were they? Mostly recluses.''

At the time, my inexperience was such that I did not quite see the drift of all this. It may be that I see it now. And, indeed, if that lexicon which is based on Holy Writ were any longer popular, one might with less difficulty define and denominate certain phenomenal men. As it is, one must turn to some authority not liable to the charge of being tinctured with the biblical element.

In a list of definitions included in the authentic translation of Plato, a list attributed to him, occurs this: "Natural Depravity: a depravity according to nature," a definition which, though savoring of Calvinism, by no means involves Calvin's dogma as to total mankind. Evidently its intent makes it applicable but to individuals. Not many are the examples of this depravity which the gallows and jail supply. At any rate, for notable instances, since these have no vulgar alloy of the brute in them, but invariably are dominated by intellectuality, one must go elsewhere. Civilization, especially if of the austerer sort, is auspicious to it. It folds itself in the mantle of respectability. It has its certain negative virtues serving as silent auxiliaries. It never allows wine to get within its guard. It is not going too far to say that it is without vices or small sins. There is a phenomenal pride in it that excludes them. It is never mercenary or avaricious.

In short, the depravity here meant partakes nothing of the sordid or sensual. It is serious, but free from acerbity. Though no flatterer of mankind it never speaks ill of it.

But the thing which in eminent instances signalizes so exceptional a nature is this: Though the man's even temper and discreet bearing would seem to intimate a mind peculiarly subject to the law of reason, not the less in heart he would seem to riot in complete exemption from that law, having apparently little to do with reason further than to employ it as an ambidexter implement for effecting the irrational. That is to say: Toward the accomplishment of an aim which in wantonness of atrocity would seem to partake of the insane, he will direct a cool judgment sagacious and sound. These men are madmen, and of the most dangerous sort, for their lunacy is not continuous, but occasional, evoked by some special object; it is protectively secretive, which is as much as to say it is self-contained, so that when, moreover, most active it is to the average mind not distinguishable from sanity, and for the reason above suggested: that whatever its aims may be—and the aim is never declared—the method and the outward proceeding are always perfectly rational.

Now something such an one was Claggart, in whom was the mania of an evil nature, not engendered by vicious training or corrupting books or licentious living, but born with him and innate, in short "a depravity according to nature."

Dark sayings are these, some will say. But why? Is it because they somewhat savor of Holy Writ in its phrase "mystery of iniquity"? If they do, such savor was far enough from being intended, for little will it commend these pages to many a reader of today.

The point of the present story turning on the hidden nature of the master-at-arms has necessitated this chapter. With an added hint or two in connection with the incident at the mess, the resumed narrative must be left to vindicate, as it may, its own credibility.

12

That Claggart's figure was not amiss, and his face, save the chin, well molded, has already been said. Of these favorable points he seemed not insensible, for he was not only neat but careful in his dress. But the form of Billy Budd was heroic; and if his face was without the intellectual look of the pallid Claggart's, not the less was it lit, like his, from within, though from a different source. The bonfire in his heart made luminous the rose-tan in his cheek.

In view of the marked contrast between the persons of the twain, it is more than probable that when the master-at-arms in the scene last given applied to the sailor the proverb "Handsome is as handsome does," he there let escape an ironic inkling, not caught by the young sailors who heard it, as to what it was that had first moved him against Billy, namely, his significant personal beauty.

Now envy and antipathy, passions irreconcilable in reason, nevertheless in fact may spring conjoined like Chang and Eng in one birth. Is Envy then such a monster? Well, though many an arraigned mortal has in hopes of mitigated penalty pleaded guilty to horrible actions, did ever anybody seriously confess to envy? Something there is in it universally felt to be more shameful than even felonious crime. And not only does everybody disown it, but the better sort are inclined to incredulity when it is in earnest imputed to an intelligent man. But since its lodgment is in the heart not the brain, no degree of intellect supplies a guarantee against it. But Claggart's was no vulgar form of the passion. Nor, as directed toward Billy Budd, did it partake of that streak of apprehensive jealousy that marred Saul's visage perturbedly brooding on the comely young David. Claggart's envy struck deeper. If askance he eyed the good looks, cheery health, and frank enjoyment of young life in Billy Budd, it was because these went along with a nature that, as Claggart magnetically felt, had in its simplicity never willed malice or experienced the reactionary bite of that serpent. To him, the spirit lodged within Billy, and looking out from his welkin eyes as from windows, that ineffability it was which made the dimple in his dyed cheek, suppled his joints, and dancing in his yellow curls made him pre-eminently the Handsome Sailor. One person excepted, the master-at-arms was perhaps the only man in the ship intellectually capable of adequately appreciating the moral phenomenon presented in Billy Budd. And the insight but intensified his passion, which assuming various secret forms within him, at times assumed that of cynic disdain, disdain of innocence—to be nothing more than innocent! Yet in an aesthetic way he saw the charm of it, the courageous free-and-easy temper of it, and fain would have shared it, but he despaired of it.

With no power to annul the elemental evil in him, though readily enough he could hide it; apprehending the good, but powerless to be it; a nature like Claggart's, surcharged with energy as such natures almost invariably are, what recourse is left to it but to recoil upon itself and, like the scorpion for which the Creator alone is responsible, act out to the end the part allotted it.

13

Passion, and passion in its profoundest, is not a thing demanding a palatial stage whereon to play its part. Down among the groundlings, among the beggars and rakers of the garbage, profound passion is enacted. And the circumstances that provoke it, however trivial or mean, are no measure of its power. In the present instance the stage is a scrubbed gun deck, and one of the external provocations a man-of-war's man's spilled soup.

Now when the master-at-arms noticed whence came that greasy fluid streaming before his feet, he must have taken it—to some extent wilfully, perhaps—not for the mere accident it assuredly was, but for the sly escape of a spontaneous feeling on Billy's part more or less answering to the antipathy on his own. In effect a foolish demonstration, he must have thought, and very harmless, like the futile kick of a heifer, which yet were the heifer a shod stallion would not be so harmless. Even so was it that into the gall of Claggart's envy he infused the vitriol of his contempt. But the incident confirmed to him certain telltale reports purveyed to his ear by "Squeak," one of his more cunning corporals, a grizzled little man, so nicknamed by the sailors on account of his squeaky voice and sharp visage ferreting about the dark corners of the lower decks after interlopers, satirically suggesting to them the idea of a rat in a cellar.

From his chief's employing him as an implicit tool in laying little traps for the worriment of the foretopman—for it was from the master-at-arms that the petty persecutions heretofore adverted to had proceeded—the corporal, having naturally enough concluded that his master could have no love for the sailor, made it his business, faithful understrapper that he was, to foment the ill blood by perverting to his chief certain innocent frolics of the good-natured foretopman, besides inventing for his mouth sundry contumelious epithets he claimed to have overheard him let fall. The master-at-arms never suspected the veracity of these reports, more especially as to the epithets, for he well knew how secretly unpopular may become a master-at-arms, at least a master-at-arms of those days, zealous in his function, and how the bluejackets shoot at him in private their raillery and wit; the nickname by which he goes among them (Jemmy Legs) implying under the form of merriment their cherished disrespect and dislike. But in view of the greediness of hate for pabulum it hardly needed a purveyor to feed Claggart's passion.

An uncommon prudence is habitual with the subtler depravity, for it has everything to hide. And in case of an injury but suspected, its secretiveness voluntarily cuts it off from enlightenment or disillusion; and, not unreluctantly, action is taken upon surmise as upon certainty. And the retaliation is apt to be in monstrous disproportion to the supposed offense; for when in anybody was revenge in its exactions aught else but an inordinate usurer? But how with Claggart's conscience? For though consciences are unlike as foreheads, every intelligence, not excluding the scriptural devils who "believe and tremble," has one. But Claggart's conscience being but the lawyer to his will, made ogres of trifles, probably arguing that the motive imputed to Billy in spilling the soup just when he did, together with the epithets alleged, these, if nothing more, made a strong case against him; nay, justified animosity into a sort of retributive righteousness. The Pharisee is the Guy Fawkes prowling in the hid chambers underlying some natures like Claggart's. And they can really form no conception of an unreciprocated malice. Probably the master-at-arms' clandestine persecution of Billy was started to try the temper of the man; but it had not developed any quality in him that enmity could make official use of or even pervert into plausible self-justification; so that the occurrence at the mess, petty if it were, was a welcome one to that peculiar conscience assigned to be the private mentor of Claggart; and, for the rest, not improbably it put him upon new experiments.

14

Not many days after the last incident narrated, something befell Billy Budd that more graveled him than aught that had previously occurred.

It was a warm night for the latitude; and the foretopman, whose watch at the time was properly below, was dozing on the uppermost deck whither he had ascended from his hot hammock, one of hundreds suspended so closely wedged together over a lower gun deck that there was little or no swing to them. He lay as in the shadow of a hillside, stretched under the lee of the booms, a piled ridge of spare spars amidships between foremast and mainmast among which the ship's largest boat, the launch, was stowed. Alongside of three other slumberers from below, he lay near that end of the booms which approaches the foremast; his station aloft on duty as a foretopman being just over the deck-station of the forecastlemen, entitling him according to usage to make himself more or less at home in that neighborhood.

Presently he was stirred into semiconsciousness by somebody, who must have previously sounded the sleep of the others, touching his shoulder, and then, as the foretopman raised his head, breathing into his ear in a quick whisper, "Slip into the lee forechains, Billy; there is something in the wind. Don't speak. Quick, I will meet you there," and disappearing.

Now Billy, like sundry other essentially good-natured ones, had some of the weaknesses inseparable from essential good nature; and among these was a reluctance, almost an incapacity of plumply saying *no* to an abrupt proposition not obviously absurd on the face of it, nor obviously unfriendly, nor iniquitous. And being of warm blood, he had not the phlegm tacitly to negative any proposition by unresponsive inaction. Like his sense of fear, his apprehension as to aught outside of the honest and natural was seldom very quick. Besides, upon the present occasion, the drowse from his sleep still hung upon him.

However it was, he mechanically rose and, sleepily wondering what could be in the wind, betook himself to the designated place, a narrow platform, one of six, outside of the high bulwarks and screened by the great deadeyes and multiple columned lanyards of the shrouds and backstays; and, in a great warship of that time, of dimensions commensurate to the hull's magnitude; a tarry balcony in short, overhanging the sea, and so secluded that one mariner of the *Bellipotent,* a nonconformist old tar of a serious turn, made it even in daytime his private oratory.

In this retired nook the stranger soon joined Billy Budd. There was no moon as yet; a haze obscured the starlight. He could not distinctly see the stranger's face. Yet from something in the outline and carriage, Billy took him, and correctly, for one of the afterguard.

"Hist! Billy," said the man, in the same quick cautionary whisper as before. "You were impressed, weren't you? Well, so was I"; and he paused, as to mark the effect. But Billy, not knowing exactly what to make of this, said nothing. Then the other: "We are not the only impressed ones, Billy. There's a gang of us. — Couldn't you — help — at a pinch?"

"What do you mean?" demanded Billy, here thoroughly shaking off his drowse.

"Hist, hist!" the hurried whisper now growing husky. "See here," and the man held up two small objects faintly twinkling in the nightlight; "see, they are yours, Billy, if you'll only —"

But Billy broke in, and in his resentful eagerness to deliver himself his vocal infirmity somewhat intruded. "D–d–damme, I don't know what you are d–d–driving at, or what you mean, but you had better g–g–go where you belong!" For the moment the fellow, as confounded, did not stir; and Billy, springing to his feet, said, "If you d–don't start, I'll t–t–toss you back over the r–rail!" There was no mistaking this, and the mysterious emissary decamped, disappearing in the direction of the main-mast in the shadow of the booms.

"Hallo, what's the matter?" here came growling from a fore-castleman awakened from his deck-doze by Billy's raised voice. And as the foretopman reappeared and was recognized by him: "Ah, Beauty, is it you? Well, something must have been the matter, for you st–st–stuttered."

"Oh," rejoined Billy, now mastering the impediment, "I found an afterguardsman in our part of the ship here, and I bid him be off where he belongs."

"And is that all you did about it, Foretopman?" gruffly demanded another, an irascible old fellow of brick-colored visage and hair who was known to his associate forecastlemen as "Red Pepper." "Such sneaks I should like to marry to the gunner's daughter!"—by that expression meaning that he would like to subject them to disciplinary castigation over a gun.

However, Billy's rendering of the matter satisfactorily accounted to these inquirers for the brief commotion, since of all the sections of a ship's company the forecastlemen, veterans for the most part and bigoted in their sea prejudices, are the most jealous in resenting territorial encroachments, especially on the part of any of the afterguard, of whom they have but a sorry opinion—chiefly landsmen, never going aloft except to reef or furl the mainsail, and in no wise competent to handle a marlinspike or turn in a deadeye, say.

15

This incident sorely puzzled Billy Budd. It was an entirely new experience, the first time in his life that he had ever been personally approached in underhand intriguing fashion. Prior to this encounter he had known nothing of the afterguardsman, the two men being stationed wide apart, one forward and aloft during his watch, the other on deck and aft.

What could it mean? And could they really be guineas, those two glittering objects the interloper had held up to his (Billy's) eyes? Where could the fellow get guineas? Why, even spare buttons are not so plentiful at sea. The more he turned the matter over, the more he was nonplussed, and made uneasy and discomfited. In his disgustful recoil from an overture which, though he but ill comprehended, he instinctively knew must involve evil of some sort, Billy Budd was like a young horse fresh from the pasture suddenly inhaling a vile whiff from some chemical factory, and by repeated snortings trying to get it out of his nostrils and lungs. This frame of mind barred all desire of holding further parley with the fellow, even were it but for the purpose of gaining some enlightenment as to his design in approaching him. And yet he was not without natural curiosity to see how such a visitor in the dark would look in broad day.

He espied him the following afternoon in his first dogwatch below, one of the smokers on that forward part of the upper gun deck allotted to the pipe. He recognized him by his general cut and build more than by his round freckled face and glassy eyes of pale blue, veiled with lashes all but white. And yet Billy was a bit uncertain whether indeed it were he—yonder chap about his own age chatting and laughing in freehearted way, leaning against a gun; a genial young fellow enough to look at, and something of a rattlebrain, to all appearance. Rather chubby too for a sailor, even an afterguardsman. In short, the last man in the world, one would think, to be overburdened with thoughts, especially those perilous thoughts that must needs belong to a conspirator in any serious project, or even to the underling of such a conspirator.

Although Billy was not aware of it, the fellow, with a side-long watchful glance, had perceived Billy first, and then noting that Billy was looking at him, thereupon nodded a familiar sort of friendly recognition as to an old acquaintance, without interrupting the talk he was engaged in with the group of smokers. A day or two afterwards, chancing in the evening promenade on a gun deck to pass Billy, he offered a flying word of good-fellowship, as it were, which by its unexpectedness, and equivocalness under the circumstances, so embarrassed Billy that he knew not how to respond to it, and let it go unnoticed.

Billy was now left more at a loss than before. The ineffectual speculations into which he was led were so disturbingly alien to him that he did his best to smother them. It never entered his mind that here was a matter which, from its extreme questionableness, it was his duty as a loyal bluejacket to report in the proper quarter. And, probably, had such a step been suggested to him, he would have been deterred from taking it by the thought, one of novice magnanimity, that it would savor overmuch of the dirty work of a telltale. He kept the thing to himself. Yet upon one occasion he could not forbear a little disburdening himself to the old Dansker, tempted thereto perhaps by the influence of a balmy night when the ship lay becalmed; the twain, silent for the most part, sitting together on deck, their heads propped against the bulwarks. But it was only a partial and anonymous account that Billy gave, the unfounded scruples above referred to preventing full disclosure to anybody. Upon hearing Billy's version, the sage Dansker seemed to divine more than he was told; and after a little meditation, during which his wrinkles were pursed as into a point, quite effacing for the time that quizzing expression his face sometimes wore: "Didn't I say so, Baby Budd?"

"Say what?" demanded Billy.

"Why, *Jemmy Legs* is *down* on you."

"And what," rejoined Billy in amazement, "has *Jemmy Legs* to do with that cracked afterguardsman?"

"Ho, it was an afterguardsman, then. A cat's-paw, a cat's-paw!" And with that exclamation, whether it had reference to a light puff of air just then coming over the calm sea, or a subtler relation to the afterguardsman, there is no telling, the old Merlin gave a twisting wrench with his black teeth at his plug of tobacco, vouchsafing no reply to Billy's impetuous question, though now repeated, for it was his wont to relapse into grim silence when interrogated in skeptical sort as to any of his sententious oracles, not always very clear ones, rather partaking of that obscurity which invests most Delphic deliverances from any quarter.

Long experience had very likely brought this old man to that bitter prudence which never interferes in aught and never gives advice.

16

Yes, despite the Dansker's pithy insistence as to the master-at-arms being at the bottom of these strange experiences of Billy on board the *Bellipotent,* the young sailor was ready to ascribe them to almost anybody but the man who, to use Billy's own expression, "always had a pleasant word for him." This is to be wondered at. Yet not so much to be wondered at. In certain matters, some sailors even in mature life remain unsophisticated enough. But a young seafarer of the disposition of our athletic foretopman is much of a child-man. And yet a child's utter innocence is but its blank ignorance, and the innocence more or less wanes as intelligence waxes. But in Billy Budd intelligence, such as it was, had advanced while yet his simple-mindedness remained for the most part unaffected. Experience is a teacher indeed; yet did Billy's years make his experience small. Besides, he had none of that intuitive knowledge of the bad which in natures not good or incompletely so foreruns experience, and therefore may pertain, as in some instances it too clearly does pertain, even to youth.

And what could Billy know of man except of man as a mere sailor? And the old-fashioned sailor, the veritable man before the mast, the sailor from boyhood up, he, though indeed of the same species as a landsman, is in some respects singularly distinct from him. The sailor is frankness, the landsman is finesse. Life is not a game with the sailor, demanding the long head—no intricate game of chess where few moves are made in straightforwardness and ends are attained by indirection, an oblique, tedious, barren game hardly worth that poor candle burnt out in playing it.

Yes, as a class, sailors are in character a juvenile race. Even their deviations are marked by juvenility, this more especially holding true with the sailors of Billy's time. Then too, certain things which apply to all sailors do more pointedly operate here and there upon the junior one. Every sailor, too, is accustomed to obey orders without debating them; his life afloat is externally ruled for him; he is not brought into that promiscuous commerce with mankind where unobstructed free agency on equal terms —equal superficially, at least—soon teaches one that unless upon occasion he exercise a distrust keen in proportion to the fairness of the appearance, some foul turn may be served him. A ruled undemonstrative distrustfulness is so habitual, not with businessmen so much as with men who know their kind in less shallow relations than business, namely, certain men of the world, that they come at last to employ it all but unconsciously; and some of them would very likely feel real surprise at being charged with it as one of their general characteristics.

17

But after the little matter at the mess Billy Budd no more found himself in strange trouble at times about his hammock or his clothes bag or what not. As to that smile that occasionally sunned him, and the pleasant passing word, these were, if not more frequent, yet if anything more pronounced than before.

But for all that, there were certain other demonstrations now. When Claggart's unobserved glance happened to light on belted Billy rolling along the upper gun deck in the leisure of the second dogwatch, exchanging passing broadsides of fun with other young promenaders in the crowd, that glance would follow the cheerful sea Hyperion with a settled meditative and melancholy expression, his eyes strangely suffused with incipient feverish tears. Then would Claggart look like the man of sorrows. Yes, and sometimes the melancholy expression would have in it a touch of soft yearning, as if Claggart could even have loved Billy but for fate and ban. But this was an evanescence, and quickly repented of, as it were, by an immitigable look, pinching and shriveling the visage into the momentary semblance of a wrinkled walnut. But sometimes catching sight in advance of the foretopman coming in his direction, he would, upon their nearing, step aside a little to let him pass, dwelling upon Billy for the moment with the glittering dental satire of a Guise. But upon any abrupt unforeseen encounter a red light would flash forth from his eye like a spark from an anvil in a dusk smithy.

That quick, fierce light was a strange one, darted from orbs which in repose were of a color nearest approaching a deeper violet, the softest of shades.

Though some of these caprices of the pit could not but be observed by their object, yet were they beyond the construing of such a nature. And the thews of Billy were hardly compatible with that sort of sensitive spiritual organization which in some cases instinctively conveys to ignorant innocence an admonition of the proximity of the malign. He thought the master-at-arms acted in a manner rather queer at times. That was all. But the occasional frank air and pleasant word went for what they purported to be, the young sailor never having heard as yet of the "too fair-spoken man."

Had the foretopman been conscious of having done or said anything to provoke the ill will of the official, it would have been different with him, and his sight might have been purged if not sharpened. As it was, innocence was his blinder.

So was it with him in yet another matter. Two minor officers, the armorer and captain of the hold, with whom he had never exchanged a word, his position in the ship not bringing him into contact with them, these men now for the first began to cast upon Billy, when they chanced to encounter him, that peculiar glance which evidences that the man from whom it comes has been some way tampered with, and to the prejudice of him upon whom the glance lights. Never did it occur to Billy as a thing to be noted or a thing suspicious, though he well knew the fact, that the armorer and captain of the hold, with the ship's yeoman, apothecary, and others of that grade, were by naval usage messmates of the master-at-arms, men with ears convenient to his confidential tongue.

But the general popularity that came from our Handsome Sailor's manly forwardness upon occasion and irresistible good nature, indicating no mental superiority tending to excite an invidious feeling, this good will on the part of most of his shipmates made him the less to concern himself about such mute aspects toward him as those whereto allusion has just been made, aspects he could not so fathom as to infer their whole import.

As to the afterguardsman, though Billy for reasons already given necessarily saw little of him, yet when the two did happen to meet, invariably came the fellow's offhand cheerful recognition, sometimes accompanied by a passing pleasant word or two. Whatever that equivocal young person's original design may really have been, or the design of which he might have been the deputy, certain it was from his manner upon these occasions that he had wholly dropped it.

It was as if his precocity of crookedness (and every vulgar villain is precocious) had for once deceived him, and the man he had sought to entrap as a simpleton had through his very simplicity ignominiously baffled him.

But shrewd ones may opine that it was hardly possible for Billy to refrain from going up to the afterguardsman and bluntly demanding to know his purpose in the initial interview so abruptly closed in the forechains. Shrewd ones may also think it but natural in Billy to set about sounding some of the other impressed men of the ship in order to discover what basis, if any, there was for the emissary's obscure suggestions as to plotting disaffection aboard. Yes, shrewd ones may so think. But something more, or rather something else than mere shrewdness is perhaps needful for the due understanding of such a character as Billy Budd's.

As to Claggart, the monomania in the man—if that indeed it were—as involuntarily disclosed by starts in the manifestations detailed, yet in general covered over by his self-contained and rational demeanor; this, like a subterranean fire, was eating its way deeper and deeper in him. Something decisive must come of it.

18

After the mysterious interview in the forechains, the one so abruptly ended there by Billy, nothing especially germane to the story occurred until the events now about to be narrated.

Elsewhere it has been said that in the lack of frigates (of course better sailers than line-of-battle ships) in the English squadron up the Straits at that period, the *Bellipotent 74* was occasionally employed not only as an available substitute for a scout, but at times on detached service of more important kind. This was not alone because of her sailing qualities, not common in a ship of her rate, but quite as much, probably, that the character of her commander, it was thought, specially adapted him for any duty where under unforeseen difficulties a prompt initiative might have to be taken in some matter demanding knowledge and ability in addition to those qualities implied in good seamanship. It was on an expedition of the latter sort, a somewhat distant one, and when the *Bellipotent* was almost at her furthest remove from the fleet, that in the latter part of an afternoon watch she unexpectedly came in sight of a ship of the enemy. It proved to be a frigate. The latter, perceiving through the glass that the weight of men and metal would be heavily against her, invoking her light heels crowded sail to get away. After a chase urged almost against hope and lasting until about the middle of the first dogwatch, she signally succeeded in effecting her escape.

Not long after the pursuit had been given up, and ere the excitement incident thereto had altogether waned away, the master-at-arms, ascending from his cavernous sphere, made his appearance cap in hand by the mainmast, respectfully waiting the notice of Captain Vere, then solitary walking the weather-side of the quarter-deck, doubtless somewhat chafed at the failure of the pursuit. The spot where Claggart stood was the place allotted to men of lesser grades seeking some more particular interview either with the officer of the deck or the captain himself. But from the latter it was not often that a sailor or petty officer of those days would seek a hearing; only some exceptional cause would, according to established custom, have warranted that.

Presently, just as the commander, absorbed in his reflections, was on the point of turning aft in his promenade, he became sensible of Claggart's presence, and saw the doffed cap held in deferential expectancy. Here be it said that Captain Vere's personal knowledge of this petty officer had only begun at the time of the ship's last sailing from home, Claggart then for the first, in transfer from a ship detained for repairs, supplying on board the *Bellipotent* the place of a previous master-at-arms disabled and ashore.

No sooner did the commander observe who it was that now deferentially stood awaiting his notice than a peculiar expression came over him. It was not unlike that which uncontrollably will flit across the countenance of one at unawares encountering a person who, though known to him indeed, has hardly been long enough known for thorough knowledge, but something in whose aspect nevertheless now for the first provokes a vaguely repellent distaste. But coming to a stand and resuming much of his wonted official manner, save that a sort of impatience lurked in the intonation of the opening word, he said "Well? What is it, Master-at-arms?"

With the air of a subordinate grieved at the necessity of being a messenger of ill tidings, and while conscientiously determined to be frank yet equally resolved upon shunning overstatement, Claggart at this invitation, or rather summons to disburden, spoke up. What he said, conveyed in the language of no uneducated man, was to the effect following, if not altogether in these words, namely, that during the chase and preparations for the possible encounter he had seen enough to convince him that at least one sailor aboard was a dangerous character in a ship mustering some who not only had taken a guilty part in the late serious troubles, but others also who, like the man in question, had entered His Majesty's service under another form than enlistment.

At this point Captain Vere with some impatience interrupted him: "Be direct, man; say *impressed men*."

Claggart made a gesture of subservience, and proceeded. Quite lately he (Claggart) had begun to suspect that on the gun decks some sort of movement prompted by the sailor in question was covertly going on, but he had not thought himself warranted in reporting the suspicion so long as it remained indistinct. But from what he had that afternoon observed in the man referred to, the suspicion of something clandestine going on had advanced to a point less removed from certainty. He deeply felt, he added, the serious responsibility assumed in making a report involving such possible consequences to the individual mainly concerned, besides tending to augment those natural anxieties which every naval commander must feel in view of extraordinary outbreaks so recent as those which, he sorrowfully said it, it needed not to name.

Now at the first broaching of the matter Captain Vere, taken by surprise, could not wholly dissemble his disquietude. But as Claggart went on, the former's aspect changed into restiveness under something in the testifier's manner in giving his testimony. However, he refrained from interrupting him. And Claggart, continuing, concluded with this: "God forbid, your honor, that the *Bellipotent*'s should be the experience of the—"

"Never mind that!" here peremptorily broke in the superior, his face altering with anger, instinctively divining the ship that the other was about to name, one in which the Nore Mutiny had assumed a singularly tragical character that for a time jeopardized the life of its commander. Under the circumstances he was indignant at the purposed allusion. When the commissioned officers themselves were on all occasions very heedful how they referred to the recent events in the fleet, for a petty officer unnecessarily to allude to them in the presence of his captain, this struck him as a most immodest presumption. Besides, to his quick sense of self-respect it even looked under the circumstances something like an attempt to alarm him. Nor at first was he without some surprise that one who so far as he had hitherto come under his notice had shown considerable tact in his function should in this particular evince such lack of it.

But these thoughts and kindred dubious ones flitting across his mind were suddenly replaced by an intuitional surmise which, though as yet obscure in form, served practically to affect his reception of the ill tidings. Certain it is that, long versed in everything pertaining to the complicated gun-deck life, which like every other form of life has its secret mines and dubious side, the side popularly disclaimed, Captain Vere did not permit himself to be unduly disturbed by the general tenor of his subordinate's report.

Furthermore, if in view of recent events prompt action should be taken at the first palpable sign of recurring insubordination, for all that, not judicious would it be, he thought, to keep the idea of lingering disaffection alive by undue forwardness in crediting an informer, even if his own subordinate, and charged among other things with police surveillance of the crew. This feeling would not perhaps have so prevailed with him were it not that upon a prior occasion the patriotic zeal officially evinced by Claggart had somewhat irritated him as appearing rather supersensible and strained. Furthermore, something even in the official's self-possessed and somewhat ostentatious manner in making his specifications strangely reminded him of a bandsman, a perjurous witness in a capital case before a court-martial ashore of which when a lieutenant he (Captain Vere) had been a member.

Now the peremptory check given to Claggart in the matter of the arrested allusion was quickly followed up by this: "You say that there is at least one dangerous man aboard. Name him."

"William Budd, a foretopman, your honor."

"William Budd!" repeated Captain Vere with unfeigned astonishment. "And mean you the man that Lieutenant Ratcliffe took from the merchantman not very long ago, the young fellow who seems to be so popular with the men—Billy, the Handsome Sailor, as they call him?"

"The same, your honor; but for all his youth and good looks, a deep one. Not for nothing does he insinuate himself into the good will of his shipmates, since at the least they will at a pinch say—all hands will—a good word for him, and at all hazards. Did Lieutenant Ratcliffe happen to tell your honor of that adroit fling of Budd's, jumping up in the cutter's bow under the merchantman's stern when he was being taken off? It is even masked by that sort of good-humored air that at heart he resents his impressment. You have but noted his fair cheek. A mantrap may be under the ruddy-tipped daisies."

Now the Handsome Sailor as a signal figure among the crew had naturally enough attracted the captain's attention from the first. Though in general not very demonstrative to his officers, he had congratulated Lieutenant Ratcliffe upon his good fortune in lighting on such a fine specimen of the *genus homo*, who in the nude might have posed for a statue of young Adam before the Fall. As to Billy's adieu to the ship *Rights-of-Man*, which the boarding lieutenant had indeed reported to him, but, in a deferential way, more as a good story than aught else, Captain Vere, though mistakenly understanding it as a satiric sally, had but thought so much the better of the impressed man for it; as a military sailor, admiring the spirit that could take an arbitrary enlistment so merrily and sensibly. The foretopman's conduct, too, so far as it had fallen under the captain's notice, had confirmed the first happy augury, while the new recruit's qualities as a "sailor-man" seemed to be such that he had thought of recommending him to the executive officer for promotion to a place that would more frequently bring him under his own observation, namely, the captaincy of the mizzentop, replacing there in the starboard watch a man not so young whom partly for that reason he deemed less fitted for the post. Be it parenthesized here that since the mizzentopmen have not to handle such breadths of heavy canvas as the lower sails on the mainmast and foremast, a young man if of the right stuff not only seems best adapted to duty there, but in fact is generally selected for the captaincy of that top, and the company under him are light hands and often but striplings. In sum, Captain Vere had from the beginning deemed Billy Budd to be what in the naval parlance of the time was called a "King's bargain": that is to say, for His Britannic Majesty's navy a capital investment at small outlay or none at all.

After a brief pause, during which the reminiscences above mentioned passed vividly through his mind and he weighed the import of Claggart's last suggestion conveyed in the phrase "mantrap under the daisies," and the more he weighed it the less reliance he felt in the informer's good faith, suddenly he turned upon him and in a low voice demanded: "Do you come to me, Master-at-arms, with so foggy a tale? As to Budd, cite me an act or spoken word of his confirmatory of what you in general charge against him. Stay," drawing nearer to him; "heed what you speak. Just now, and in a case like this, there is a yardarm-end for the false witness."

"Ah, your honor!" sighed Claggart, mildly shaking his shapely head as in sad deprecation of such unmerited severity of tone. Then, bridling—erecting himself as in virtuous self-assertion— he circumstantially alleged certain words and acts which collectively, if credited, led to presumptions mortally inculpating Budd. And for some of these averments, he added, substantiating proof was not far.

With gray eyes impatient and distrustful essaying to fathom to the bottom Claggart's calm violet ones, Captain Vere again heard him out; then for the moment stood ruminating. The mood he evinced, Claggart—himself for the time liberated from the other's scrutiny—steadily regarded with a look difficult to render: a look curious of the operation of his tactics, a look such as might have been that of the spokesman of the envious children of Jacob deceptively imposing upon the troubled patriarch the blood-dyed coat of young Joseph.

Though something exceptional in the moral quality of Captain Vere made him, in earnest encounter with a fellow man, a veritable touchstone of that man's essential nature, yet now as to Claggart and what was really going on in him his feeling partook less of intuitional conviction than of strong suspicion clogged by strange dubieties. The perplexity he evinced proceeded less from aught touching the man informed against— as Claggart doubtless opined—than from considerations how best to act in regard to the informer. At first, indeed, he was naturally for summoning that substantiation of his allegations which Claggart said was at hand. But such a proceeding would result in the matter at once getting abroad, which in the present stage of it, he thought, might undesirably affect the ship's company. If Claggart was a false witness—that closed the affair. And therefore, before trying the accusation, he would first practically test the accuser; and he thought this could be done in a quiet, undemonstrative way.

The measure he determined upon involved a shifting of the scene, a transfer to a place less exposed to observation than the broad quarter-deck. For although the few gun-room officers there at the time had, in due observance of naval etiquette, withdrawn to leeward the moment Captain Vere had begun his promenade on the deck's weather-side; and though during the colloquy with Claggart they of course ventured not to diminish the distance; and though throughout the interview Captain Vere's voice was far from high, and Claggart's silvery and low; and the wind in the cordage and the wash of the sea helped the more to put them beyond earshot; nevertheless, the interview's continuance already had attracted observation from some topmen aloft and other sailors in the waist or further forward.

Having determined upon his measures, Captain Vere forthwith took action. Abruptly turning to Claggart, he asked, "Master-at-arms, is it now Budd's watch aloft?"

"No, your honor."

Whereupon, "Mr. Wilkes!" summoning the nearest midshipman. "Tell Albert to come to me." Albert was the captain's hammock-boy, a sort of sea valet in whose discretion and fidelity his master had much confidence. The lad appeared.

"You know Budd, the foretopman?"

"I do, sir."

"Go find him. It is his watch off. Manage to tell him out of earshot that he is wanted aft. Contrive it that he speaks to nobody. Keep him in talk yourself. And not till you get well aft here, not till then let him know that the place where he is wanted is my cabin. You understand. Go.—Master-at-arms, show yourself on the decks below, and when you think it time for Albert to be coming with his man, stand by quietly to follow the sailor in."

19   Billy kills Claggart

Now when the foretopman found himself in the cabin, closeted there, as it were, with the captain and Claggart, he was surprised enough. But it was a surprise unaccompanied by apprehension or distrust. To an immature nature essentially honest and humane, forewarning intimations of subtler danger from one's kind come tardily if at all. The only thing that took shape in the young sailor's mind was this: Yes, the captain, I have always thought, looks kindly upon me. Wonder if he's going to make me his coxswain. I should like that. And maybe now he is going to ask the master-at-arms about me.

"Shut the door there, sentry," said the commander; "stand without, and let nobody come in.—Now, Master-at-arms, tell this man to his face what you told of him to me," and stood prepared to scrutinize the mutually confronting visages.

With the measured step and calm collected air of an asylum physician approaching in the public hall some patient beginning to show indications of a coming paroxysm, Claggart deliberately advanced within short range of Billy and, mesmerically looking him in the eye, briefly recapitulated the accusation.

Not at first did Billy take it in. When he did, the rose-tan of his cheek looked struck as by white leprosy. He stood like one impaled and gagged. Meanwhile the accuser's eyes, removing not as yet from the blue dilated ones, underwent a phenomenal change, their wonted rich violet color blurring into a muddy purple. Those lights of human intelligence, losing human expression, were gelidly protruding like the alien eyes of certain uncatalogued creatures of the deep. The first mesmeristic glance was one of serpent fascination; the last was as the paralyzing lurch of the torpedo fish.

"Speak, man!" said Captain Vere to the transfixed one, struck by his aspect even more than by Claggart's. "Speak! Defend yourself!" Which appeal caused but a strange dumb gesturing and gurgling in Billy; amazement at such an accusation so suddenly sprung on inexperienced nonage; this, and, it may be, horror of the accuser's eyes, serving to bring out his lurking defect and in this instance for the time intensifying it into a convulsed tongue-tie; while the intent head and entire form straining forward in an agony of ineffectual eagerness to obey the injunction to speak and defend himself, gave an expression to the face like that of a condemned vestal priestess in the moment of being buried alive, and in the first struggle against suffocation.

Though at the time Captain Vere was quite ignorant of Billy's liability to vocal impediment, he now immediately divined it, since vividly Billy's aspect recalled to him that of a bright young schoolmate of his whom he had once seen struck by much the

same startling impotence in the act of eagerly rising in the class
to be foremost in response to a testing question put to it by the
master. Going close up to the young sailor, and laying a soothing
hand on his shoulder, he said, "There is no hurry, my boy.
Take your time, take your time." Contrary to the effect intended,
these words so fatherly in tone, doubtless touching Billy's heart
to the quick, prompted yet more violent efforts at utterance—
efforts soon ending for the time in confirming the paralysis, and
bringing to his face an expression which was as a crucifixion to
behold. The next instant, quick as the flame from a discharged
cannon at night, his right arm shot out, and Claggart dropped
to the deck. Whether intentionally or but owing to the young
athlete's superior height, the blow had taken effect full upon
the forehead, so shapely and intellectual-looking a feature in the
master-at-arms; so that the body fell over lengthwise, like a
heavy plank tilted from erectness. A gasp or two, and he lay
motionless.

"Fated boy," breathed Captain Vere in tone so low as to be
almost a whisper, "what have you done! But here, help me."

The twain raised the felled one from the loins up into a sitting
position. The spare form flexibly acquiesced, but inertly. It was
like handling a dead snake. They lowered it back. Regaining
erectness, Captain Vere with one hand covering his face stood
to all appearance as impassive as the object at his feet. Was he
absorbed in taking in all the bearings of the event and what
was best not only now at once to be done, but also in the sequel?
Slowly he uncovered his face; and the effect was as if the moon
emerging from eclipse should reappear with quite another aspect
than that which had gone into hiding. The father in him, manifested towards Billy thus far in the scene, was replaced by the
military disciplinarian. In his official tone he bade the foretopman retire to a stateroom aft (pointing it out), and there remain
till thence summoned. This order Billy in silence mechanically
obeyed. Then going to the cabin door where it opened on the

quarter-deck, Captain Vere said to the sentry without, "Tell somebody to send Albert here." When the lad appeared, his master so contrived it that he should not catch sight of the prone one. "Albert," he said to him, "tell the surgeon I wish to see him. You need not come back till called."

When the surgeon entered—a self-poised character of that grave sense and experience that hardly anything could take him aback—Captain Vere advanced to meet him, thus unconsciously intercepting his view of Claggart, and, interrupting the other's wonted ceremonious salutation, said, "Nay. Tell me how it is with yonder man," directing his attention to the prostrate one.

The surgeon looked, and for all his self-command somewhat started at the abrupt revelation. On Claggart's always pallid complexion, thick black blood was now oozing from nostril and ear. To the gazer's professional eye it was unmistakably no living man that he saw.

"Is it so, then?" said Captain Vere, intently watching him. "I thought it. But verify it." Whereupon the customary tests confirmed the surgeon's first glance, who now, looking up in unfeigned concern, cast a look of intense inquisitiveness upon his superior. But Captain Vere, with one hand to his brow, was standing motionless. Suddenly, catching the surgeon's arm convulsively, he exclaimed, pointing down to the body, "It is the divine judgment on Ananias! Look!"

Disturbed by the excited manner he had never before observed in the *Bellipotent*'s captain, and as yet wholly ignorant of the affair, the prudent surgeon nevertheless held his peace, only again looking an earnest interrogatory as to what it was that had resulted in such a tragedy.

But Captain Vere was now again motionless, standing absorbed in thought. Again starting, he vehemently exclaimed, "Struck dead by an angel of God! Yet the angel must hang!"

At these passionate interjections, mere incoherences to the listener as yet unapprised of the antecedents, the surgeon was profoundly discomposed. But now, as recollecting himself, Captain Vere in less passionate tone briefly related the circumstances leading up to the event. "But come; we must dispatch," he added. "Help me to remove him" (meaning the body) "to yonder compartment," designating one opposite that where the foretopman remained immured. Anew disturbed by a request that, as implying a desire for secrecy, seemed unaccountably strange to him, there was nothing for the subordinate to do but comply.

"Go now," said Captain Vere with something of his wonted manner. "Go now. I presently shall call a drumhead court. Tell the lieutenants what has happened, and tell Mr. Mordant" (meaning the captain of marines), "and charge them to keep the matter to themselves."

20

Full of disquietude and misgiving, the surgeon left the cabin. Was Captain Vere suddenly affected in his mind, or was it but a transient excitement, brought about by so strange and extraordinary a tragedy? As to the drumhead court, it struck the surgeon as impolitic, if nothing more. The thing to do, he thought, was to place Billy Budd in confinement, and in a way dictated by usage, and postpone further action in so extraordinary a case to such time as they should rejoin the squadron, and then refer it to the admiral. He recalled the unwonted agitation of Captain Vere and his excited exclamations, so at variance with his normal manner. Was he unhinged?

But assuming that he is, it is not so susceptible of proof. What then can the surgeon do? No more trying situation is conceivable than that of an officer subordinate under a captain whom he suspects to be not mad, indeed, but yet not quite unaffected in his intellect. To argue his order to him would be insolence. To resist him would be mutiny.

In obedience to Captain Vere, he communicated what had happened to the lieutenants and captain of marines, saying nothing as to the captain's state. They fully shared his own surprise and concern. Like him too, they seemed to think that such a matter should be referred to the admiral.

21

Who in the rainbow can draw the line where the violet tint ends and the orange tint begins? Distinctly we see the difference of the colors, but where exactly does the one first blendingly enter into the other? So with sanity and insanity. In pronounced cases there is no question about them. But in some supposed cases, in various degrees supposedly less pronounced, to draw the exact line of demarcation few will undertake, though for a fee becoming considerate some professional experts will. There is nothing namable but that some men will, or undertake to, do it for pay.

Whether Captain Vere, as the surgeon professionally and privately surmised, was really the sudden victim of any degree of aberration, every one must determine for himself by such light as this narrative may afford.

That the unhappy event which has been narrated could not have happened at a worse juncture was but too true. For it was close on the heel of the suppressed insurrections, an aftertime very critical to naval authority, demanding from every English sea commander two qualities not readily interfusable—prudence and rigor. Moreover, there was something crucial in the case.

In the jugglery of circumstances preceding and attending the event on board the *Bellipotent,* and in the light of that martial code whereby it was formally to be judged, innocence and guilt personified in Claggart and Budd in effect changed places. In a legal view the apparent victim of the tragedy was he who had sought to victimize a man blameless; and the indisputable deed of the latter, navally regarded, constituted the most heinous of military crimes. Yet more. The essential right and wrong involved in the matter, the clearer that might be, so much the worse for the responsibility of a loyal sea commander, inasmuch as he was not authorized to determine the matter on that primitive basis.

Small wonder then that the *Bellipotent*'s captain, though in general a man of rapid decision, felt that circumspectness not less then promptitude was necessary. Until he could decide upon his course, and in each detail; and not only so, but until the concluding measure was upon the point of being enacted, he deemed it advisable, in view of all the circumstances, to guard as much as possible against publicity. Here he may or may not have erred. Certain it is, however, that subsequently in the confidential talk of more than one or two gun rooms and cabins he was not a little criticized by some officers, a fact imputed by his friends and vehemently by his cousin Jack Denton to professional jealousy of Starry Vere. Some imaginative ground for invidious comment there was. The maintenance of secrecy in the matter, the confining all knowledge of it for a time to the place where the homicide occurred, the quarter-deck cabin; in these particulars lurked some resemblance to the policy adopted in those tragedies of the palace which have occurred more than once in the capital founded by Peter the Barbarian.

The case indeed was such that fain would the *Bellipotent*'s captain have deferred taking any action whatever respecting it further than to keep the foretopman a close prisoner till the ship rejoined the squadron and then submitting the matter to the judgment of his admiral.

But a true military officer is in one particular like a true monk. Not with more of self-abnegation will the latter keep his vows of monastic obedience than the former his vows of allegiance to martial duty.

Feeling that unless quick action was taken on it, the deed of the foretopman, so soon as it should be known on the gun decks, would tend to awaken any slumbering embers of the Nore among the crew, a sense of the urgency of the case overruled in Captain Vere every other consideration. But though a conscientious disciplinarian, he was no lover of authority for mere authority's sake. Very far was he from embracing opportunities for monopolizing to himself the perils of moral responsibility, none at least that could properly be referred to an official superior or shared with him by his official equals or even subordinates. So thinking, he was glad it would not be at variance with usage to turn the matter over to a summary court of his own officers, reserving to himself, as the one on whom the ultimate accountability would rest, the right of maintaining a supervision of it, or formally or informally interposing at need. Accordingly a drumhead court was summarily convened, he electing the individuals composing it: the first lieutenant, the captain of marines, and the sailing master.

In associating an officer of marines with the sea-lieutenant and the sailing master in a case having to do with a sailor, the commander perhaps deviated from general custom. He was prompted thereto by the circumstance that he took that soldier to be a judicious person, thoughtful, and not altogether incapable of grappling with a difficult case unprecedented in his prior experience. Yet even as to him he was not without some latent misgiving, for withal he was an extremely good-natured man, an enjoyer of his dinner, a sound sleeper, and inclined to obesity—a man who though he would always maintain his manhood in battle might not prove altogether reliable in a moral dilemma involving aught of the tragic. As to the first lieutenant and the sailing master, Captain Vere could not but be aware that though honest natures, of approved gallantry upon occasion, their intelligence was mostly confined to the matter of active seamanship and the fighting demands of their profession.

The court was held in the same cabin where the unfortunate affair had taken place. This cabin, the commander's, embraced the entire area under the poop deck. Aft, and on either side, was a small stateroom, the one now temporarily a jail and the other a dead-house, and a yet smaller compartment, leaving a space between expanding forward into a goodly oblong of length coinciding with the ship's beam. A skylight of moderate dimension was overhead, and at each end of the oblong space were two sashed porthole windows easily convertible back into embrasures for short carronades.

All being quickly in readiness, Billy Budd was arraigned, Captain Vere necessarily appearing as the sole witness in the case, and as such temporarily sinking his rank, though singularly maintaining it in a matter apparently trivial, namely, that he testified from the ship's weather-side, with that object having caused the court to sit on the lee-side. Concisely he narrated all that had led up to the catastrophe, omitting nothing in Claggart's accusation and deposing as to the manner in which the prisoner had received it. At this testimony the three officers glanced with no little surprise at Billy Budd, the last man they would have suspected either of the mutinous design alleged by Claggart or the undeniable deed he himself had done. The first lieutenant, taking judicial primacy and turning toward the prisoner, said, "Captain Vere has spoken. Is it or is it not as Captain Vere says?"

In response came syllables not so much impeded in the utterance as might have been anticipated. They were these: "Captain Vere tells the truth. It is just as Captain Vere says, but it is not as the master-at-arms said. I have eaten the King's bread and I am true to the King."

"I believe you, my man," said the witness, his voice indicating a suppressed emotion not otherwise betrayed.

"God will bless you for that, your honor!" not without stammering said Billy, and all but broke down. But immediately he was recalled to self-control by another question, to which with the same emotional difficulty of utterance he said, "No, there was no malice between us. I never bore malice against the master-at-arms. I am sorry that he is dead. I did not mean to kill him. Could I have used my tongue I would not have struck him. But he foully lied to my face and in presence of my captain, and I had to say something, and I could only say it with a blow, God help me!"

In the impulsive aboveboard manner of the frank one the court saw confirmed all that was implied in words that just previously had perplexed them, coming as they did from the testifier to the tragedy and promptly following Billy's impassioned disclaimer of mutinous intent—Captain Vere's words, "I believe you, my man."

Next it was asked of him whether he knew of or suspected aught savoring of incipient trouble (meaning mutiny, though the explicit term was avoided) going on in any section of the ship's company.

The reply lingered. This was naturally imputed by the court to the same vocal embarrassment which had retarded or obstructed previous answers. But in main it was otherwise here, the question immediately recalling to Billy's mind the interview with the afterguardsman in the forechains. But an innate repugnance to playing a part at all approaching that of an informer against one's own shipmates—the same erring sense of uninstructed honor which had stood in the way of his reporting the matter at the time, though as a loyal man-of-war's man it was incumbent on him, and failure so to do, if charged against him and proven, would have subjected him to the heaviest of penalties; this, with the blind feeling now his that nothing really was being hatched, prevailed with him. When the answer came it was a negative.

"One question more," said the officer of marines, now first speaking and with a troubled earnestness. "You tell us that what the master-at-arms said against you was a lie. Now why should he have so lied, so maliciously lied, since you declare there was no malice between you?"

At that question, unintentionally touching on a spiritual sphere wholly obscure to Billy's thoughts, he was nonplussed, evincing a confusion indeed that some observers, such as can readily be imagined, would have construed into involuntary evidence of hidden guilt. Nevertheless, he strove some way to answer, but all at once relinquished the vain endeavor, at the same time turning an appealing glance towards Captain Vere as deeming him his best helper and friend. Captain Vere, who had been seated for a time, rose to his feet, addressing the interrogator. "The question you put to him comes naturally enough. But how can he rightly answer it?—or anybody else, unless indeed it be he who lies within there," designating the compartment where lay the corpse. "But the prone one there will not rise to our summons. In effect, though, as it seems to me, the point you make is hardly material. Quite aside from any conceivable motive actuating the master-at-arms, and irrespective of the provocation to the blow, a martial court must needs in the present case confine its attention to the blow's consequence, which consequence justly is to be deemed not otherwise than as the striker's deed."

This utterance, the full significance of which it was not at all likely that Billy took in, nevertheless caused him to turn a wistful interrogative look towards the speaker, a look in its dumb expressiveness not unlike that which a dog of generous breed might turn upon his master, seeking in his face some elucidation of a previous gesture ambiguous to the canine intelligence. Nor was the same utterance without marked effect upon the three officers, more especially the soldier. Couched in it seemed to them a meaning unanticipated, involving a prejudgment on the speaker's part. It served to augment a mental disturbance previously evident enough.

The soldier once more spoke, in a tone of suggestive dubiety addressing at once his associates and Captain Vere: "Nobody is present—none of the ship's company, I mean—who might shed lateral light, if any is to be had, upon what remains mysterious in this matter."

"That is thoughtfully put," said Captain Vere; "I see your drift. Ay, there is a mystery; but, to use a scriptural phrase, it is a 'mystery of iniquity,' a matter for psychologic theologians to discuss. But what has a military court to do with it? Not to add that for us any possible investigation of it is cut off by the lasting tongue-tie of—him—in yonder," again designating the mortuary stateroom. "The prisoner's deed—with that alone we have to do."

To this, and particularly the closing reiteration, the marine soldier, knowing not how aptly to reply, sadly abstained from saying aught. The first lieutenant, who at the outset had not unnaturally assumed primacy in the court, now overrulingly instructed by a glance from Captain Vere, a glance more effective than words, resumed that primacy. Turning to the prisoner, "Budd," he said, and scarce in equable tones, "Budd, if you have aught further to say for yourself, say it now."

Upon this the young sailor turned another quick glance toward Captain Vere; then, as taking a hint from that aspect, a hint confirming his own instinct that silence was now best, replied to the lieutenant, "I have said all, sir."

The marine—the same who had been the sentinel without the cabin door at the time that the foretopman, followed by the master-at-arms, entered it—he, standing by the sailor throughout these judicial proceedings, was now directed to take him back to the after compartment originally assigned to the prisoner and his custodian. As the twain disappeared from view, the three officers, as partially liberated from some inward constraint associated with Billy's mere presence, simultaneously stirred in their seats. They exchanged looks of troubled indecision, yet feeling that decide they must and without long delay. For Captain Vere, he for the time stood—unconsciously with his back toward them, apparently in one of his absent fits—gazing out from a sashed porthole to windward upon the monotonous blank of the twilight sea. But the court's silence continuing, broken only at moments by brief consultations, in low earnest tones, this served to arouse him and energize him. Turning, he to-and-fro paced the cabin athwart; in the returning ascent to windward climbing the slant deck in the ship's lee roll, without knowing it symbolizing thus in his action a mind resolute to surmount difficulties even if against primitive instincts strong as the wind and the sea. Presently he came to a stand before the three. After scanning their faces he stood less as mustering his thoughts for expression than as one inly deliberating how best to put them to well-meaning men not intellectually mature, men with whom it was necessary to demonstrate certain principles that were axioms to himself. Similar impatience as to talking is perhaps one reason that deters some minds from addressing any popular assemblies.

When speak he did, something, both in the substance of what he said and his manner of saying it, showed the influence of unshared studies modifying and tempering the practical training of an active career. This, along with his phraseology, now and then was suggestive of the grounds whereon rested that imputation of a certain pedantry socially alleged against him by certain naval men of wholly practical cast, captains who nevertheless would frankly concede that His Majesty's navy mustered no more efficient officer of their grade than Starry Vere.

What he said was to this effect: "Hitherto I have been but the witness, little more; and I should hardly think now to take another tone, that of your coadjutor for the time, did I not perceive in you—at the crisis too—a troubled hesitancy, proceeding, I doubt not, from the clash of military duty with moral scruple—scruple vitalized by compassion. For the compassion, how can I otherwise than share it? But, mindful of paramount obligations, I strive against scruples that may tend to enervate decision. Not, gentlemen, that I hide from myself that the case *determines what is right or wrong*

is an exceptional one. Speculatively regarded, it well might be referred to a jury of casuists. But for us here, acting not as casuists or moralists, it is a case practical, and under martial law practically to be dealt with.

"But your scruples: do they move as in a dusk? Challenge them. Make them advance and declare themselves. Come now; do they import something like this: If, mindless of palliating circumstances, we are bound to regard the death of the master-at-arms as the prisoner's deed, then does that deed constitute a capital crime whereof the penalty is a mortal one? But in natural justice is nothing but the prisoner's overt act to be considered? How can we adjudge to summary and shameful death a fellow creature innocent before God, and whom we feel to be so?—Does that state it aright? You sign sad assent. Well, I too feel that, the full force of that. It is Nature. But do these buttons that we wear attest that our allegiance is to Nature? No, to the King. Though the ocean, which is inviolate Nature primeval, though this be the element where we move and have our being as sailors, yet as the King's officers lies our duty in a sphere correspondingly natural? So little is that true, that in receiving our commissions we in the most important regards ceased to be natural free agents. When was is declared are we the commissioned fighters previously consulted? We fight at command. If our judgments approve the war, that is but co-incidence. So in other particulars. So now. For suppose condemnation to follow these present proceedings. Would it be so much we ourselves that would condemn as it would be martial law operating through us? For that law and the rigor of it, we are not responsible. Our vowed responsibility is in this: That however pitilessly that law may operate in any instances, we nevertheless adhere to it and administer it.

"But the exceptional in the matter moves the hearts within you. Even so too is mine moved. But let not warm hearts betray heads that should be cool. Ashore in a criminal case, will an upright judge allow himself off the bench to be waylaid by some tender kinswoman of the accused seeking to touch him with her tearful plea? Well, the heart here, sometimes the feminine in man, is as that piteous woman, and hard though it be, she must here be ruled out."

He paused, earnestly studying them for a moment; then resumed.

"But something in your aspect seems to urge that it is not solely the heart that moves in you, but also the conscience, the private conscience. But tell me whether or not, occupying the position we do, private conscience should not yield to that imperial one formulated in the code under which alone we officially proceed?"

Here the three men moved in their seats, less convinced than agitated by the course of an argument troubling but the more the spontaneous conflict within.

Perceiving which, the speaker paused for a moment; then abruptly changing his tone, went on.

"To steady us a bit, let us recur to the facts. — In wartime at sea a man-of-war's man strikes his superior in grade, and the blow kills. Apart from its effect the blow itself is, according to the Articles of War, a capital crime. Furthermore—"

"Ay, sir," emotionally broke in the officer of marines, "in one sense it was. But surely Budd purposed neither mutiny nor homicide."

"Surely not, my good man. And before a court less arbitrary and more merciful than a martial one, that plea would largely extenuate. At the Last Assizes it shall acquit. But how here? We proceed under the law of the Mutiny Act. In feature no child can resemble his father more than that Act resembles in spirit the thing from which it derives—War. In His Majesty's service—in this ship, indeed—there are Englishmen forced to fight for the King against their will. Against their conscience, for aught we know. Though as their fellow creatures some of us may appreciate their position, yet as navy officers what reck we of it? Still less recks the enemy. Our impressed men he would fain cut down in the same swath with our volunteers. As regards the enemy's naval conscripts, some of whom may even share our own abhorrence of the regicidal French Directory, it is the same on our side. War looks but to the frontage, the appearance. And the Mutiny Act, War's child, takes after the father. Budd's intent or non-intent is nothing to the purpose.

"But while, put to it by those anxieties in you which I cannot but respect, I only repeat myself—while thus strangely we prolong proceedings that should be summary—the enemy may be sighted and an engagement result. We must do; and one of two things must we do—condemn or let go."

"Can we not convict and yet mitigate the penalty?" asked the sailing master, here speaking, and falteringly, for the first.

"Gentlemen, were that clearly lawful for us under the circumstances, consider the consequences of such clemency. The people" (meaning the ship's company) "have native sense; most of them are familiar with our naval usage and tradition; and how would they take it? Even could you explain to them—which our official position forbids—they, long molded by arbitrary discipline, have not that kind of intelligent responsiveness that might qualify them to comprehend and discriminate. No, to the people the foretopman's deed, however it be worded in the announcement, will be plain homicide committed in a flagrant act of mutiny. What penalty for that should follow, they know. But it does not follow. *Why?* they will ruminate. You know what sailors are. Will they not revert to the recent outbreak at the Nore? Ay. They know the well-founded alarm—the panic it struck throughout England. Your clement sentence they would account pusillanimous. They would think that we flinch, that we are afraid of them—afraid of practicing a lawful rigor singularly demanded at this juncture, lest it should provoke new troubles. What shame to us such a conjecture on their part, and how deadly to discipline. You see then, whither, prompted by duty and the law, I steadfastly drive. But I beseech you, my friends, do not take me amiss. I feel as you do for this unfortunate boy. But did he know our hearts, I take him to be of that generous nature that he would feel even for us on whom in this military necessity so heavy a compulsion is laid."

With that, crossing the deck he resumed his place by the sashed porthole, tacitly leaving the three to come to a decision. On the cabin's opposite side the troubled court sat silent. Loyal lieges, plain and practical, though at bottom they dissented from some points Captain Vere had put to them, they were without the faculty, hardly had the inclination, to gainsay one whom they felt to be an earnest man, one too not less their superior in mind than in naval rank. But it is not improbable that even such of his words as were not without influence over them, less came home to them than his closing appeal to their instinct as sea officers: in the forethought he threw out as to the practical consequences to discipline, considering the unconfirmed tone of the fleet at the time, should a man-of-war's man's violent killing at sea of a superior in grade be allowed to pass for aught else than a capital crime demanding prompt infliction of the penalty.

Not unlikely they were brought to something more or less akin to that harassed frame of mind which in the year 1842 actuated the commander of the U.S. brig-of-war *Somers* to resolve, under the so-called Articles of War, Articles modeled upon the English Mutiny Act, to resolve upon the execution at sea of a midshipman and two sailors as mutineers designing the seizure of the brig. Which resolution was carried out though in a time of peace and within not many days' sail of home. An act vindicated by a naval court of inquiry subsequently convened ashore. History, and here cited without comment. True, the circumstances on board the *Somers* were different from those on board the *Bellipotent*. But the urgency felt, well-warranted or otherwise, was much the same.

Says a writer whom few know, "Forty years after a battle it is easy for a noncombatant to reason about how it ought to have been fought. It is another thing personally and under fire to have to direct the fighting while involved in the obscuring smoke of it. Much so with respect to other emergencies involving considerations both practical and moral, and when it is imperative promptly to act. The greater the fog the more it imperils the steamer, and speed is put on though at the hazard of running somebody down. Little ween the snug card players in the cabin of the responsibilities of the sleepless man on the bridge."

In brief, Billy Budd was formally convicted and sentenced to be hung at the yardarm in the early morning watch, it being now night. Otherwise, as is customary in such cases, the sentence would forthwith have been carried out. In wartime on the field or in the fleet, a mortal punishment decreed by a drumhead court—on the field sometimes decreed by but a nod from the general—follows without delay on the heel of conviction, without appeal.

22

Telling Billy

It was Captain Vere himself who of his own motion communicated the finding of the court to the prisoner, for that purpose going to the compartment where he was in custody and bidding the marine there to withdraw for the time.

Beyond the communication of the sentence, what took place at this interview was never known. But in view of the character of the twain briefly closeted in that stateroom, each radically sharing in the rarer qualities of our nature—so rare indeed as to be all but incredible to average minds however much cultivated—some conjectures may be ventured.

It would have been in consonance with the spirit of Captain Vere should he on this occasion have concealed nothing from the condemned one—should he indeed have frankly disclosed to him the part he himself had played in bringing about the decision, at the same time revealing his actuating motives. On Billy's side it is not improbable that such a confession would have been received in much the same spirit that prompted it. Not without a sort of joy, indeed, he might have appreciated the brave opinion of him implied in his captain's making such a confidant of him. Nor, as to the sentence itself, could he have been insensible that it was imparted to him as to one not afraid to die. Even more may have been. Captain Vere in the end may have developed the passion sometimes latent under an exterior stoical or indifferent. He was old enough to have been Billy's father. The austere devotee of military duty, letting himself melt back into what remains primeval in our formalized humanity, may in the end have caught Billy to his heart, even as Abraham may have caught young Isaac on the brink of resolutely offering him up in obedience to the exacting behest. But there is no telling the sacrament, seldom if in any case revealed to the gadding world, wherever under circumstances at all akin to those here attempted to be set forth two of great Nature's nobler order embrace. There is privacy at the time, inviolable to the survivor; and holy oblivion, the sequel to each diviner magnanimity, providentially covers all at last.

The first to encounter Captain Vere in act of leaving the compartment was the senior lieutenant. The face he beheld, for the moment one expressive of the agony of the strong, was to that officer, though a man of fifty, a startling revelation. That the condemned one suffered less than he who mainly had effected the condemnation was apparently indicated by the former's exclamation in the scene soon perforce to be touched upon.

23

Of a series of incidents within a brief term rapidly following each other, the adequate narration may take up a term less brief, especially if explanation or comment here and there seem requisite to the better understanding of such incidents. Between the entrance into the cabin of him who never left it alive, and him who when he did leave it left it as one condemned to die; between this and the closeted interview just given, less than an hour and a half had elapsed. It was an interval long enough, however, to awaken speculations among no few of the ship's company as to what it was that could be detaining in the cabin the master-at-arms and the sailor; for a rumor that both of them had been seen to enter it and neither of them had been seen to emerge, this rumor had got abroad upon the gun decks and in the tops, the people of a great warship being in one respect like villagers, taking microscopic note of every outward movement or non-movement going on. When therefore, in weather not at all tempestuous, all hands were called in the second dogwatch, a summons under such circumstances not usual in those hours, the crew were not wholly unprepared for some announcement extraordinary, one having connection too with the continued absence of the two men from their wonted haunts.

There was a moderate sea at the time; and the moon, newly risen and near to being at its full, silvered the white spar deck wherever not blotted by the clear-cut shadows horizontally thrown of fixtures and moving men. On either side of the quarter-deck the marine guard under arms was drawn up; and Captain Vere, standing in his place surrounded by all the wardroom officers, addressed his men. In so doing, his manner showed neither more nor less than that properly pertaining to his supreme position aboard his own ship. In clear terms and concise he told them what had taken place in the cabin: that the master-at-arms was dead, that he who had killed him had been already tried by a summary court and condemned to death, and that the execution would take place in the early morning watch. The word *mutiny* was not named in what he said. He refrained too from making the occasion an opportunity for any preachment as to the maintenance of discipline, thinking perhaps that under existing circumstances in the navy the consequence of violating discipline should be made to speak for itself.

Their captain's announcement was listened to by the throng of standing sailors in a dumbness like that of a seated congregation of believers in hell listening to the clergyman's announcement of his Calvinistic text.

At the close, however, a confused murmur went up. It began to wax. All but instantly, then, at a sign, it was pierced and suppressed by shrill whistles of the boatswain and his mates. The word was given to about ship.

To be prepared for burial Claggart's body was delivered to certain petty officers of his mess. And here, not to clog the sequel with lateral matters, it may be added that at a suitable hour, the master-at-arms was committed to the sea with every funeral honor properly belonging to his naval grade.

In this proceeding as in every public one growing out of the tragedy, strict adherence to usage was observed. Nor in any point could it have been at all deviated from, either with respect to Claggart or Billy Budd, without begetting undesirable speculations in the ship's company, sailors, and more particularly men-of-war's men, being of all men the greatest sticklers for usage. For similar cause, all communication between Captain Vere and the condemned one ended with the closeted interview already given, the latter being now surrendered to the ordinary routine preliminary to the end. His transfer under guard from the captain's quarters was effected without unusual precautions—at least no visible ones. If possible, not to let the men so much as surmise that their officers anticipate aught amiss from them is the tacit rule in a military ship. And the more that some sort of trouble should really be apprehended, the more do the officers keep that apprehension to themselves, though not the less unostentatious vigilance may be augmented. In the present instance, the sentry placed over the prisoner had strict orders to let no one have communication with him but the chaplain. And certain unobtrusive measures were taken absolutely to insure this point.

24

In a seventy-four of the old order the deck known as the upper gun deck was the one covered over by the spar deck, which last, though not without its armament, was for the most part exposed to the weather. In general it was at all hours free from hammocks; those of the crew swinging on the lower gun deck and berth deck, the latter being not only a dormitory but also the place for the stowing of the sailors' bags, and on both sides lined with the large chests or movable pantries of the many messes of the men.

On the starboard side of the *Bellipotent's* upper gun deck, behold Billy Budd under sentry lying prone in irons in one of the bays formed by the regular spacing of the guns comprising the batteries on either side. All these pieces were of the heavier caliber of that period. Mounted on lumbering wooden carriages, they were hampered with cumbersome harness of breeching and strong side-tackles for running them out. Guns and carriages, together with the long rammers and shorter linstocks lodged in loops overhead—all these, as customary, were painted black; and the heavy hempen breechings, tarred to the same tint, wore the like livery of the undertakers. In contrast with the funereal hue of these surroundings, the prone sailor's exterior apparel, white jumper and white duck trousers, each more or less soiled, dimly glimmered in the obscure light of the bay like a patch of discolored snow in early April lingering at some upland cave's black mouth. In effect he is already in his shroud, or the garments that shall serve him in lieu of one. Over him, but scarce illuminating him, two battle lanterns swing from two massive beams of the deck above. Fed with the oil supplied by the war contractors (whose gains, honest or otherwise, are in every land an anticipated portion of the harvest of death), with flickering splashes of dirty yellow light they pollute the pale moonshine all but ineffectually struggling in obstructed flecks through the open ports from which the tampioned cannon protrude. Other lanterns at intervals serve but to bring out somewhat the obscurer bays which, like small confessionals or side-chapels in a cathedral, branch from the long dim-vistaed broad aisle between the two batteries of that covered tier.

Such was the deck where now lay the Handsome Sailor. Through the rose-tan of his complexion no pallor could have shown. It would have taken days of sequestration from the winds and the sun to have brought about the effacement of that. But the skeleton in the cheekbone at the point of its angle was just beginning delicately to be defined under the warm-tinted skin. In fervid hearts self-contained, some brief experiences devour our human tissue as secret fire in a ship's hold consumes cotton in the bale.

But now lying between the two guns, as nipped in the vice of fate, Billy's agony, mainly proceeding from a generous young heart's virgin experience of the diabolical incarnate and effective in some men—the tension of that agony was over now. It survived not the something healing in the closeted interview with Captain Vere. Without movement, he lay as in a trance, that adolescent expression previously noted as his taking on something akin to the look of a slumbering child in the cradle when the warm hearth-glow of the still chamber at night plays on the dimples that at whiles mysteriously form in the cheek, silently coming and going there. For now and then in the gyved one's trance a serene happy light born of some wandering reminiscence or dream would diffuse itself over his face, and then wane away only anew to return.

The chaplain, coming to see him and finding him thus, and perceiving no sign that he was conscious of his presence, attentively regarded him for a space, then slipping aside, withdrew for the time, peradventure feeling that even he, the minister of Christ, though receiving his stipend from Mars, had no consolation to proffer which could result in a peace transcending that which he beheld. But in the small hours he came again.

And the prisoner, now awake to his surroundings, noticed his approach, and civilly, all but cheerfully, welcomed him. But it was to little purpose that in the interview following, the good man sought to bring Billy Budd to some godly understanding that he must die, and at dawn. True, Billy himself freely referred to his death as a thing close at hand; but it was something in the way that children will refer to death in general, who yet among their other sports will play a funeral with hearse and mourners.

Not that like children Billy was incapable of conceiving what death really is. No, but he was wholly without irrational fear of it, a fear more prevalent in highly civilized communities than those so-called barbarous ones which in all respects stand nearer to unadulterate Nature. And, as elsewhere said, a barbarian Billy radically was—as much so, for all the costume, as his countrymen the British captives, living trophies, made to march in the Roman triumph of Germanicus. Quite as much so as those later barbarians, young men probably, and picked specimens among the earlier British converts to Christianity, at least nominally such, taken to Rome (as today converts from lesser isles of the sea may be taken to London), of whom the Pope of that time, admiring the strangeness of their personal beauty so unlike the Italian stamp, their clear ruddy complexion and curled flaxen locks, exclaimed, "Angles" (meaning *English,* the modern derivative), "Angles, do you call them? And is it because they look so like angels?" Had it been later in time, one would think that the Pope had in mind Fra Angelico's seraphs, some of whom, plucking apples in gardens of the Hesperides, have the faint rosebud complexion of the more beautiful English girls.

If in vain the good chaplain sought to impress the young barbarian with ideas of death akin to those conveyed in the skull, dial, and crossbones on old tombstones, equally futile to all appearance were his efforts to bring home to him the thought of salvation and a Savior. Billy listened, but less out of awe or reverence, perhaps, than from a certain natural politeness, doubt-less at bottom regarding all that in much the same way that most mariners of his class take any discourse abstract or out of the common tone of the workaday world. And this sailor way of taking clerical discourse is not wholly unlike the way in which the primer of Christianity, full of transcendent miracles, was received long ago on tropic isles by any superior *savage,* so-called—a Tahitian, say, of Captain Cook's time or shortly after that time. Out of natural courtesy he received, but did not appropriate. It was like a gift placed in the palm of an outreached hand upon which the fingers do not close.

But the *Bellipotent*'s chaplain was a discreet man possessing the good sense of a good heart. So he insisted not in his vocation here. At the instance of Captain Vere, a lieutenant had apprised him of pretty much everything as to Billy; and since he felt that innocence was even a better thing than religion wherewith to go to Judgment, he reluctantly withdrew; but in his emotion not without first performing an act strange enough in an En-glishman, and under the circumstances yet more so in any regular priest. Stooping over, he kissed on the fair cheek his fellow man, a felon in martial law, one whom though on the confines of death he felt he could never convert to a dogma; nor for all that did he fear for his future.

Marvel not that having been made acquainted with the young sailor's essential innocence the worthy man lifted not a finger to avert the doom of such a martyr to martial discipline. So to do would not only have been as idle as invoking the desert, but would also have been an audacious transgression of the bounds of his function, one as exactly prescribed to him by military law as that of the boatswain or any other naval officer. Bluntly put, a chaplain is the minister of the Prince of Peace serving in the host of the God of War—Mars. As such, he is as incongruous as a musket would be on the altar at Christmas. Why, then, is he there? Because he indirectly subserves the purpose attested by the cannon; because too he lends the sanction of the religion of the meek to that which practically is the abrogation of everything but brute Force.

25

The night so luminous on the spar deck, but otherwise on the cavernous ones below, levels so like the tiered galleries in a coal mine—the luminous night passed away. But like the prophet in the chariot disappearing in heaven and dropping his mantle to Elisha, the withdrawing night transferred its pale robe to the breaking day. A meek, shy light appeared in the East, where stretched a diaphanous fleece of white furrowed vapor. That light slowly waxed. Suddenly *eight bells* was struck aft, responded to by one louder metallic stroke from forward. It was four o'clock in the morning. Instantly the silver whistles were heard summoning all hands to witness punishment. Up through the great hatchways rimmed with racks of heavy shot the watch below came pouring, overspreading with the watch already on deck the space between the mainmast and foremast including that occupied by the capacious launch and the black booms tiered on either side of it, boat and booms making a summit of observation for the powder-boys and younger tars. A different group comprising one watch of topmen leaned over the rail of that sea balcony, no small one in a seventy-four, looking down on the crowd below. Man or boy, none spake but in whisper, and few spake at all. Captain Vere—as before, the central figure among the assembled commissioned officers—stood nigh the break of the poop-deck facing forward. Just below him on the quarter-deck the marines in full equipment were drawn up much as at the scene of the promulgated sentence.

At sea in the old time, the execution by halter of a military sailor was generally from the foreyard. In the present instance, for special reasons the mainyard was assigned. Under an arm of that yard the prisoner was presently brought up, the chaplain attending him. It was noted at the time, and remarked upon afterwards, that in this final scene the good man evinced little or nothing of the perfunctory. Brief speech indeed he had with the condemned one, but the genuine Gospel was less on his tongue than in his aspect and manner towards him. The final preparations personal to the latter being speedily brought to an end by two boatswain's mates, the consummation impended. Billy stood facing aft. At the penultimate moment, his words, his only ones, words wholly unobstructed in the utterance, were these: "God bless Captain Vere!" Syllables so unanticipated coming from one with the ignominious hemp about his neck —a conventional felon's benediction directed aft towards the quarters of honor; syllables too delivered in the clear melody of a singing bird on the point of launching from the twig—had a phenomenal effect, not unenhanced by the rare personal beauty of the young sailor, spiritualized now through late experiences so poignantly profound.

Without volition, as it were, as if indeed the ship's populace were but the vehicles of some vocal current-electric, with one voice from alow and aloft came a resonant sympathetic echo: "God bless Captain Vere!" And yet at that instant Billy alone must have been in their hearts, even as in their eyes.

At the pronounced words and the spontaneous echo that voluminously rebounded them, Captain Vere, either through stoic self-control or a sort of momentary paralysis induced by emotional shock, stood erectly rigid as a musket in the ship-armorer's rack.

The hull, deliberately recovering from the periodic roll to leeward, was just regaining an even keel when the last signal, a preconcerted dumb one, was given. At the same moment it chanced that the vapory fleece hanging low in the East was shot through with a soft glory as of the fleece of the Lamb of God seen in mystical vision, and simultaneously therewith, watched by the wedged mass of upturned faces, Billy ascended; and, ascending, took the full rose of the dawn.

In the pinioned figure arrived at the yard-end, to the wonder of all no motion was apparent, none save that created by the slow roll of the hull in moderate weather, so majestic in a great ship ponderously cannoned.

26   *How Billy reacted to hanging*

When some days afterwards, in reference to the singularity just mentioned, the purser, a rather ruddy, rotund person more accurate as an accountant than profound as a philosopher, said at mess to the surgeon, "What testimony to the force lodged in will power," the latter, saturnine, spare, and tall, one in whom a discreet causticity went along with a manner less genial than polite, replied, "Your pardon, Mr. Purser. In a hanging scientifically conducted—and under special orders I myself directed how Budd's was to be effected—any movement following the completed suspension and originating in the body suspended, such movement indicates mechanical spasm in the muscular system. Hence the absence of that is no more attributable to will power, as you call it, than to horsepower—begging your pardon."

"But this muscular spasm you speak of, is not that in a degree more or less invariable in these cases?"

"Assuredly so, Mr. Purser."

"How then, my good sir, do you account for its absence in this instance?"

"Mr. Purser, it is clear that your sense of the singularity in this matter equals not mine. You account for it by what you call will power—a term not yet included in the lexicon of science. For me, I do not, with my present knowledge, pretend to account for it at all. Even should we assume the hypothesis that at the first touch of the halyards the action of Budd's heart, intensified by extraordinary emotion at its climax, abruptly stopped—much like a watch when in carelessly winding it up you strain at the finish, thus snapping the chain—even under that hypothesis how account for the phenomenon that followed?"

"You admit, then, that the absence of spasmodic movement was phenomenal."

"It was phenomenal, Mr. Purser, in the sense that it was an appearance the cause of which is not immediately to be assigned."

"But tell me, my dear sir," pertinaciously continued the other, "was the man's death effected by the halter, or was it a species of euthanasia?"

"*Euthanasia,* Mr. Purser, is something like your *will power:* I doubt its authenticity as a scientific term—begging your pardon again. It is at once imaginative and metaphysical—in short, Greek.—But," abruptly changing his tone, "there is a case in the sick bay that I do not care to leave to my assistants. Beg your pardon, but excuse me." And rising from the mess he formally withdrew.

27

The silence at the moment of execution and for a moment or two continuing thereafter, a silence but emphasized by the regular wash of the sea against the hull or the flutter of a sail caused by the helmsman's eyes being tempted astray, this emphasized silence was gradually disturbed by a sound not easily to be verbally rendered. Whoever has heard the freshet-wave of a torrent suddenly swelled by pouring showers in tropical mountains, showers not shared by the plain; whoever has heard the first muffled murmur of its sloping advance through precipitous woods may form some conception of the sound now heard. The seeming remoteness of its source was because of its murmurous indistinctness, since it came from close by, even from the men massed on the ship's open deck. Being inarticulate, it was dubious in significance further than it seemed to indicate some capricious revulsion of thought or feeling such as mobs ashore are liable to, in the present instance possibly implying a sullen revocation on the men's part of their involuntary echoing of Billy's benediction. But ere the murmur had time to wax into clamor it was met by a strategic command, the more telling that it came with abrupt unexpectedness: "Pipe down the starboard watch, Boatswain, and see that they go."

Shrill as the shriek of the sea hawk, the silver whistles of the boatswain and his mates pierced that ominous low sound, dissipating it; and yielding to the mechanism of discipline the throng was thinned by one-half. For the remainder, most of them were set to temporary employments connected with trimming the yards and so forth, business readily to be got up to serve occasion by any officer of the deck.

Now each proceeding that follows a mortal sentence pronounced at sea by a drumhead court is characterized by promptitude not perceptibly merging into hurry, though bordering that. The hammock, the one which had been Billy's bed when alive, having already been ballasted with shot and otherwise prepared to serve for his canvas coffin, the last offices of the sea undertakers, the sailmaker's mates, were now speedily completed. When everything was in readiness a second call for all hands, made necessary by the strategic movement before mentioned, was sounded, and now to witness burial.

The details of this closing formality it needs not to give. But when the tilted plank let slide its freight into the sea, a second strange human murmur was heard, blended now with another inarticulate sound proceeding from certain larger seafowl who, their attention having been attracted by the peculiar commotion in the water resulting from the heavy sloped dive of the shotted hammock into the sea, flew screaming to the spot. So near the hull did they come, that the stridor or bony creak of their gaunt double-jointed pinions was audible. As the ship under light airs passed on, leaving the burial spot astern, they still kept circling it low down with the moving shadow of their outstretched wings and the croaked requiem of their cries.

Upon sailors as superstitious as those of the age preceding ours, men-of-war's men too who had just beheld the prodigy of repose in the form suspended in air, and now foundering in the deeps; to such mariners the action of the seafowl, though dictated by mere animal greed for prey, was big with no prosaic significance. An uncertain movement began among them, in which some encroachment was made. It was tolerated but for a moment. For suddenly the drum beat to quarters, which familiar sound happening at least twice every day, had upon the present occasion a signal peremptoriness in it. True martial discipline long continued superinduces in average man a sort of impulse whose operation at the official word of command much resembles in its promptitude the effect of an instinct.

The drumbeat dissolved the multitude, distributing most of them along the batteries of the two covered gun decks. There, as wonted, the guns' crews stood by their respective cannon erect and silent. In due course the first officer, sword under arm and standing in his place on the quarter-deck, formally received the successive reports of the sworded lieutenants commanding the sections of batteries below; the last of which reports being made, the summed report he delivered with the customary salute to the commander. All this occupied time, which in the present case was the object in beating to quarters at an hour prior to the customary one. That such variance from usage was authorized by an officer like Captain Vere, a martinet as some deemed him, was evidence of the necessity for unusual action implied in what he deemed to be temporarily the mood of his men. "With mankind," he would say, "forms, measured forms, are everything; and that is the import couched in the story of Orpheus with his lyre spellbinding the wild denizens of the wood." And this he once applied to the disruption of forms going on across the Channel and the consequences thereof.

At this unwonted muster at quarters, all proceeded as at the regular hour. The band on the quarter-deck played a sacred air, after which the chaplain went through the customary morning service. That done, the drum beat the retreat; and toned by music and religious rites subserving the discipline and purposes of war, the men in their wonted orderly manner dispersed to the places allotted them when not at the guns.

And now it was full day. The fleece of low-hanging vapor had vanished, licked up by the sun that late had so glorified it. And the circumambient air in the clearness of its serenity was like smooth white marble in the polished block not yet removed from the marble-dealer's yard.

28

The symmetry of form attainable in pure fiction cannot so readily be achieved in a narration esssentially having less to do with fable than with fact. Truth uncompromisingly told will always have its ragged edges; hence the conclusion of such a narration is apt to be less finished than an architectural finial.

How it fared with the Handsome Sailor during the year of the Great Mutiny has been faithfully given. But though properly the story ends with his life, something in way of sequel will not be amiss. Three brief chapters will suffice.

In the general rechristening under the Directory of the craft originally forming the navy of the French monarchy, the *St. Louis* line-of-battle ship was named the *Athée* (the *Atheist*). Such a name, like some other substituted ones in the Revolutionary fleet, while proclaiming the infidel audacity of the ruling power, was yet, though not so intended to be, the aptest name, if one consider it, ever given to a warship; far more so indeed than the *Devastation,* the *Erebus* (the *Hell*), and similar names bestowed upon fighting ships.

On the return passage to the English fleet from the detached cruise during which occurred the events already recorded, the *Bellipotent* fell in with the *Athée.* An engagement ensued, during which Captain Vere, in the act of putting his ship alongside the enemy with a view of throwing his boarders across her bulwarks, was hit by a musket ball from a porthole of the enemy's main cabin. More than disabled, he dropped to the deck and was carried below to the same cockpit where some of his men already lay. The senior lieutenant took command. Under him the enemy was finally captured, and though much crippled was by rare good fortune successfully taken into Gibraltar, an English port not very distant from the scene of the fight. There, Captain Vere with the rest of the wounded was put ashore. He lingered for some days, but the end came. Unhappily he was cut off too early for the Nile and Trafalgar. The spirit that 'spite its philosophic austerity may yet have indulged in the most secret of all passions, ambition, never attained to the fulness of fame.

Not long before death, while lying under the influence of that magical drug which, soothing the physical frame, mysteriously operates on the subtler element in man, he was heard to murmur words inexplicable to his attendant: "Billy Budd, Billy Budd." That these were not the accents of remorse would seem clear from what the attendant said to the *Bellipotent*'s senior officer of marines, who, as the most reluctant to condemn of the members of the drumhead court, too well knew, though here he kept the knowledge to himself, who Billy Budd was.

29

Some few weeks after the execution, among other matters under the head of "News from the Mediterranean," there appeared in a naval chronicle of the time, an authorized weekly publication, an account of the affair. It was doubtless for the most part written in good faith, though the medium, partly rumor, through which the facts must have reached the writer served to deflect and in part falsify them. The account was as follows:

"On the tenth of the last month a deplorable occurrence took place on board H.M.S. *Bellipotent*. John Claggart, the ship's master-at-arms, discovering that some sort of plot was incipient among an inferior section of the ship's company, and that the ringleader was one William Budd; he, Claggart, in the act of arraigning the man before the captain, was vindictively stabbed to the heart by the suddenly drawn sheath knife of Budd.

"The deed and the implement employed sufficiently suggest that though mustered into the service under an English name the assassin was no Englishman, but one of those aliens adopting English cognomens whom the present extraordinary necessities of the service have caused to be admitted into it in considerable numbers.

"The enormity of the crime and the extreme depravity of the criminal appear the greater in view of the character of the victim, a middle-aged man respectable and discreet, belonging to that minor official grade, the petty officers, upon whom, as none know better than the commissioned gentlemen, the efficiency of His Majesty's navy so largely depends. His function was a responsible one, at once onerous and thankless; and his fidelity in it the greater because of his strong patriotic impulse. In this instance as in so many other instances in these days, the character of this unfortunate man signally refutes, if refutation were needed, that peevish saying attributed to the late Dr. Johnson, that patriotism is the last refuge of a scoundrel.

"The criminal paid the penalty of his crime. The promptitude of the punishment has proved salutary. Nothing amiss is now apprehended aboard H.M.S. *Bellipotent*."

The above, appearing in a publication now long ago superannuated and forgotten, is all that hitherto has stood in human record to attest what manner of men respectively were John Claggart and Billy Budd.

30

Everything is for a term venerated in navies. Any tangible object associated with some striking incident of the service is converted into a monument. The spar from which the foretopman was suspended was for some few years kept trace of by the blue-jackets. Their knowledge followed it from ship to dockyard and again from dockyard to ship, still pursuing it even when at last reduced to a mere dockyard boom. To them a chip of it was as a piece of the Cross. Ignorant though they were of the secret facts of the tragedy, and not thinking but that the penalty was somehow unavoidably inflicted from the naval point of view, for all that, they instinctively felt that Billy was a sort of man as incapable of mutiny as of wilful murder. They recalled the fresh young image of the Handsome Sailor, that face never deformed by a sneer or subtler vile freak of the heart within. This impression of him was doubtless deepened by the fact that he was gone, and in a measure mysteriously gone. On the gun decks of the *Bellipotent* the general estimate of his nature and its unconscious simplicity eventually found rude utterance from another foretopman, one of his own watch, gifted, as some sailors are, with an artless *poetic* temperament. The tarry hand made some lines which, after circulating among the shipboard crews for a while, finally got rudely printed at Portsmouth as a ballad. The title given to it was the sailor's.

BILLY IN THE DARBIES

Good of the chaplain to enter Lone Bay
And down on his marrowbones here and pray
For the likes just o' me, Billy Budd. — But, look:
Through the port comes the moonshine astray!
It tips the guard's cutlass and silvers this nook;
But 'twill die in the dawning of Billy's last day.
A jewel-block they'll make of me tomorrow,
Pendant pearl from the yardarm-end
Like the eardrop I gave to Bristol Molly —
O, 'tis me, not the sentence they'll suspend.
Ay, ay, all is up; and I must up too,
Early in the morning, aloft from alow.
On an empty stomach now never it would do.
They'll give me a nibble — bit o' biscuit ere I go.

Sure, a messmate will reach me the last parting cup;
But, turning heads away from the hoist and the belay,
Heaven knows who will have the running of me up!
No pipe to those halyards.—But aren't it all sham?
A blur's in my eyes; it is dreaming that I am.
A hatchet to my hawser? All adrift to go?
The drum roll to grog, and Billy never know?
But Donald he has promised to stand by the plank;
So I'll shake a friendly hand ere I sink.
But—no! It is dead then I'll be, come to think.
I remember Taff the Welshman when he sank.
And his cheek it was like the budding pink.
But me they'll lash in hammock, drop me deep.
Fathoms down, fathoms down, how I'll dream fast asleep.
I feel it stealing now. Sentry, are you there?
Just ease these darbies at the wrist,
And roll me over fair,
I am sleepy, and the oozy weeds about me twist.

ADAM SMITH was born in 1723 in Kircaldy, Scotland, not far from Edinburgh. When he was three years old, he was abducted by gypsies, but was later rescued. Smith studied philosophy at the University of Glasgow and then won a scholarship to Oxford. After returning to Kircaldy, he began to give public lectures in Edinburgh, and this led to Smith's appointment in 1751 as professor of logic at the University of Glasgow. A year later, Smith was promoted to a professorship of moral philosophy. He was elected dean of the faculty, and in 1759 he published his first book, *The Theory of Moral Sentiments*. The success of his book brought Smith an invitation to serve as tutor to the Duke of Buccleuch, with the promise of travel to Europe, so Smith resigned from Glasgow and went to France, Switzerland, and London, meeting Voltaire, Edmund Burke, Samuel Johnson, Edward Gibbon, and Benjamin Franklin en route. In 1767 he came home and spent the next ten years writing *The Wealth of Nations* (1776). Smith died in 1790.

A selection from *The Wealth of Nations,* edited by Edwin Cannan. Publisher: The Modern Library, Random House, Inc., 1965. From pages lvii and lviii and Book I, Chapters 1–8.

Wealth of Nations

INTRODUCTION AND PLAN OF THE WORK

The annual labour of every nation is the fund which supplies it with all the necessaries and conveniencies of life which it annually consumes, and which consist always either in the immediate produce of that labour, or in what is purchased with that produce from other nations.

According, therefore, as this produce, or what is purchased with it, bears a greater or smaller proportion to the number of those who are to consume it, the nation will be better or worse supplied with all the necessaries and conveniencies for which it has occasion.

But this proportion must in every nation be regulated by two different circumstances; first, by the skill, dexterity, and judgment with which its labour is generally applied; and, secondly, by the proportion between the number of those who are employed in useful labour, and that of those who are not so employed. Whatever be the soil, climate, or extent of territory of any particular nation, the abundance or scantiness of its annual supply must, in that particular situation, depend upon those two circumstances.

The abundance or scantiness of this supply too seems to depend more upon the former of those two circumstances than upon the latter. Among the savage nations of hunters and fishers, every individual who is able to work, is more or less employed in useful labour, and endeavours to provide, as well as he can, the necessaries and conveniencies of life, for himself, or such of his family or tribe as are either too old, or too young, or too infirm to go hunting and fishing. Such nations, however, are so miserably poor, that from mere want, they are frequently reduced, or, at least, think themselves reduced, to the necessity sometimes of directly destroying, and sometimes of abandoning their infants, their old people, and those afflicted with lingering diseases, to perish with hunger, or to be devoured by wild beasts. Among civilized and thriving nations, on the contrary, though a great number of people do not labour at all, many of whom consume the produce of ten times, frequently of a hundred times more labour than the greater part of those who work; yet the produce of the whole labour of the society is so great, that all are often abundantly supplied, and a workman, even of the lowest and poorest order, if he is frugal and industrious, may enjoy a greater share of the necessaries and conveniencies of life than it is possible for any savage to acquire.

The causes of this improvement in the productive powers of labour, and the order, according to which its produce is naturally distributed among the different ranks and conditions of men in the society, make the subject of . . . this Inquiry. . . .

CHAPTER I
Of the Division of Labour

The greatest improvement in the productive powers of labour, and the greater part of the skill, dexterity, and judgment with which it is anywhere directed, or applied, seem to have been the effects of the division of labour.

The effects of the division of labour, in the general business of society, will be more easily understood, by considering in what manner it operates in some particular manufactures. It is commonly supposed to be carried furthest in some very trifling ones; not perhaps that it really is carried further in them than in others of more importance; but in those trifling manufactures which are destined to supply the small wants of but a small number of people, the whole number of workmen must necessarily be small; and those employed in every different branch of the work can often be collected into the same workhouse, and placed at once under the view of the spectator. In those great manufactures, on the contrary, which are destined to supply the great wants of the great body of the people, every different branch of the work employs so great a number of workmen, that it is impossible to collect them all into the same workhouse. We can seldom see more, at one time, than those employed in one single branch. Though in such manufactures, therefore, the work may really be divided into a much greater number of parts, than in those of a more trifling nature, the division is not near so obvious, and has accordingly been much less observed.

To take an example, therefore, from a very trifling manufacture; but one in which the division of labour has been very often taken notice of, the trade of the pin-maker; a workman not educated to this business (which the division of labour has rendered a distinct trade), nor acquainted with the use of the machinery employed in it (to the invention of which the same division of labour has probably given occasion), could scarce, perhaps, with his utmost industry, make one pin in a day, and certainly could not make twenty. But in the way in which this business is now carried on, not only the whole work is a peculiar trade, but it is divided into a number of branches, of which the greater part are likewise peculiar trades. One man draws out the wire, another straights it, a third cuts it, a fourth points it, a fifth grinds it at the top for receiving the head; to make the head requires two or three distinct operations; to put it on, is a peculiar business, to whiten the pins is another; it is even a trade by itself to put them into the paper; and the important business of making a pin is, in this manner, divided into about eighteen distinct operations, which, in some manufactories, are all performed by distinct hands, though in others the same man will sometimes perform two or three of them. I have seen a small manufactory of this kind where ten men only were employed, and where some of them consequently performed two or three distinct operations. But though they were very poor, and therefore but indifferently accommodated with the necessary machinery, they could, when they exerted themselves, make among them about twelve pounds of pins in a day. There are in a pound upwards of four thousand pins of a middling size. Those ten persons, therefore, could make among them upwards of forty-eight thousand pins in a day. Each person, therefore, making a tenth part of forty-eight thousand pins, might be considered as making four thousand eight hundred pins in a day. But if they had all wrought separately and independently, and without any of them having been educated to this peculiar business, they certainly could not each of them have made twenty, perhaps not one pin in a day; that is, certainly, not the two hundred and fortieth, perhaps not the four thousand eight hundredth part of what they are at present capable of performing, in consequence of a proper division and combination of their different operations.

In every other art and manufacture, the effects of the division of labour are similar to what they are in this very trifling one; though, in many of them, the labour can neither be so much subdivided, nor reduced to so great a simplicity of operation. The division of labour, however, so far as it can be introduced, occasions, in every art, a proportionable increase of the productive powers of labour. The separation of different trades and employments from one another seems to have taken place in consequence of this advantage. This separation too is generally carried furthest in those countries which enjoy the highest degree of industry and improvement; what is the work of one man in a rude state of society, being generally that of several in an improved one. In every improved society, the farmer is generally nothing but a farmer; the manufacturer, nothing but a manufacturer. The labour too which is necessary to produce any one complete manufacture, is almost always divided among a great number of hands. How many different trades are employed in each branch of the linen and woollen manufactures, from the growers of the flax and the wool, to the bleachers and smoothers of the linen, or to the dyers and dressers of the cloth! The nature of agriculture, indeed, does not admit of so many subdivisions of labour, nor of so complete a separation of one business from another, as manufactures. It is impossible to separate so entirely, the business of the grazier from that of the corn-farmer, as the trade of the carpenter is commonly separated from that of the smith. The spinner is almost always a distinct person from the weaver; but the ploughman, the harrower, the sower of the seed, and the reaper of the corn, are often the same. The occasions for those different sorts of labour returning with the different seasons of the year, it is impossible that one man should be constantly employed in any one of them. This impossibility of making so complete and entire a separation of all the different branches of labour employed in agriculture, is perhaps the reason why the improvement of the productive powers of labour in this art, does not always keep pace with their improvement in manufactures. The most opulent nations, indeed, generally excel all their neighbours in agriculture as well as in manufactures; but they are commonly more distinguished by their superiority in the latter than in the former. Their lands are in general better cultivated, and having more labour and expence bestowed upon them, produce more in proportion to the extent and natural fertility of the ground. But this superiority of produce is seldom much more than in proportion to the superiority of labour and expence. In agriculture, the labour of the rich country is not always much more productive than that of the poor; or, at least, it is never so much more productive, as it commonly is in manufactures. The corn of the rich country, therefore, will not always, in the same degree of goodness, come cheaper to market than that of the poor. The corn of Poland, in the same degree of goodness, is as cheap as that of France, notwithstanding the superior opulence and improvement of the latter country. The corn of France is, in the corn provinces, fully as good, and in most years nearly about the same price with the corn of England, though, in opulence and improvement, France is perhaps inferior to England. The corn-lands of England, however, are better cultivated than those of France, and the corn-lands of France are said to be much better cultivated than those of Poland. But though the poor country, notwithstanding the inferiority of its cultivation, can, in some measure, rival the rich in the cheapness and goodness of its corn, it can pretend to no such competition in its manufactures; at least if those manufactures suit the soil, climate, and situation of the rich country. The silks of France are better and cheaper than those of England, because the silk manufacture, at least under the present high duties upon the importation of raw silk, does not so well suit the climate of England as that of France. But the hard-ware and the coarse woollens of England are beyond all comparison superior to those of France, and much cheaper too in the same degree of goodness. In Poland there are said to be scarce any manufactures of any kind, a few of those coarser household manufactures excepted, without which no country can well subsist.

This great increase of the quantity of work, which, in consequence of the division of labour, the same number of people are capable of performing, is owing to three different circumstances; first, to the increase of dexterity in every particular workman; secondly, to the saving of the time which is commonly lost in passing from one species of work to another; and lastly, to the invention of a great number of machines which facilitate and abridge labour, and enable one man to do the work of many.

First, the improvement of the dexterity of the workman necessarily increases the quantity of the work he can perform; and the division of labour, by reducing every man's business to some one simple operation, and by making this operation the sole employment of his life, necessarily increases very much the dexterity of the workman. A common smith, who, though accustomed to handle the hammer, has never been used to make nails, if upon some particular occasion he is obliged to attempt it, will scarce, I am assured, be able to make above two or three hundred nails in a day, and those too very bad ones. A smith who has been accustomed to make nails, but whose sole or principal business has not been that of a nailer, can seldom with his utmost diligence make more than eight hundred or a thousand nails in a day. I have seen several boys under twenty years of age who had never exercised any other trade but that of making nails, and who, when they exerted themselves, could make, each of them, upwards of two thousand three hundred nails in a day. The making of a nail, however, is by no means one of the simplest operations. The same person blows the bellows, stirs or mends the fire as there is occasion, heats the iron, and forges every part of the nail: In forging the head too he is obliged to change his tools. The different operations into which the making of a pin, or of a metal button, is subdivided, are all of them much more simple, and the dexterity of the person, of whose life it has been the sole business to perform them, is usually much greater. The rapidity with which some of the operations of those manufactures are performed, exceeds what the human hand could, by those who had never seen them, be supposed capable of acquiring.

Secondly, the advantage which is gained by saving the time commonly lost in passing from one sort of work to another, is much greater than we should at first view be apt to imagine it. It is impossible to pass very quickly from one kind of work to another, that is carried on in a different place, and with quite different tools. A country weaver, who cultivates a small farm, must lose a good deal of time in passing from his loom to the field, and from the field to his loom. When the two trades can be carried on in the same workhouse, the loss of time is no doubt much less. It is even in this case, however, very considerable. A man commonly saunters a little in turning his hand from one sort of employment to another. When he first begins the new work he is seldom very keen and hearty; his mind, as they say, does not go to it, and for some time he rather trifles than applies to good purpose. The habit of sauntering and of indolent careless application, which is naturally, or rather necessarily acquired by every country workman who is obliged to change his work and his tools every half hour, and to apply his hand in twenty different ways almost every day of his life, renders him almost always slothful and lazy, and incapable of any vigourous application even on the most pressing occasions. Independent, therefore, of his deficiency in point of dexterity, this cause alone must always reduce considerably the quantity of work which he is capable of performing.

Thirdly, and lastly, everybody must be sensible how much labour is facilitated and abridged by the application of proper machinery. It is unnecessary to give any example. I shall only observe, therefore, that the invention of all those machines by which labour is so much facilitated and abridged, seems to have been originally owing to the division of labour. Men are much more likely to discover easier and readier methods of attaining any object, when the whole attention of their minds is directed towards that single object, than when it is dissipated among a great variety of things. But in consequence of the division of labour, the whole of every man's attention comes naturally to be directed towards some one very simple object. It is naturally to be expected, therefore, that some one or other of those who are employed in each particular branch of labour should soon find out easier and readier methods of performing their own particular work, wherever the nature of it admits of such improvement. A great part of the machines made use of in those manufactures in which labour is most subdivided, were originally the inventions of common workmen, who, being each of them employed in some very simple operation, naturally turned their thoughts towards finding out easier and readier methods of performing it. Whoever has been much accustomed to visit such manufactures, must frequently have been shown very pretty machines, which were the inventions of such workmen, in order to facilitate and quicken their own particular part of the work. In the first fire engines, a boy was constantly employed to open and shut alternately the communication between the boiler and the cylinder, according as the piston either ascended or descended. One of those boys, who loved to play with his companions, observed that, by tying a string from the handle of the valve which opened this communication to another part of the machine, the valve would open and shut without his assistance, and leave him at liberty to divert himself with his play-fellows. One of the greatest improvements that has been made upon this machine, since it was first invented, was in this manner the discovery of a boy who wanted to save his own labour.

All the improvements in machinery, however, have by no means been the inventions of those who had occasion to use the machines. Many improvements have been made by the ingenuity of the makers of the machines, when to make them became the business of a peculiar trade; and some by that of those who are called philosophers or men of speculation, whose trade it is not to do anything, but to observe everything; and who, upon that account, are often capable of combining together the powers of the most distant and dissimilar objects. In the progress of society, philosophy or speculation becomes, like every other employment, the principal or sole trade and occupation of a particular class of citizens. Like every other employment too, it is subdivided into a great number of different branches, each of which affords occupation to a peculiar tribe or class of philosophers; and this subdivision of employment in philosophy, as well as in every other business, improves dexterity, and saves time. Each individual becomes more expert in his own peculiar branch, more work is done upon the whole, and the quantity of science is considerably increased by it.

It is the great multiplication of the productions of all the different arts, in consequence of the division of labour, which occasions, in a well-governed society, that universal opulence which extends itself to the lowest ranks of the people. Every workman has a great quantity of his own work to dispose of beyond what he himself has occasion for; and every other workman being exactly in the same situation, he is enabled to exchange a great quantity of his own goods for a great quantity, or, what comes to the same thing, for the price of a great quantity of theirs. He supplies them abundantly with what they have occasion for, and they accommodate him as amply with what he has occasion for, and a general plenty diffuses itself through all the different ranks of the society.

Observe the accommodation of the most common artificer or day-labourer in a civilized and thriving country, and you will perceive that the number of people of whose industry a part, though but a small part, has been employed in procuring him this accommodation, exceeds all computation. The woollen coat, for example, which covers the day-labourer, as coarse and rough as it may appear, is the produce of the joint labour of a great multitude of workmen. The shepherd, the sorter of the wool, the wool-comber or carder, the dyer, the scribbler, the spinner, the weaver, the fuller, the dresser, with many others, must all join their different arts in order to complete even this homely production. How many merchants and carriers, besides, must have been employed in transporting the materials from some of those workmen to others who often live in a very distant part of the country! How much commerce and navigation in particular, how many ship-builders, sailors, sail-makers, rope-makers, must have been employed in order to bring together the different drugs made use of by the dyer, which often come from the remotest corners of the world! What a variety of labour too is necessary in order to produce the tools of the meanest of those workmen! To say nothing of such complicated machines as the ship of the sailor, the mill of the fuller, or even the loom of the weaver, let us consider only what a variety of labour is requisite in order to form that very simple machine, the shears with which the shepherd clips the wool. The miner, the builder of the furnace for smelting the ore, the feller of the timber, the burner of the charcoal to be made use of in the smelting-house, the brick-maker, the brick-layer, the workmen who attend the furnace, the mill-wright, the forger, the smith, must all of them join their different arts in order to produce them. Were we to examine, in the same manner, all the different parts of his dress and household furniture, the coarse linen shirt which he wears next to his skin, the shoes which cover his feet, the bed which he lies on, and all the different parts which compose it, the kitchen-grate at which he prepares his victuals, the coals which he makes use of for that purpose, dug from the bowels of the earth, and brought to him perhaps by a long sea and a long land carriage, all the other utensils of his kitchen, all the furniture of his table, the knives and forks, the earthen or pewter plates upon which he serves up and divides his victuals, the different hands employed in preparing his bread and his beer, the glass window which lets in the heat and the light, and keeps out the wind and the rain, with all the knowledge and art requisite for preparing that beautiful and happy invention, without which these northern parts of the world could scarce have afforded a very comfortable habitation, together with the tools of all the different workmen employed in producing those different conveniencies; if we examine, I say, all these things, and consider what a variety of labour is employed about each of them, we shall be sensible that without the assistance and co-operation of many thousands, the very meanest person in a civilized country could not be provided, even according to, what we very falsely imagine, the easy and simple manner in which he is commonly accommodated. Compared, indeed, with the more extravagant luxury of the great, his accommodation must no doubt appear extremely simple and easy; and yet it may be true, perhaps, that the accommodation of a European prince does not always so much exceed that of an industrious and frugal peasant, as the accommodation of the latter exceeds that of many an African king, the absolute master of the lives and liberties of ten thousand naked savages.

CHAPTER II
Of the Principle Which Gives Occasion to the Division of Labour

This division of labour, from which so many advantages are derived, is not originally the effect of any human wisdom, which foresees and intends that general opulence to which it gives occasion. It is the necessary, though very slow and gradual, consequence of a certain propensity in human nature which has in view no such extensive utility; the propensity to truck, barter, and exchange one thing for another.

Whether this propensity be one of those original principles in human nature, of which no further account can be given; or whether, as seems more probable, it be the necessary consequence of the faculties of reason and speech, it belongs not to our present subject to enquire. It is common to all men, and to be found in no other race of animals, which seem to know neither this nor any other species of contracts. Two greyhounds, in running down the same hare, have sometimes the appearance of acting in some sort of concert. Each turns her towards his companion, or endeavours to intercept her when his companion turns her towards himself. This, however, is not the effect of any contract, but of the accidental concurrence of their passions in the same object at that particular time. Nobody ever saw a dog make a fair and deliberate exchange of one bone for another with another dog. Nobody ever saw one animal by its gestures and natural cries signify to another, this is mine, that yours; I am willing to give this for that. When an animal wants to obtain something either of a man or of another animal, it has no other means of persuasion but to gain the favour of those whose service it requires. A puppy fawns upon its dam, and a spaniel endeavours by a thousand attractions to engage the attention of its master who is at dinner, when it wants to be fed by him. Man sometimes uses the same arts with his brethren, and when he has no other means of engaging them to act according to his inclinations, endeavours by every servile and fawning attention to obtain their good will. He has not time, however, to do this upon every occasion. In civilized society he stands at all times in need of the co-operation and assistance of great multitudes, while his whole life is scarce sufficient to gain the friendship of a few persons. In almost every other race of animals each individual, when it is grown up to maturity, is entirely independent, and in its natural state has occasion for the assistance of no other living creature. But man has almost constant occasion for the help of his brethren, and it is in vain for him to expect it from their benevolence only. He will be more likely to prevail if he can interest their self-love in his favour, and show them that it is for their own advantage to do for him what he requires of them. Whoever offers to another a bargain of any kind, proposes to do this. Give me that which I want, and you shall have this which you want, is the meaning of every such offer; and it is in this manner that we obtain from one another the far greater part of those good offices which we stand in need of. It is not from the benevolence of the butcher, the brewer, or the baker, that we expect our dinner, but from their regard to their own interest. We address ourselves, not to their humanity but to their self-love, and never talk to them of our own necessities but of their advantages. Nobody but a beggar chooses to depend chiefly upon the benevolence of his fellow-citizens. Even a beggar does not depend upon it entirely. The charity of well-disposed people, indeed, supplies him with the whole fund of his subsistence. But though this principle ultimately provides him with all the necessaries of life which he has occasion for, it neither does nor can provide him with them as he has occasion for them. The greater part of his occasional wants are supplied in the same manner as those of other people, by treaty, by barter, and by purchase. With the money which one man gives him he purchases food. The old clothes which another bestows upon him he exchanges for other old clothes which suit him better, or for lodging, or for food, or for money, with which he can buy either food, clothing, or lodging, as he has occasion.

As it is by treaty, by barter, and by purchase, that we obtain from one another the greater part of those mutual good offices which we stand in need of, so it is this same trucking disposition which originally gives occasion to the division of labour. In a tribe of hunters or shepherds a particular person makes bows and arrows, for example, with more readiness and dexterity than any other. He frequently exchanges them for cattle or for venison with his companions; and he finds at last that he can in this manner get more cattle and venison, than if he himself went to the field to catch them. From a regard to his own interest, therefore, the making of bows and arrows grows to be his chief business, and he becomes a sort of armourer. Another excels in making the frames and covers of their little huts or moveable houses. He is accustomed to be of use in this way to his neighbours, who reward him in the same manner with cattle and with venison, till at last he finds it his interest to dedicate himself entirely to this employment, and to become a sort of house-carpenter. In the same manner a third becomes a smith or a brazier; a fourth a tanner or dresser of hides or skins, the principal part of the clothing of savages. And thus the certainty of being able to exchange all that surplus part of the produce of his own labour, which is over and above his own consumption, for such parts of the produce of other men's labour as he may have occasion for, encourages every man to apply himself to a particular occupation, and to cultivate and bring to perfection whatever talent or genius he may possess for that particular species of business.

The difference of natural talents in different men is, in reality, much less than we are aware of; and the very different genius which appears to distinguish men of different professions, when grown up to maturity, is not upon many occasions so much the cause, as the effect of the division of labour. The difference between the most dissimilar characters, between a philosopher and a common street porter, for example, seems to arise not so much from nature, as from habit, custom, and education. When they came into the world, and for the first six or eight years of their existence, they were, perhaps, very much alike, and neither their parents nor play-fellows could perceive any remarkable difference. About that age, or soon after, they come to be employed in very different occupations. The difference of talents comes then to be taken notice of, and widens by degrees, till at last the vanity of the philosopher is willing to acknowledge scarce any resemblance. But without the disposition to truck, barter, and exchange, every man must have procured to himself every necessary and conveniency of life which he wanted. All must have had the same duties to perform, and the same work to do, and there could have been no such difference of employment as could alone give occasion to any great difference of talents.

As it is this disposition which forms that difference of talents, so remarkable among men of different professions, so it is this same disposition which renders that difference useful. Many tribes of animals acknowledged to be all of the same species, derive from nature a much more remarkable distinction of genius, than what, antecedent to custom and education, appears to take place among men. By nature a philosopher is not in genius and disposition half so different from a street porter, as a mastiff is from a greyhound, or a greyhound from a spaniel, or this last from a shepherd's dog. Those different tribes of animals, however, though all of the same species, are of scarce any use to one another. The strength of the mastiff is not in the least supported either by the swiftness of the greyhound, or by the sagacity of the spaniel, or by the docility of the shepherd's dog. The effects of those different geniuses and talents, for want of the power or disposition to barter and exchange, cannot be brought into a common stock, and do not in the least contribute to the better accommodation and conveniency of the species. Each animal is still obliged to support and defend itself, separately and independently, and derives no sort of advantage from that variety of talents with which nature has distinguished its fellows. Among men, on the contrary, the most dissimilar geniuses are of use to one another; the different produces of their respective talents, by the general disposition to truck, barter, and exchange, being brought, as it were, into a common stock, where every man may purchase whatever part of the produce of other men's talents he has occasion for.

CHAPTER III

That the Division of Labour is Limited by the Extent of the Market

As it is the power of exchanging that gives occasion to the division of labour, so the extent of this division must always be limited by the extent of that power, or, in other words, by the extent of the market. When the market is very small, no person can have any encouragement to dedicate himself entirely to one employment, for want of the power to exchange all that surplus part of the produce of his own labour, which is over and above his own consumption, for such parts of the produce of other men's labour as he has occasion for.

There are some sorts of industry, even of the lowest kind, which can be carried on nowhere but in a great town. A porter, for example, can find employment and subsistence in no other place. A village is by much too narrow a sphere for him; even an ordinary market town is scarce large enough to afford him constant occupation. In the lone houses and very small villages which are scattered about in so deserted a country as the Highlands of Scotland, every farmer must be butcher, baker, and brewer for his own family. In such situations we can scarce expect to find even a smith, a carpenter, or a mason, within less than twenty miles of another of the same trade. The scattered families that live at eight or ten miles distance from the nearest of them, must learn to perform themselves a great number of little pieces of work, for which, in more populous countries, they would call in the assistance of those workmen. Country workmen are almost everywhere obliged to apply themselves to all the different branches of industry that have so much affinity to one another as to be employed about the same sort of materials. A country carpenter deals in every sort of work that is made of wood; a country smith in every sort of work that is made of iron. The former is not only a carpenter, but a joiner, a cabinet maker, and even a carver in wood, as well as a wheelwright, a ploughwright, a cart and wagon maker. The employments of the latter are still more various. It is impossible there should be such a trade as even that of a nailer in the remote and inland parts of the Highlands of Scotland. Such a workman at the rate of a thousand nails a day, and three hundred working days in the year, will make three hundred thousand nails in the year. But in such a situation it would be impossible to dispose of one thousand, that is, of one day's work in the year.

As by means of water-carriage a more extensive market is opened to every sort of industry than what land-carriage alone can afford it, so it is upon the seacoast, and along the banks of navigable rivers, that industry of every kind naturally begins to subdivide and improve itself, and it is frequently not till a long time after that those improvements extend themselves to the inland parts of the country. A broad-wheeled wagon, attended by two men, and drawn by eight horses, in about six weeks' time carries and brings back between London and Edinburgh near four ton weight of goods. In about the same time a ship navigated by six or eight men, and sailing between the ports of London and Leith, frequently carries and brings back two hundred ton weight of goods. Six or eight men, therefore, by the help of water-carriage, can carry and bring back in the same time the same quantity of goods between London and Edinburgh, as fifty broad-wheeled wagons, attended by a hundred men, and drawn by four hundred horses. Upon two hundred tons of goods, therefore, carried by the cheapest land-carriage from London to Edinburgh, there must be charged the maintenance of a hundred men for three weeks, and both the maintenance, and, what is nearly equal to the maintenance, the wear and tear of four hundred horses as well as of fifty great wagons. Whereas, upon the same quantity of goods carried by water, there is to be charged only the maintenance of six or eight men, and the wear and tear of a ship of two hundred tons burden, together with the value of the superior risk, or the difference of the insurance between land and water-carriage. Were there no other communication between those two places, therefore, but by land-carriage, as no goods could be transported from the one to the other, except such whose price was very considerable in proportion to their weight, they could carry on but a small part of that commerce which at present subsists between them, and consequently could give but a small part of that encouragement which they at present mutually afford to each other's industry. There could be little or no commerce of any kind between the distant parts of the world. What goods could bear the expence of land-carriage between London and Calcutta? Or if there were any so precious as to be able to support this expence, with what safety could they be transported through the territories of so many barbarous nations? Those two cities, however, at present carry on a very considerable commerce with each other, and by mutually affording a market, give a good deal of encouragement to each other's industry.

Since such, therefore, are the advantages of water-carriage, it is natural that the first improvements of art and industry should be made where this conveniency opens the whole world for a market to the produce of every sort of labour, and that they should always be much later in extending themselves into the inland parts of the country. The inland parts of the country can for a long time have no other market for the greater part of their goods, but the country which lies round about them, and separates them from the seacoast, and the great navigable rivers. The extent of their market, therefore, must for a long time be in proportion to the riches and populousness of that country, and consequently their improvement must always be posterior to the improvement of that country. In our North American colonies the plantations have constantly followed either the sea-coast or the banks of navigable rivers, and have scarce anywhere extended themselves to any considerable distance from both.

The nations that, according to the best authenticated history, appear to have been first civilized, were those that dwelt round the coast of the Mediterranean Sea. That sea, by far the greatest inlet that is known in the world, having no tides, nor consequently any waves except such as are caused by the wind only, was, by the smoothness of its surface, as well as by the multitude of its islands, and the proximity of its neighbouring shores, extremely favourable to the infant navigation of the world; when, from their ignorance of the compass, men were afraid to quit the view of the coast, and from the imperfection of the art of ship-building, to abandon themselves to the boisterous waves of the ocean. To pass beyond the pillars of Hercules, that is, to sail out of the Straits of Gibraltar, was, in the ancient world, long considered as a most wonderful and dangerous exploit of navigation. It was late before even the Phenicians and Carthaginians, the most skilful navigators and ship-builders of those old times, attempted it, and they were for a long time the only nations that did attempt it.

Of all the countries on the coast of the Mediterranean Sea, Egypt seems to have been the first in which either agriculture or manufactures were cultivated and improved to any considerable degree. Upper Egypt extends itself nowhere above a few miles from the Nile, and in Lower Egypt that great river breaks itself into many different canals, which, with the assistance of a little art, seem to have afforded a communication by water-carriage, not only between all the great towns, but between all the considerable villages, and even to many farmhouses in the country; nearly in the same manner as the Rhine and the Maese do in Holland at present. The extent and easiness of this inland navigation was probably one of the principal causes of the early improvement of Egypt.

The improvements in agriculture and manufactures seem likewise to have been of very great antiquity in the provinces of Bengal in the East Indies, and in some of the eastern provinces of China; though the great extent of this antiquity is not authenticated by any histories of whose authority we, in this part of the world, are well assured. In Bengal the Ganges and several other great rivers form a great number of navigable canals in the same manner as the Nile does in Egypt. In the eastern provinces of China, too, several great rivers form, by their different branches, a multitude of canals, and by communicating with one another afford an inland navigation much more extensive than that either of the Nile or the Ganges, or perhaps than both of them put together. It is remarkable that neither the ancient Egyptians, nor the Indians, nor the Chinese, encouraged foreign commerce, but seem all to have derived their great opulence from this inland navigation.

All the inland parts of Africa, and all that part of Asia which lies any considerable way north of the Euxine and Caspian seas, the ancient Scythia, the modern Tartary and Siberia, seem in all ages of the world to have been in the same barbarous and uncivilized state in which we find them at present. The sea of Tartary is the frozen ocean which admits of no navigation, and though some of the greatest rivers in the world run through that country, they are at too great a distance from one another to carry commerce and communication through the greater part of it. There are in Africa none of those great inlets, such as the Baltic and Adriatic seas in Europe, the Mediterranean and Euxine seas in both Europe and Asia, and the gulfs of Arabia, Persia, India, Bengal, and Siam, in Asia, to carry maritime commerce into the interior parts of that great continent: and the great rivers of Africa are at too great a distance from one another to give occasion to any considerable inland navigation. The commerce besides which any nation can carry on by means of a river which does not break itself into any great number of branches or canals, and which runs into another territory before it reaches the sea, can never be very considerable; because it is always in the power of the nations who possess that other territory to obstruct the communication between the upper country and the sea. The navigation of the Danube is of very little use to the different states of Bavaria, Austria, and Hungary, in comparison of what it would be if any of them possessed the whole of its course till it falls into the Black Sea.

CHAPTER IV
Of the Origin and Use of Money

When the division of labour has been once thoroughly established, it is but a very small part of a man's wants which the produce of his own labour can supply. He supplies the far greater part of them by exchanging that surplus part of the produce of his own labour, which is over and above his own consumption, for such parts of the produce of other men's labour as he has occasion for. Every man thus lives by exchanging, or becomes in some measure a merchant, and the society itself grows to be what is properly a commercial society.

But when the division of labour first began to take place, this power of exchanging must frequently have been very much clogged and embarrassed in its operations. One man, we shall suppose, has more of a certain commodity than he himself has occasion for, while another has less. The former consequently would be glad to dispose of, and the latter to purchase, a part of this superfluity. But if this latter should chance to have nothing that the former stands in need of, no exchange can be made between them. The butcher has more meat in his shop than he himself can consume, and the brewer and the baker would each of them be willing to purchase a part of it. But they have nothing to offer in exchange, except the different productions of their respective trades, and the butcher is already provided with all the bread and beer which he has immediate occasion for. No exchange can, in this case, be made between them. He cannot be their merchant, nor they his customers; and they are all of them thus mutually less serviceable to one another. In order to avoid the inconveniency of such situations, every prudent man in every period of society, after the first establishment of the division of labour, must naturally have endeavoured to manage his affairs in such a manner, as to have at all times by him, besides the peculiar produce of his own industry, a certain quantity of some one commodity or other, such as he imagined few people would be likely to refuse in exchange for the produce of their industry.

Many different commodities, it is probable, were successively both thought of and employed for this purpose. In the rude ages of society, cattle are said to have been the common instrument of commerce; and, though they must have been a most inconvenient one, yet in old times we find things were frequently valued according to the number of cattle which had been given in exchange for them. The armour of Diomede, says Homer, cost only nine oxen; but that of Glaucus cost a hundred oxen. Salt is said to be the common instrument of commerce and exchanges in Abyssinia; a species of shells in some parts of the coast of India; dried cod at Newfoundland; tobacco in Virginia; sugar in some of our West India colonies; hides or dressed leather in some other countries; and there is at this day a village in Scotland where it is not uncommon, I am told, for a workman to carry nails instead of money to the baker's shop or the ale-house.

In all countries, however, men seem at last to have been determined by irresistible reasons to give the preference, for this employment, to metals above every other commodity. Metals cannot only be kept with as little loss as any other commodity, scarce anything being less perishable than they are, but they can likewise, without any loss, be divided into any number of parts, as by fusion those parts can easily be reunited again; a quality which no other equally durable commodities possess, and which more than any other quality renders them fit to be the instruments of commerce and circulation. The man who wanted to buy salt, for example, and had nothing but cattle to give in exchange for it, must have been obliged to buy salt to the value of a whole ox, or a whole sheep, at a time. He could seldom buy less than this, because what he was to give for it could seldom be divided without loss; and if he had a mind to buy more, he must, for the same reasons, have been obliged to buy double or triple the quantity, the value, to wit, of two or three oxen, or of two or three sheep. If, on the contrary, instead of sheep or oxen, he had metals to give in exchange for it, he could easily proportion the quantity of the metal to the precise quantity of the commodity which he had immediate occasion for.

Different metals have been made use of by different nations for this purpose. Iron was the common instrument of commerce among the ancient Spartans; copper among the ancient Romans; and gold and silver among all rich and commercial nations.

Those metals seem originally to have been made use of for this purpose in rude bars, without any stamp or coinage. Thus we are told by Pliny, upon the authority of Timaeus, an ancient historian, that, till the time of Servius Tullius, the Romans had no coined money, but made use of unstamped bars of copper, to purchase whatever they had occasion for. These rude bars, therefore, performed at this time the function of money.

The use of metals in this rude state was attended with two very considerable inconveniencies; first with the trouble of weighing; and, secondly, with that of assaying them. In the precious metals, where a small difference in the quantity makes a great difference in the value, even the business of weighing, with proper exactness, requires at least very accurate weights and scales. The weighing of gold in particular is an operation of some nicety. In the coarser metals, indeed, where a small error would be of little consequence, less accuracy would, no doubt, be necessary. Yet we should find it excessively troublesome, if every time a poor man had occasion either to buy or sell a farthing's worth of goods, he was obliged to weigh the farthing. The operation of assaying is still more difficult, still more tedious, and, unless a part of the metal is fairly melted in the crucible, with proper dissolvents, any conclusion that can be drawn from it is extremely uncertain. Before the institution of coined money, however, unless they went through this tedious and difficult operation, people must always have been liable to the grossest frauds and impositions, and instead of a pound weight of pure silver, or pure copper, might receive in exchange for their goods an adulterated composition of the coarsest and cheapest materials, which had, however, in their outward appearance, been made to resemble those metals. To prevent such abuses, to facilitate exchanges, and thereby to encourage all sorts of industry and commerce, it had been found necessary, in all countries that have made any considerable advances towards improvement, to affix a public stamp upon certain quantities of such particular metals, as were in those countries commonly made use of to purchase goods. Hence the origin of coined money, and of those public offices called mints; institutions exactly of the same nature with those of the aulnagers and stampmasters of woollen and linen cloth. All of them are equally meant to ascertain, by means of a public stamp, the quantity and uniform goodness of those different commodities when brought to market. . . .

It is in this manner that money has become in all civilized nations the universal instrument of commerce, by the intervention of which goods of all kinds are bought and sold, or exchanged for one another.

What are the rules which men naturally observe in exchanging them either for money or for one another, I shall now proceed to examine. These rules determine what may be called the relative or exchangeable value of goods.

The word VALUE, it is to be observed, has two different meanings, and sometimes expresses the utility of some particular object, and sometimes the power of purchasing other goods which the possession of that object conveys. The one may be called "value in use"; the other, "value in exchange." The things which have the greatest value in use have frequently little or no value in exchange; and on the contrary, those which have the greatest value in exchange have frequently little or no value in use. Nothing is more useful than water; but it will purchase scarce anything; scarce anything can be had in exchange for it. A diamond, on the contrary, has scarce any value in use; but a very great quantity of other goods may frequently be had in exchange for it.

In order to investigate the principles which regulate the exchangeable value of commodities, I shall endeavour to show,

First, what is the real measure of this exchangeable value; or, wherein consists the real price of all commodities.

Secondly, what are the different parts of which this real price is composed or made up.

And, lastly, what are the different circumstances which sometimes raise some or all of these different parts of price above, and sometimes sink them below, their natural or ordinary rate; or, what are the causes which sometimes hinder the market price, that is, the actual price of commodities, from coinciding exactly with what may be called their natural price. . . .

CHAPTER V

Of the Real and Nominal Price of Commodities, or of Their Price in Labour, and Their Price in Money

Every man is rich or poor according to the degree in which he can afford to enjoy the necessaries, conveniencies, and amusements of human life. But after the division of labour has once thoroughly taken place, it is but a very small part of these with which a man's own labour can supply him. The far greater part of them he must derive from the labour of other people, and he must be rich or poor according to the quantity of that labour which he can command, or which he can afford to purchase. The value of any commodity, therefore, to the person who possesses it, and who means not to use or consume it himself, but to exchange it for other commodities, is equal to the quantity of labour which it enables him to purchase or command. Labour, therefore, is the real measure of the exchangeable value of all commodities.

The real price of everything, what everything really costs to the man who wants to acquire it, is the toil and trouble of acquiring it. What everything is really worth to the man who has acquired it, and who wants to dispose of it or exchange it for something else, is the toil and trouble which it can save to himself, and which it can impose upon other people. What is bought with money or with goods is purchased by labour, as much as what we acquire by the toil of our own body. That money or those goods indeed save us this toil. They contain the value of a certain quantity of labour which we exchange for what is supposed at the time to contain the value of an equal quantity. Labour was the first price, the original purchase-money that was paid for all things. It was not by gold or by silver, but by labour, that all the wealth of the world was originally purchased; and its value, to those who possess it, and who want to exchange it for some new productions, is precisely equal to the quantity of labour which it can enable them to purchase or command.

Wealth, as Mr. Hobbes says, is power. But the person who either acquires, or succeeds to a great fortune, does not necessarily acquire or succeed to any political power, either civil or military. His fortune may, perhaps, afford him the means of acquiring both, but the mere possession of that fortune does not necessarily convey to him either. The power which that possession immediately and directly conveys to him, is the power of purchasing; a certain command over all the labour, or over all the produce of labour which is then in the market. His fortune is greater or less, precisely in proportion to the extent of this power; or to the quantity either of other men's labour, or, what is the same thing, of the produce of other men's labour, which it enables him to purchase or command. The exchangeable value of everything must always be precisely equal to the extent of this power which it conveys to its owner.

But though labour be the real measure of the exchangeable value of all commodities, it is not that by which their value is commonly estimated. It is often difficult to ascertain the proportion between two different quantities of labour. The time spent in two different sorts of work will not always alone de-

termine this proportion. The different degrees of hardship endured, and of ingenuity exercised, must likewise be taken into
account. There may be more labour in an hour's hard work than
in two hours' easy business; or in an hour's application to a
trade which it cost ten years' labour to learn, than in a month's
industry at an ordinary and obvious employment. But it is not
easy to find any accurate measure either of hardship or ingenuity.
In exchanging indeed the different productions of different sorts
of labour for one another, some allowance is commonly made
for both. It is adjusted, however, not by any accurate measure,
but by the haggling and bargaining of the market, according
to that sort of rough equality which, though not exact, is sufficient for carrying on the business of common life.

Every commodity, besides, is more frequently exchanged for,
and thereby compared with, other commodities than with labour. It is more natural, therefore, to estimate its exchangeable
value by the quantity of some other commodity than by that
of the labour which it can purchase. The greater part of people
too understand better what is meant by a quantity of a particular
commodity, than by a quantity of labour. The one is a plain
palpable object; the other an abstract notion, which, though it
can be made sufficiently intelligible, is not altogether so natural
and obvious.

But when barter ceases, and money has become the common
instrument of commerce, every particular commodity is more
frequently exchanged for money than for any other commodity.
The butcher seldom carries his beef or his mutton to the baker,
or the brewer, in order to exchange them for bread or for beer;
but he carries them to the market, where he exchanges them
for money, and afterwards exchanges that money for bread and
for beer. The quantity of money which he gets for them regulates
too the quantity of bread and beer which he can afterwards
purchase. It is more natural and obvious to him, therefore, to
estimate their value by the quantity of money, the commodity

for which he immediately exchanges them, than by that of bread and beer, the commodities for which he can exchange them only by the intervention of another commodity; and rather to say that his butcher's meat is worth threepence or fourpence a pound, than that it is worth three or four pounds of bread, or three or four quarts of small beer. Hence it comes to pass, that the exchangeable value of every commodity is more frequently estimated by the quantity of money, than by the quantity either of labour or of any other commodity which can be had in exchange for it.

Gold and silver, however, like every other commodity, vary in their value, are sometimes cheaper and sometimes dearer, sometimes of easier and sometimes of more difficult purchase. The quantity of labour which any particular quantity of them can purchase or command, or the quantity of other goods which it will exchange for, depends always upon the fertility or barrenness of the mines which happen to be known about the time when such exchanges are made. The discovery of the abundant mines of America reduced, in the sixteenth century, the value of gold and silver in Europe to about a third of what it had been before. As it cost less labour to bring those metals from the mine to the market, so when they were brought thither they could purchase or command less labour; and this revolution in their value, though perhaps the greatest, is by no means the only one of which history gives some account. But as a measure of quantity, such as the natural foot, fathom, or handful, which is continually varying in its own quantity, can never be an accurate measure of the quantity of other things; so a commodity which is itself continually varying in its own value, can never be an accurate measure of the value of other commodities. Equal quantities of labour, at all times and places, may be said to be of equal value to the labourer. In his ordinary state of health, strength, and spirits; in the ordinary degree of his skill and dexterity, he must always lay down the same portion of his ease, his liberty, and his happiness. The price which he pays must always be the same, whatever may be the quantity of goods which he receives in return for it. Of these, indeed, it may sometimes purchase a greater and sometimes a smaller quantity; but it is their value which varies, not that of the labour which purchases them. At all times and places that is dear which it is difficult to come at, or which it costs much labour to acquire; and that cheap which is to be had easily, or with very little labour. Labour alone, therefore, never varying in its own value, is alone the ultimate and real standard by which the value of all commodities can at all times and places be estimated and compared. It is their real price; money is their nominal price only.

But though equal quantities of labour are always of equal value to the labourer, yet to the person who employs him they appear sometimes to be of greater and sometimes of smaller value. He purchases them sometimes with a greater and sometimes with a smaller quantity of goods, and to him the price of labour seems to vary like that of all other things. It appears to him dear in the one case, and cheap in the other. In reality, however, it is the goods which are cheap in the one case, and dear in the other.

In this popular sense, therefore, labour, like commodities, may be said to have a real and a nominal price. Its real price may be said to consist in the quantity of the necessaries and conveniencies of life which are given for it; its nominal price, in the quantity of money. The labourer is rich or poor, is well or ill rewarded, in proportion to the real, not to the nominal price of his labour. . . .

CHAPTER VI
Of the Component Parts of the Price of Commodities

In that early and rude state of society which precedes both the accumulation of stock and the appropriation of land, the proportion between the quantities of labour necessary for acquiring different objects seems to be the only circumstance which can afford any rule for exchanging them for one other. If among a nation of hunters, for example, it usually costs twice the labour to kill a beaver which it does to kill a deer, one beaver should naturally exchange for or be worth two deer. It is natural that what is usually the produce of two days' or two hours' labour, should be worth double of what is usually the produce of one day's or one hour's labour.

If the one species of labour should be more severe than the other, some allowance will naturally be made for this superior hardship; and the produce of one hour's labour in the one way may frequently exchange for that of two hours' labour in the other.

Or if the one species of labour requires an uncommon degree of dexterity and ingenuity, the esteem which men have for such talents will naturally give a value to their produce, superior to what would be due to the time employed about it. Such talents can seldom be acquired but in consequence of long application, and the superior value of their produce may frequently be no more than a reasonable compensation for the time and labour which must be spent in acquiring them. In the advanced state of society, allowances of this kind, for superior hardship and superior skill, are commonly made in the wages of labour; and something of the same kind must probably have taken place in its earliest and rudest period.

In this state of things, the whole produce of labour belongs to the labourer; and the quantity of labour commonly employed in acquiring or producing any commodity is the only circumstance which can regulate the quantity of labour which it ought commonly to purchase, command, or exchange for.

As soon as stock has accumulated in the hands of particular persons, some of them will naturally employ it in setting to work industrious people, whom they will supply with materials and subsistence, in order to make a profit by the sale of their work, or by what their labour adds to the value of the materials.

In exchanging the complete manufacture either for money, for labour, or for other goods, over and above what may be sufficient to pay the price of the materials, and the wages of the workmen, something must be given for the profits of the undertaker of the work who hazards his stock in this adventure. The value which the workmen add to the materials, therefore, resolves itself in this case into two parts, of which the one pays their wages, the other the profits of their employer upon the whole stock of materials and wages which he advanced. He could have no interest to employ them, unless he expected from the sale of their work something more than what was sufficient to replace his stock to him; and he could have no interest to employ a great stock rather than a small one, unless his profits were to bear some proportion to the extent of his stock.

The profits of stock, it may perhaps be thought, are only a different name for the wages of a particular sort of labour, the labour of inspection and direction. They are, however, altogether different, are regulated by quite sufficient principles, and bear no proportion to the quantity, the hardship, or the ingenuity of this supposed labour of inspection and direction. They are regulated altogether by the value of the stock employed, and are greater or smaller in proportion to the extent of this stock. Let us suppose, for example, that in some particular place, where the common annual profits of manufacturing stock are ten percent, there are two different manufactures, in each of which twenty workmen are employed at the rate of fifteen pounds a year each, or at the expence of three hundred a year in each manufactory. Let us suppose too, that the coarse materials annually wrought up in the one cost only seven hundred pounds, while the finer materials in the other cost seven thousand. The capital annually employed in the one will in this case amount only to one thousand pounds; whereas that employed in the other will amount to seven thousand three hundred pounds. At the rate of ten percent, therefore, the undertaker of the one will expect a yearly profit of about one hundred pounds only; while that of the other will expect about seven hundred and thirty pounds. But though their profits are so very different, their labour of inspection and direction may be either altogether or very nearly the same. In many great works, almost the whole labour of this kind is committed to some principal clerk. His wages properly express the value of this labour of inspection and direction. Though in settling them some regard is had commonly, not only to his labour and skill, but to the trust which is reposed in him, yet they never bear any regular proportion to the capital of which he oversees the management; and the owner of this capital, though he is thus discharged of almost all labour, still expects that his profits should bear a regular proportion to his capital. In the price of commodities, therefore, the profits of stock constitute a component part altogether different from the wages of labour, and regulated by quite different principles.

In this state of things, the whole produce of labour does not always belong to the labourer. He must in most cases share it with the owner of the stock which employs him. Neither is the quantity of labour commonly employed in acquiring or producing any commodity the only circumstance which can regulate the quantity which it ought commonly to purchase, command, or exchange for. An additional quantity, it is evident, must be due for the profits of the stock which advanced the wages and furnished the materials of that labour.

As soon as the land of any country has all become private property, the landlords, like all other men, love to reap where they never sowed, and demand a rent even for its natural produce. The wood of the forest, the grass of the field, and all the natural fruits of the earth, which, when land was in common, cost the labourer only the trouble of gathering them, come, even to him, to have an additional price fixed upon them. He must give up to the landlord a portion of what his labour either collects or produces. This portion, or, what comes to the same thing, the price of this portion, constitutes the rent of land, and in the price of the greater part of commodities makes a third component part.

The real value of all the different component parts of price, it must be observed, is measured by the quantity of labour which they can, each of them, purchase or command. Labour measures the value not only of that part of price which resolves itself into labour, but of that which resolves itself into rent, and of that which resolves itself into profit.

In every society the price of every commodity finally resolves itself into some one or other, or all of those three parts; and in every improved society, all the three enter more or less, as component parts, into the price of the far greater part of commodities. . . .

Chapter VII
Of the Natural and Market Price of Commodities

There is in every society or neighbourhood an ordinary or average rate both of wages and profit in every different employment of labour and stock. This rate is naturally regulated, as I shall show hereafter, partly by the general circumstances of the society, their riches or poverty, their advancing, stationary, or declining condition; and partly by the particular nature of each employment.

There is likewise in every society or neighbourhood an ordinary or average rate of rent, which is regulated too, as I shall show hereafter, partly by the general circumstances of the society or neighbourhood in which the land is situated, and partly by the natural or improved fertility of the land.

These ordinary or average rates may be called the natural rates of wages, profit, and rent, at the time and place in which they commonly prevail.

When the price of any commodity is neither more nor less than what is sufficient to pay the rent of the land, the wages of the labour, and the profits of the stock employed in raising, preparing, and bringing it to market, according to their natural rates, the commodity is then sold for what may be called its natural price.

The commodity is then sold precisely for what it is worth, or for what it really costs the person who brings it to market; for though in common language what is called the prime cost of any commodity does not comprehend the profit of the person who is to sell it again, yet if he sells it at a price which does not allow him the ordinary rate of profit in his neighbourhood, he is evidently a loser by the trade; since by employing his stock in some other way he might have made that profit. His profit, besides, is his revenue, the proper fund of his subsistence. As, while he is preparing and bringing the goods to market, he advances to his workmen their wages, or their subsistence; so he advances to himself, in the same manner, his own subsistence, which is generally suitable to the profit which he may reasonably expect from the sale of his goods. Unless they yield him this profit, therefore, they do not repay him what they may very properly be said to have really cost him.

Though the price, therefore, which leaves him this profit, is not always the lowest at which a dealer may sometimes sell his goods, it is the lowest at which he is likely to sell them for any considerable time; at least where there is perfect liberty, or where he may change his trade as often as he pleases.

The actual price at which any commodity is commonly sold is called its market price. It may either be above, or below, or exactly the same with its natural price.

The market price of every particular commodity is regulated by the proportion between the quantity which is actually brought to market, and the demand of those who are willing to pay the natural price of the commodity, or the whole value of the rent, labour, and profit, which must be paid in order to bring it thither. Such people may be called the effectual demanders, and their demand the effectual demand, since it may be sufficient to effectuate the bringing of the commodity to market. It is different from the absolute demand. A very poor man may be said in some sense to have a demand for a coach and six; he might like to have it; but his demand is not an effectual demand, as the commodity can never be brought to market in order to satisfy it.

When the quantity of any commodity which is brought to market falls short of the effectual demand, all those who are willing to pay the whole value of the rent, wages, and profit, which must be paid in order to bring it thither, cannot be supplied with the quantity which they want. Rather than want it altogether, some of them will be willing to give more. A competition will immediately begin among them, and the market price will rise more or less above the natural price, according as either the greatness of the deficiency, or the wealth and wanton luxury of the competitors, happen to animate more or less the eagerness of the competition. Among competitors of equal wealth and luxury the same deficiency will generally occasion a more or less eager competition, according as the acquisition or the commodity happens to be of more or less importance to them. Hence the exorbitant price of the necessaries of life during the blockade of a town or in a famine.

When the quantity brought to market exceeds the effectual demand, it cannot be all sold to those who are willing to pay the whole value of the rent, wages, and profit, which must be paid in order to bring it thither. Some part must be sold to those who are willing to pay less, and the low price which they give for it must reduce the price of the whole. The market price will sink more or less below the natural price, according as the greatness of the excess increases more or less the competition of the sellers, or according as it happens to be more or less important to them to get immediately rid of the commodity. The same excess in the importation of perishable will occasion a much greater competition than in that of durable commodities; in the importation of oranges, for example, than in that of old iron.

When the quantity brought to market is just sufficient to supply the effectual demand and no more, the market price naturally comes to be either exactly, or as nearly as can be judged of, the same with the natural price. The whole quantity upon hand can be disposed of for this price, and cannot be disposed of for more. The competition of the different dealers obliges them all to accept of this price, but does not oblige them to accept of less.

The quantity of every commodity brought to market naturally suits itself to the effectual demand. It is the interest of all those who employ their land, labour, or stock, in bringing any commodity to market, that the quantity never should exceed the effectual demand; and it is the interest of all other people that it never should fall short of that demand.

If at any time it exceeds the effectual demand, some of the component parts of its price must be paid below their natural rate. If it is rent, the interest of the landlords will immediately prompt them to withdraw a part of their land; and if it is wages or profit, the interest of the labourers in the one case, and of their employers in the other, will prompt them to withdraw a part of their labour or stock from this employment. The quantity brought to market will soon be no more than sufficient to supply the effectual demand. All the different parts of its price will rise to their natural rate, and the whole price to its natural price.

If, on the contrary, the quantity brought to market should at any time fall short of the effectual demand, some of the component parts of its price must rise above their natural rate. If it is rent, the interest of all other landlords will naturally prompt them to prepare more land for the raising of this commodity; if it is wages or profit, the interest of all other labourers and dealers will soon prompt them to employ more labour and stock in preparing and bringing it to market. The quantity brought thither will soon be sufficient to supply the effectual demand. All the different parts of its price will soon sink to their natural rate, and the whole price to its natural price.

The natural price, therefore, is, as it were, the central price, to which the prices of all commodities are continually gravitating. Different accidents may sometimes keep them suspended a good deal above it, and sometimes force them down even somewhat below it. But whatever may be the obstacles which hinder them from settling in this center of repose and continuance, they are constantly tending towards it. . . .

But though the market price of every particular commodity is in this manner continually gravitating, if one may say so, towards the natural price, yet sometimes particular accidents, sometimes natural causes, and sometimes particular regulations of police, may, in many commodities, keep up the market price, for a long time together, a good deal above the natural price.

When by an increase in the effectual demand, the market price of some particular commodity happens to rise a good deal above the natural price, those who employ their stocks in supplying that market are generally careful to conceal this change. If it was commonly known, their great profit would tempt so many new rivals to employ their stocks in the same way, that, the effectual demand being fully supplied, the market price would soon be reduced to the natural price, and perhaps for some time even below it. If the market is at a great distance from the residence of those who supply it, they may sometimes be able to keep the secret for several years together, and may so long enjoy their extraordinary profits without any new rivals. Secrets of this kind, however, it must be acknowledged, can seldom be long kept; and the extraordinary profit can last very little longer than they are kept.

Secrets in manufactures are capable of being longer kept than secrets in trade. A dyer who has found the means of producing a particular colour with materials which cost only half the price of those commonly made use of, may, with good management, enjoy the advantage of his discovery as long as he lives, and even leave it as a legacy to his posterity. His extraordinary gains arise from the high price which is paid for this private labour. They properly consist in the high wages of that labour. But as they are repeated upon every part of his stock, and as their whole amount bears, upon that account, a regular proportion to it, they are commonly considered as extraordinary profits of stock.

Such enhancements of the market price are evidently the effects of particular accidents, of which, however, the operation may sometimes last for many years together.

Some natural productions require such a singularity of soil and situation, that all the land in a great country, which is fit for producing them, may not be sufficient to supply the effectual demand. The whole quantity brought to market, therefore, may be disposed of to those who are willing to give more than what is sufficient to pay the rent of the land which produced them, together with the wages of the labour, and the profits of the stock which were employed in preparing and bringing them to market, according to their natural rates. Such commodities may continue for whole centuries together to be sold at this high price; and that part of it which resolves itself into the rent of land is in this case the part which is generally paid above its natural rate. The rent of the land which affords such singular and esteemed productions, like the rent of some vineyards in France of a peculiarly happy soil and situation, bears no regular proportion to the rent of other equally fertile and equally well-cultivated land in its neighbourhood. The wages of the labour and the profits of the stock employed in bringing such commodities to market, on the contrary, are seldom out of their natural proportion to those of the other employments of labour and stock in their neighbourhood.

Such enhancements of the market price are evidently the effect of natural causes which may hinder the effectual demand from ever being fully supplied, and which may continue, therefore, to operate forever.

A monopoly granted either to an individual or to a trading company has the same effect as a secret in trade or manufactures. The monopolists, by keeping the market constantly under-stocked, by never fully supplying the effectual demand, sell their commodities much above the natural price, and raise their emol-uments, whether they consist in wages or profit, greatly above their natural rate.

The price of monopoly is upon every occasion the highest which can be got. The natural price, or the price of free com-petition, on the contrary, is the lowest which can be taken, not upon every occasion indeed, but for any considerable time to-gether. The one is upon every occasion the highest which can be squeezed out of the buyers, or which, it is supposed, they will consent to give; the other is the lowest which the sellers can commonly afford to take, and at the same time continue their business.

The exclusive privileges of corporations, statutes of appren-ticeship, and all those laws which restrain, in particular em-ployments, the competition to a smaller number than might otherwise go into them, have the same tendency, though in a less degree. They are a sort of enlarged monopolies, and may frequently, for ages together, and in whole classes of employ-ments, keep up the market price of particular commodities above the natural price, and maintain both the wages of the labour and the profits of the stock employed about them somewhat above their natural rate.

Such enhancements of the market price may last as long as the regulations of police which give occasion to them.

The market price of any particular commodity, though it may continue long above, can seldom continue long below its natural price. Whatever part of it was paid below the natural rate, the persons whose interest it affected would immediately feel the loss, and would immediately withdraw either so much land, or so much labour, or so much stock, from being employed about it, that the quantity brought to market would soon be no more than sufficient to supply the effectual demand. Its market price, therefore, would soon rise to the natural price. This at least would be the case where there was perfect liberty.

The same statutes of apprenticeship and other corporation laws indeed, which, when a manufacture is in prosperity, enable the workman to raise his wages a good deal above their natural rate, sometimes oblige him, when it decays, to let them down a good deal below it. As in the one case they exclude many people from his employment, so in the other they exclude him from many employments. The effect of such regulations, however, is not near so durable in sinking the workman's wages below, as in raising them above, their natural rate. Their operation in the one way may endure for many centuries, but in the other it can last no longer than the lives of some of the workmen who were bred to the business in the time of its prosperity. When they are gone, the number of those who are afterwards educated to the trade will naturally suit itself to the effectual demand. The police must be as violent as that of Indostan or ancient Egypt (where every man was bound by a principle of religion to follow the occupation of his father, and was supposed to commit the most horrid sacrilege if he changed it for another), which can in any particular employment, and for several generations together, sink either the wages of labour or the profits of stock below their natural rate.

This is all that I think necessary to be observed at present concerning the deviations, whether occasional or permanent, of the market price of commodities from the natural price. . . .

CHAPTER VIII
Of the Wages of Labour

The produce of labour constitutes the natural recompence or wages of labour.

In that original state of things, which precedes both the appropriation of land and the accumulation of stock, the whole produce of labour belongs to the labourer. He has neither landlord nor master to share with him.

Had this state continued, the wages of labour would have augmented with all those improvements in its productive powers, to which the division of labour gives occasion. All things would gradually have become cheaper. They would have been produced by a smaller quantity of labour; and as the commodities produced by equal quantities of labour would naturally in this state of things be exchanged for one another, they would have been purchased likewise with the produce of a smaller quantity. . . .

But this original state of things, in which the labourer enjoyed the whole produce of his own labour, could not last beyond the first introduction of the appropriation of land and the accumulation of stock. It was at an end, therefore, long before the most considerable improvements were made in the productive powers of labour, and it would be to no purpose to trace further what might have been its effect upon the recompence or wages of labour.

As soon as land becomes private property, the landlord demands a share of almost all the produce which the labourer can either raise, or collect from it. His rent makes the first deduction from the produce of the labour which is employed upon land.

It seldom happens that the person who tills the ground has wherewithal to maintain himself till he reaps the harvest. His maintenance is generally advanced to him from the stock of a master, the farmer who employs him, and who would have no interest to employ him, unless he was to share in the produce of his labour, or unless his stock was to be replaced to him with a profit. This profit makes a second deduction from the produce of the labour which is employed upon land.

The produce of almost all other labour is liable to the like deduction of profit. In all arts and manufactures the greater part of the workmen stand in need of a master to advance them the materials of their work, and their wages and maintenance till it be completed. He shares in the produce of their labour, or in the value which it adds to the materials upon which it is bestowed; and in this share consists his profit. . . .

What are the common wages of labour, depends everywhere upon the contract usually made between those two parties, whose interests are by no means the same. The workmen desire to get as much, the masters to give as little as possible. The former are disposed to combine in order to raise, the latter in order to lower the wages of labour.

It is not, however, difficult to foresee which of the two parties must, upon all ordinary occasions, have the advantage in the dispute, and force the other into a compliance with their terms. The masters, being fewer in number, can combine much more easily; and the law, besides, authorises, or at least does not prohibit their combinations, while it prohibits those of the workmen. We have no acts of parliament against combining to lower the price of work; but many against combining to raise it. In all such disputes the masters can hold out much longer. A landlord, a farmer, a master manufacturer, or merchant, though they did not employ a single workman, could generally live a year or two upon the stocks which they have already acquired. Many workmen could not subsist a week, few could subsist a month, and scarce any a year without employment. In the longrun the workman may be as necessary to his master as his master is to him, but the necessity is not so immediate.

We rarely hear, it has been said, of the combinations of masters, though frequently of those of workmen. But whoever imagines, upon this account, that masters rarely combine, is as ignorant of the world as of the subject. Masters are always and everywhere in a sort of tacit, but constant and uniform combination, not to raise the wages of labour above their actual rate. To violate this combination is everywhere a most unpopular action, and a sort of reproach to a master among his neighbours and equals. We seldom, indeed, hear of this combination, because it is the usual, and one may say, the natural state of things which nobody ever hears of. Masters too sometimes enter into particular combinations to sink the wages of labour even below this rate. These are always conducted with the utmost silence and secrecy, till the moment of execution, and when the workmen yield, as they sometimes do, without resistance, though severely felt by them, they are never heard of by other people. Such combinations, however, are frequently resisted by a contrary defensive combination of the workmen; who sometimes too, without any provocation of this kind, combine of their own accord to raise the price of their labour. Their usual pretences are, sometimes the high price of provisions; sometimes the great profit which their masters make by their work. But whether their combinations be offensive or defensive, they are always abundantly heard of. In order to bring the point to a speedy decision, they have always recourse to the loudest clamour, and sometimes to the most shocking violence and outrage. They are desperate, and act with the folly and extravagance of desperate men, who must either starve, or frighten their masters into an immediate compliance with their demands. The masters upon these occasions are just as clamourous upon the other side, and never cease to call aloud for the assistance of the civil magistrate, and the rigourous execution of those laws which have been enacted with so much severity against the combinations of servants, labourers, and journeymen. The workmen, accordingly, very seldom derive any advantage from the violence of those tumultuous combinations, which, partly from the interposition of the civil magistrate, partly from the superior steadiness of the masters, partly from the necessity which the greater part of the workmen are under of submitting for the sake of present subsistence, generally end in nothing, but the punishment or ruin of the ring-leaders.

But though in disputes with their workmen, masters must generally have the advantage, there is, however, a certain rate below which it seems impossible to reduce, for any considerable time, the ordinary wages even of the lowest species of labour.

A man must always live by his work, and his wages must at least be sufficient to maintain him. They must even upon most occasions be somewhat more; otherwise it would be impossible for him to bring up a family, and the race of such workmen could not last beyond the first generation.

WILLIAM SHAKESPEARE's birth date is uncertain, but he was baptized in 1564 in Stratford-on-Avon, England. Many of the details of Shakespeare's life are unknown or contested. His father was a shopkeeper and glover who was a prominent local citizen, serving Stratford as a burgess, an alderman, and as bailiff. William Shakespeare was educated only at the local grammar school, where he studied Latin and most likely read the plays of Terence and Plautus. He married in 1582 and had three children. It is unclear when and how Shakespeare went to London and began working in the theater, but by 1594 he had joined the Lord Chamberlain's Company of players as an actor, a playwright, and a shareholder. *The Comedy of Errors,* probably first performed in 1591, was one of Shakespeare's earliest plays; his latest dates to 1613. He enjoyed some degree of prosperity, purchasing one of the largest homes in Stratford in 1597 and acquiring 107 acres of farmland in 1602. Shakespeare's plays were published in his lifetime, but none with his approval. He died in 1616.

From *The Tragedy of Antony and Cleopatra,* edited by George Wyllys Benedict. Publisher: The MacMillan Company, 1926.

Antony and Cleopatra

CHARACTERS

MARK ANTONY
OCTAVIUS CAESAR } Triumvirs
M. AEMILIUS LEPIDUS
SEXTUS POMPEIUS

Friends to Antony:
DOMITIUS ENOBARBUS
VENTIDIUS
EROS
SCARUS
DERCETAS
DEMETRIUS
PHILO

Friends to Caesar:
MAECENAS
AGRIPPA
DOLABELLA
PROCULEIUS
THYREUS
GALLUS

MENAS, MENECRATES, VARRIUS: Friends to Pompey

TAURUS, Lieutenant-General to Caesar
CANIDIUS, Lieutenant-General to Antony
SILIUS, an Officer under Ventidius
EUPHRONIUS, a Schoolmaster
A SOOTHSAYER · A CLOWN

Attendants on Cleopatra:
ALEXAS
MARDIAN
SELEUCUS
DIOMEDES

CLEOPATRA, Queen of Egypt
OCTAVIA, Sister to Caesar, and wife to Antony
CHARMIAN, IRAS: Attendants on Cleopatra

Officers, Soldiers, Messengers, and other Attendants

SCENE: *In several parts of the Roman Empire*

173

ACT I

SCENE ONE—*Alexandria. A room in* CLEOPATRA'*s palace.*

Enter DEMETRIUS *and* PHILO.

PHILO: Nay, but this dotage of our general's
 O'erflows the measure. Those his goodly eyes,
 That o'er the files and musters of the war
 Have glow'd like plated Mars, now bend, now turn,
 The office and devotion of their view
 Upon a tawny front; his captain's heart,
 Which in the scuffles of great fights hath burst
 The buckles on his breast, reneges all temper,[1]
 And is become the bellows and the fan
 To cool a gipsy's lust.

Flourish. Enter ANTONY, CLEOPATRA, *her Ladies, the train,
with Eunuchs fanning her.*

      Look, where they come!
 Take but good note, and you shall see in him
 The triple pillar of the world transform'd
 Into a strumpet's fool. Behold and see.
CLEOPATRA: If it be love indeed, tell me how much.
ANTONY: There's beggary in the love that can be reckon'd.
CLEOPATRA: I'll set a bourn how far to be belov'd.
ANTONY: Then must thou needs find out new heaven, new
  earth.

Enter a MESSENGER.

MESSENGER: News, my good lord, from Rome.
ANTONY: Grates me: the
  sum.

---

[1] [*reneges all temper:* denies all moderation.]

CLEOPATRA: Nay, hear them, Antony.
Fulvia perchance is angry; or, who knows
If the scarce-bearded Caesar have not sent
His powerful mandate to you: "Do this, or this;
Take in that kingdom, and enfranchise that;
Perform't, or else we damn thee."
ANTONY: How, my love!
CLEOPATRA: Perchance! nay, and most like.
You must not stay here longer, your dismission
Is from Caesar; therefore hear it, Antony.
Where's Fulvia's process?—Caesar's, I would say. Both?
Call in the messengers. As I am Egypt's queen,
Thou blushest, Antony, and that blood of thine
Is Caesar's homager; else so thy cheek pays shame
When shrill-tongu'd Fulvia scolds. The messengers!
ANTONY: Let Rome in Tiber melt, and the wide arch
Of the rang'd empire fall! Here is my space.
Kingdoms are clay; our dungy earth alike
Feeds beast as man; the nobleness of life
Is to do thus, when such a mutual pair   [*Embracing.*]
And such a twain can do't, in which I bind,
On pain of punishment, the world to wit
We stand up peerless.
CLEOPATRA: Excellent falsehood!
Why did he marry Fulvia, and not love her?
I'll seem the fool I am not; Antony
Will be himself.
ANTONY: But stirr'd by Cleopatra.
Now, for the love of Love and her soft hours,
Let's not confound the time with conference harsh.
There's not a minute of our lives should stretch
Without some pleasure now. What sport to-night?
CLEOPATRA: Hear the ambassadors.
ANTONY: Fie, wrangling queen!
Whom everything becomes, to chide, to laugh,
To weep; whose every passion fully strives

To make itself, in thee, fair and admir'd!
No messenger but thine; and all alone
To-night we'll wander through the streets and note
The qualities of people. Come, my queen;
Last night you did desire it.—Speak not to us.
   Exeunt [ANTONY *and* CLEOPATRA] *with their train.*

DEMETRIUS: Is Caesar with Antonius priz'd so slight?
PHILO: Sir, sometimes, when he is not Antony,
 He come too short of that great property
 Which still should go with Antony.
DEMETRIUS: I am full sorry
 That he approves the common liar, who
 Thus speaks of him at Rome; but I will hope
 Of better deeds to-morrow. Rest you happy! *Exeunt.*

   SCENE TWO—*The same. Another room.*

Enter ENOBARBUS, LAMPRIUS, *a* SOOTHSAYER, RANNIUS,
LUCILIUS, CHARMIAN, IRAS, MARDIAN *the Eunuch, and* ALEXAS.

CHARMIAN: Lord Alexas, sweet Alexas, most anything Alexas,
 almost most absolute Alexas, where's the soothsayer that
 you prais'd so to the Queen? O, that I knew this husband,
 which, you say, must charge his horns with garlands!
ALEXAS: Soothsayer!
SOOTHSAYER: Your will?
CHARMIAN: Is this the man? Is't you, sir, that know things?
SOOTHSAYER: In nature's infinite book of secrecy
 A little I can read.
ALEXAS: Show him your hand.
ENOBARBUS: Bring in the banquet quickly; wine enough
 Cleopatra's health to drink.
CHARMIAN: Good sir, give me good fortune.
SOOTHSAYER: I make not, but foresee.

CHARMIAN: Pray, then, foresee me one.

SOOTHSAYER: You shall be yet far fairer than you are.

CHARMIAN: He means in flesh.

IRAS: No, you shall paint when you are old.

CHARMIAN: Wrinkles forbid!

ALEXAS: Vex not his prescience; be attentive.

CHARMIAN: Hush!

SOOTHSAYER: You shall be more beloving than beloved.

CHARMIAN: I had rather heat my liver with drinking.

ALEXAS: Nay, hear him.

CHARMIAN: Good now, some excellent fortune! Let me be married to three kings in a forenoon, and widow them all. Let me have a child at fifty, to whom Herod of Jewry may do homage. Find me to marry me with Octavius Caesar, and companion me with my mistress.

SOOTHSAYER: You shall outlive the lady whom you serve.

CHARMIAN: O excellent! I love long life better than figs.

SOOTHSAYER: You have seen and proved a fairer former fortune
Than that which is to approach.

CHARMIAN: Then belike my children shall have no names.
Prithee, how many boys and wenches must I have?

SOOTHSAYER: If every of your wishes had a womb,
And fertile every wish, a million.

CHARMIAN: Out, fool! I forgive thee for a witch.

ALEXAS: You think none but your sheets are privy to your wishes.

CHARMIAN: Nay, come, tell Iras hers.

ALEXAS: We'll know all our fortunes.

ENOBARBUS: Mine and most of our fortunes to-night shall be—drunk to bed.

IRAS: There's a palm presages chastity, if nothing else.

CHARMIAN: E'en as the o'erflowing Nilus presageth famine.

IRAS: Go, you wild bedfellow, you cannot soothsay.

CHARMIAN: Nay, if an oily palm be not a fruitful prognostication, I cannot scratch mine ear. Prithee, tell her but a work-a-day fortune.

SOOTHSAYER: Your fortunes are alike.

IRAS: But how, but how? Give me particulars.

SOOTHSAYER: I have said.

IRAS: Am I not an inch of fortune better than she?

CHARMIAN: Well, if you were but an inch of fortune better than I, where would you choose it?

IRAS: Not in my husband's nose.

CHARMIAN: Our worser thoughts heavens mend! Alexas,—come, his fortune, his fortune! O, let him marry a woman that cannot go, sweet Isis, I beseech thee! and let her die too, and give him a worse! and let worse follow worse, till the worst of all follow him laughing to his grave, fifty-fold a cuckold! Good Isis, hear me this prayer, though thou deny me a matter of more weight; good Isis, I beseech thee!

IRAS: Amen. Dear goddess, hear that prayer of the people! for, as it is a heart-breaking to see a handsome man loose-wiv'd, so it is a deadly sorrow to behold a foul knave uncuckolded; therefore, dear Isis, keep decorum, and fortune him accordingly!

CHARMIAN: Amen.

ALEXAS: Lo, now, if it lay in their hands to make me a cuckold, they would make themselves whores, but they'd do't!

Enter CLEOPATRA.

ENOBARBUS: Hush! here comes Antony.

CHARMIAN: Not he; the Queen.

CLEOPATRA: Saw you my lord?

ENOBARBUS: No, lady.

CLEOPATRA: Was he not here?

CHARMIAN: No, madam.

CLEOPATRA: He was dispos'd to mirth, but on the sudden
  A Roman thought hath struck him. Enobarbus!

ENOBARBUS: Madam?

CLEOPATRA: Seek him, and bring him hither. Where's Alexas?

ALEXAS: Here, at your service. My lord approaches.

Enter ANTONY *with a* MESSENGER [*and* Attendants].

CLEOPATRA: We will not look upon him. Go with us.
                                        Exeunt [CLEOPATRA *and train*].

MESSENGER: Fulvia thy wife first came into the field.
ANTONY: Against my brother Lucius?
MESSENGER: Ay;
    But soon that war had end, and the time's state,
    Made friends of them, jointing their force 'gainst Caesar;
    Whose better issue in the war, from Italy,
    Upon the first encounter, drave them.
ANTONY: Well, what worst?
MESSENGER: The nature of bad news infects the teller.
ANTONY: When it concerns the fool or coward. On:
    Things that are past are done with me. 'Tis thus;
    Who tells me true, though in his tale lie death,
    I hear him as he flatter'd.
MESSENGER: Labienus—
    This is stiff news—hath, with his Parthian force,
    Extended Asia from Euphrates;
    His conquering banner shook from Syria
    To Lydia and to Ionia,
    Whilst—
ANTONY: Antony, thou wouldst say,—
MESSENGER: O, my lord!
ANTONY: Speak to me home, mince not the general tongue.
    Name Cleopatra as she is call'd in Rome;
    Rail thou in Fulvia's phrase; and taunt my faults
    With such full license as both truth and malice
    Have power to utter. O, then we bring forth weeds
    When our quick minds lie still; and our ills told us
    Is as our earing. Fare thee well a while.

MESSENGER: At your noble pleasure.   *Exit.*

ANTONY: From Sicyon, ho, the news! Speak there!

[FIRST ATTENDANT]: The man from Sicyon,—is there such an
    one?

[SECOND ATTENDANT]: He stays upon your will.

ANTONY: Let him appear.
    These strong Egyptian fetters I must break,
    Or lose myself in dotage.

Enter another MESSENGER *with a letter.*
                    What are you?

SECOND MESSENGER: Fulvia thy wife is dead!

ANTONY: Where died she?

SECOND MESSENGER: In Sicyon:
    Her length of sickness, with what else more serious
    Importeth thee to know, this bears.   [*Gives a letter.*]

ANTONY: .   Forbear me.
                    [*Exit* SECOND MESSENGER.]

    There's a great spirit gone! Thus did I desire it.
    What our contempts doth often hurl from us,
    We wish it ours again; the present pleasure,
    By revolution low'ring, does become
    The opposite of itself. She's good, being gone;
    The hand could pluck her back that shov'd her on.
    I must from this enchanting queen break off;
    Ten thousand harms, more than the ills I know,
    My idleness doth hatch.

Re-enter ENOBARBUS.
                    How now! Enobarbus!

ENOBARBUS: What's your pleasure, sir?

ANTONY: I must with haste from hence.

ENOBARBUS: Why, then, we kill all our women. We see how
    mortal an unkindness is to them; if they suffer our de-
    parture, death's the word.

ANTONY: I must be gone.

ENOBARBUS: Under a compelling occasion, let women die. It were pity to cast them away for nothing; though, between them and a great cause, they should be esteemed nothing. Cleopatra, catching but the least noise of this, dies instantly; I have seen her die twenty times upon far poorer moment. I do think there is mettle in Death, which commits some loving act upon her, she hath such a celerity in dying.

ANTONY: She is cunning past man's thought.

ENOBARBUS: Alack, sir, no; her passions are made of nothing but the finest part of pure love. We cannot call her winds and waters sighs and tears; they are greater storms and tempests than almanacs can report. This cannot be cunning in her; if it be, she makes a shower of rain as well as Jove.

ANTONY: Would I had never seen her!

ENOBARBUS: O, sir, you had then left unseen a wonderful piece of work; which not to have been blest withal would have discredited your travel.

ANTONY: Fulvia is dead.

ENOBARBUS: Sir?

ANTONY: Fulvia is dead.

ENOBARBUS: Fulvia!

ANTONY: Dead.

ENOBARBUS: Why, sir, give the gods a thankful sacrifice. When it pleaseth their deities to take the wife of a man from him, it shows to man the tailors of the earth; comforting therein, that when old robes are worn out, there are members to make new. If there were no more women but Fulvia, then had you indeed a cut, and the case to be lamented. This grief is crown'd with consolation; your old smock brings forth a new petticoat: and indeed the tears live in an onion that should water this sorrow.

ANTONY: The business she hath broached in the state
Cannot endure my absence.

ENOBARBUS: And the business you have broached here cannot
    be without you; especially that of Cleopatra's, which wholly
    depends on your abode.
ANTONY: No more light answers. Let our officers
    Have notice what we purpose. I shall break
    The cause of our expedience to the Queen,
    And get her leave to part. For not alone
    The death of Fulvia, with more urgent touches,
    Do strongly speak to us; but the letters too
    Of many our contriving friends in Rome
    Petition us at home. Sextus Pompeius
    Hath given the dare to Caesar, and commands
    The empire of the sea. Our slippery people,
    Whose love is never link'd to the deserver
    Till his deserts are past, begin to throw
    Pompey the Great and all his dignities
    Upon his son; who, high in name and power,
    Higher than both in blood and life, stands up
    For the main soldier; whose quality, going on,
    The sides o' the world may danger. Much is breeding,
    Which, like the courser's hair, hath yet but life,
    And not a serpent's poison. Say, our pleasure,
    To such whose place is under us, requires
    Our quick remove from hence.
ENOBARBUS: I shall do't.   *[Exeunt.]*

SCENE THREE—*The same. Another room.*

Enter CLEOPATRA, CHARMIAN, IRAS, *and* ALEXAS.

CLEOPATRA: Where is he?
CHARMIAN: I did not see him since.
CLEOPATRA: See where he is, who's with him, what he does.
    I did not send you. If you find him sad,
    Say I am dancing; if in mirth, report
    That I am sudden sick. Quick, and return. *[Exit* ALEXAS.*]*

CHARMIAN: Madam, methinks, if you did love him dearly,
  You do not hold the method to enforce
  The like from him.
CLEOPATRA: What should I do, I do not?
CHARMIAN: In each thing give him way, cross him in nothing.
CLEOPATRA: Thou teachest like a fool: the way to lose him.
CHARMIAN: Tempt him not so too far; I wish, forbear.
  In time we hate that which we often fear.

Enter ANTONY.

  But here comes Antony.
CLEOPATRA: I am sick and sullen.
ANTONY: I am sorry to give breathing to my purpose,—
CLEOPATRA: Help me away, dear Charmian; I shall fall.
  It cannot be thus long, the sides of nature
  Will not sustain it.
ANTONY: Now, my dearest queen,—
CLEOPATRA: Pray you, stand farther from me.
ANTONY: What's the matter?
CLEOPATRA: I know, by that same eye, there's some good news.
  What says the married woman? You may go.
  Would she had never given you leave to come!
  Let her not say 'tis I that keep you here;
  I have no power upon you; hers you are.
ANTONY: The gods best know,—
CLEOPATRA: O, never was there queen
  So mightily betrayed! Yet at the first
  I saw the treasons planted.
ANTONY: Cleopatra,—
CLEOPATRA: Why should I think you can be mine and true,
  Though you in swearing shake the throned gods,
  Who have been false to Fulvia? Riotous madness,
  To be entangled with those mouth-made vows,
  Which break themselves in swearing!
ANTONY: Most sweet queen,—

CLEOPATRA: Nay, pray you, seek no colour for your going,
But bid farewell, and go. When you sued staying,
Then was the time for words; no going then;
Eternity was in our lips and eyes,
Bliss in our brows' bent; none our parts so poor,
But was a race of heaven. They are so still,
Or thou, the greatest soldier of the world,
Art turn'd the greatest liar.
ANTONY: How now, lady!
CLEOPATRA: I would I had thy inches; thou shouldst know
There were a heart in Egypt.
ANTONY: Hear me, Queen.
The strong necessity of time commands
Our services a while; but my full heart
Remains in use with you. Our Italy
Shines o'er with civil swords; Sextus Pompeius
Makes his approaches to the port of Rome;
Equality of two domestic powers
Breed scrupulous faction; the hated, grown to strength,
Are newly grown to love; the condemn'd Pompey,
Rich in his father's honour, creeps apace
Into the hearts of such as have not thrived
Upon the present state, whose numbers threaten;
And quietness, grown sick of rest, would purge
By any desperate change. My more particular,
And that which most with you should safe my going,
Is Fulvia's death.
CLEOPATRA: Though age from folly could not give me freedom,
It does from childishness. Can Fulvia die?
ANTONY: She's dead, my queen.
Look here, and at thy sovereign leisure read
The garboils[2] she awak'd: at the last, best;
See when and where she died.
CLEOPATRA: O most false love!

---

[2] [*garboils:* disturbances.]

Where be the sacred vials thou shouldst fill
With sorrowful water? Now I see, I see,
In Fulvia's death, how mine receiv'd shall be.
ANTONY: Quarrel no more, but be prepar'd to know
  The purposes I bear; which are, or cease,
  As you shall give the advice. By the fire
  That quickens Nilus' slime, I go from hence
  Thy soldier, servant; making peace or war
  As thou affects.
CLEOPATRA: Cut my lace, Charmian, come!
  But let it be; I am quickly ill and well,
  So Antony loves.
ANTONY: My precious queen, forbear;
  And give true evidence to his love, which stands
  An honourable trial.
CLEOPATRA: So Fulvia told me.
  I prithee, turn aside and weep for her;
  Then bid adieu to me, and say the tears
  Belong to Egypt. Good now, play one scene
  Of excellent dissembling; and let it look
  Like perfect honour.
ANTONY: You'll heat my blood. No more.
CLEOPATRA: You can do better yet; but this is meetly.[3]
ANTONY: Now, by my sword,—
CLEOPATRA: And target.—Still he mends;
  But this is not the best. Look, prithee, Charmian,
  How this Herculean Roman does become
  The carriage of his chafe.
ANTONY: I'll leave you, lady.
CLEOPATRA: Courteous lord, one word.
  Sir, you and I must part, but that's not it;
  Sir, you and I have lov'd, but there's not it;
  That you know well. Something it is I would,—
  O, my oblivion is a very Antony,

---

[3] [*meetly:* suitable.]

And I am all forgotten.
ANTONY: But that your royalty
   Holds idleness your subject, I should take you
   For idleness itself.
CLEOPATRA: 'Tis sweating labour
   To bear such idleness so near the heart
   As Cleopatra this. But, sir, forgive me,
   Since my becomings kill me when they do not
   Eye well to you. Your honour calls you hence;
   Therefore be deaf to my unpitied folly,
   And all the gods go with you! Upon your sword
   Sit laurell'd victory, and smooth success
   Be strew'd before your feet!
ANTONY: Let us go. — Come;
   Our separation so abides, and flies,
   That thou, residing here, goes yet with me,
   And I, hence fleeting, here remain with thee.
   Away!   *Exeunt.*

SCENE FOUR — *Rome.* CAESAR's *house.*

Enter OCTAVIUS CAESAR, *reading a letter,* LEPIDUS, *and their train.*

CAESAR: You may see, Lepidus, and henceforth know,
   It is not Caesar's natural vice to hate
   Our great competitor. From Alexandria
   This is the news: he fishes, drinks, and wastes
   The lamps of night in revel; is not more man-like
   Than Cleopatra; nor the queen of Ptolemy
   More womanly than he; hardly gave audience, or
   Vouchsaf'd to think he had partners. You shall find there
   A man who is the abstract of all faults
   That all men follow.
LEPIDUS: I must not think there are
   Evils enow to darken all his goodness.

His faults in him seem as the spots of heaven,
More fiery by night's blackness; hereditary,
Rather than purchas'd; what he cannot change,
Than what he chooses.
CAESAR: You are too indulgent. Let's grant it is not
Amiss to tumble on the bed of Ptolemy;
To give a kingdom for a mirth; to sit
And keep the turn of tippling with a slave;
To reel the streets at noon, and stand the buffet
With knaves that smell of sweat: say this becomes him,—
As his composure must be rare indeed
Whom these things cannot blemish,—yet must Antony
No way excuse his soils, when we do bear
So great weight in his lightness. If he fill'd
His vacancy with his voluptuousness,
Full surfeits and the dryness of his bones
Call on him for't; but to confound such time
That drums him from his sport and speaks as loud
As his own state and ours, 'tis to be chid
As we rate boys, who, being mature in knowledge,
Pawn their experience to their present pleasure,
And so rebel to judgement.

Enter a MESSENGER.

LEPIDUS: Here's more news.
MESSENGER: Thy biddings have been done; and every hour,
Most noble Caesar, shalt thou have report
How 'tis abroad. Pompey is strong at sea;
And it appears he is belov'd of those
That only have fear'd Caesar. To the ports
The discontents repair; and men's reports
Give him much wrong'd.
CAESAR: I should have known no less.
It hath been taught us from the primal state,
That he which is was wish'd until he were;
And the ebb'd man, ne'er loved till ne'er worth love,

Comes dear'd by being lack'd. This common body,
Like to a vagabond flag upon the stream,
Goes to and back, lackeying the varying tide,
To rot itself with motion.

MESSENGER: Caesar, I bring thee word,
Menecrates and Menas, famous pirates,
Makes the sea serve them, which they ear and wound
With keels of every kind. Many hot inroads
They make in Italy; the borders maritime
Lack blood to think on't, and flush youth revolt.
No vessel can peep forth, but 'tis as soon
Taken as seen; for Pompey's name strikes more
Than could his war resisted.

CAESAR: Antony,
Leave thy lascivious wassails. When thou once
Was beaten from Modena, where thou slew'st
Hirtius and Pansa, consuls, at thy heel
Did famine follow; whom thou fought'st against,
Though daintily brought up, with patience more
Than savages could suffer. Thou didst drink
The stale[4] of horses, and the gilded puddle
Which beasts would cough at; thy palate then did deign
The roughest berry on the rudest hedge;
Yea, like the stag, when snow the pasture sheets,
The barks of trees thou brows'd; on the Alps
It is reported thou didst eat strange flesh,
Which some did die to look on; and all this—
It wounds thine honour that I speak it now—
Was borne so like a soldier, that thy cheek
So much as lank'd not.

LEPIDUS: 'Tis pity of him.

CAESAR: Let his shames quickly
Drive him to Rome. 'Tis time we twain
Did show ourselves i' the field, and to that end

---

[4] [*stale:* urine.]

Assemble we immediate council. Pompey
Thrives in our idleness.

LEPIDUS: To-morrow, Caesar,
I shall be furnish'd to inform you rightly
Both what by sea and land I can be able
To front this present time.

CAESAR: Till which encounter,
It is my business too. Farewell.

LEPIDUS: Farewell, my lord. What you shall know meantime
Of stirs abroad, I shall beseech you, sir,
To let me be partaker.

CAESAR: Doubt not, sir;
I knew it for my bond.   *Exeunt.*

SCENE FIVE—*Alexandria.* CLEOPATRA's *palace.*

Enter CLEOPATRA, CHARMIAN, IRAS, *and* MARDIAN.

CLEOPATRA: Charmian!

CHARMIAN: Madam?

CLEOPATRA: Ha, ha!
Give me to drink mandragora.

CHARMIAN: Why, madam?

CLEOPATRA: That I might sleep out this great gap of time
My Antony is away.

CHARMIAN: You think of him too much.

CLEOPATRA: O, 'tis treason!

CHARMIAN: Madam, I trust not so.

CLEOPATRA: Thou, eunuch Mardian!

MARDIAN: What's your Highness' pleasure?

CLEOPATRA: Not now to hear thee sing; I take no pleasure
In aught an eunuch has. 'Tis well for thee,
That, being unseminar'd, thy freer thoughts
May not fly forth of Egypt. Hast thou affections?

MARDIAN: Yes, gracious madam.

CLEOPATRA: Indeed!

MARDIAN: Not in deed, madam, for I can do nothing
But what indeed is honest to be done;
Yet have I fierce affections, and think
What Venus did with Mars.

CLEOPATRA: O Charmian,
Where think'st thou he is now? Stands he, or sits he?
Or does he walk? Or is he on his horse?
O happy horse, to bear the weight of Antony!
Do bravely, horse! for wot'st thou whom thou mov'st?
The demi-Atlas of this earth, the arm
And burgonet of men. He's speaking now,
Or murmuring, "Where's my serpent of old Nile?"
For so he calls me. Now I feed myself
With most delicious poison. Think on me,
That am with Phoebus' amorous pinches black,
And wrinkled deep in time? Broad-fronted Caesar,
When thou wast here above the ground, I was
A morsel for a monarch; and great Pompey
Would stand and make his eyes grow in my brow;
There would he anchor his aspect and die
With looking on his life.

Enter ALEXAS.

ALEXAS: Sovereign of Egypt, hail!

CLEOPATRA: How much unlike art thou Mark Antony!
Yet, coming from him, that great medicine hath
With his tinct gilded thee.
How goes it with my brave Mark Antony?

ALEXAS: Last thing he did, dear queen,
He kiss'd,—the last of many doubled kisses,—
This orient pearl. His speech sticks in my heart.

CLEOPATRA: Mine ear must pluck it thence.

ALEXAS: "Good friend," quoth he,
"Say, the firm Roman to great Egypt sends
This treasure of an oyster; at whose foot,
To mend the petty present, I will piece
Her opulent throne with kingdoms. All the East,
Say thou, shall call her mistress." So he nodded,
And soberly did mount an arm-gaunt steed,
Who neigh'd so high that what I would have spoke
Was beastly dumb'd by him.

CLEOPATRA: What, was he sad or merry?

ALEXAS: Like to the time o' the year between the extremes
Of hot and cold, he was nor sad nor merry.

CLEOPATRA: O well-divided disposition! Note him,
Note him, good Charmian, 'tis the man; but note him:
He was not sad, for he would shine on those
That make their looks by his; he was not merry,
Which seem'd to tell them his remembrance lay
In Egypt with his joy; but between both.
O heavenly mingle! Be'st thou sad or merry,
The violence of either thee becomes,
So does it no man else. Met'st thou my posts?

ALEXAS: Ay, madam, twenty several messengers:
Why do you send so thick?

CLEOPATRA: Who's born that day
When I forget to send to Antony,
Shall die a beggar. Ink and paper, Charmian.
Welcome, my good Alexas. Did I, Charmian,
Ever love Caesar so?

CHARMIAN: O that brave Caesar!

CLEOPATRA: Be chok'd with such another emphasis!
Say, the brave Antony!

CHARMIAN: The valiant Caesar!

CLEOPATRA: By Isis, I will give thee bloody teeth,
If thou with Caesar paragon again
My man of men.

CHARMIAN: By your most gracious pardon,
  I sing but after you.
CLEOPATRA: My salad days,
  When I was green in judgement; cold in blood,
  To say as I said then! But, come, away;
  Get me ink and paper.
  He shall have every day a several greeting,
  Or I'll unpeople Egypt.   *Exeunt.*

ACT II

SCENE ONE—*Messina.* POMPEY'*s house.*

Enter POMPEY, MENECRATES, *and* MENAS, *in warlike manner.*

POMPEY: If the great gods be just, they shall assist
  The deeds of justest men.
MENECRATES: Know, worthy Pompey,
  That what they do delay, they not deny.
POMPEY: Whiles we are suitors to their throne, decays
  The thing we sue for.
MENECRATES: We, ignorant of ourselves,
  Beg often our own harms, which the wise powers
  Deny us for our good; so find we profit
  By losing of our prayers.
POMPEY: I shall do well.
  The people love me, and the sea is mine;
  My powers are crescent, and my auguring hope
  Says it will come to the full. Mark Antony
  In Egypt sits at dinner, and will make
  No wars without-doors. Caesar gets money where
  He loses hearts. Lepidus flatters both,
  Of both is flatter'd; but he neither loves,
  Nor either cares for him.
MENAS: Caesar and Lepidus
  Are in the field; a mighty strength they carry.
POMPEY: Where have you this? 'Tis false.
MENAS: From Silvius, sir.
POMPEY: He dreams. I know they are in Rome together,
  Looking for Antony. But all the charms of love,
  Salt Cleopatra, soften thy wan'd lip!
  Let witchcraft join with beauty, lust with both!
  Tie up the libertine in a field of feasts,
  Keep his brain fuming; Epicurean cooks
  Sharpen with cloyless sauce his appetite;

That sleep and feeding may prorogue[5] his honour
Even till a Lethe'd dulness!

Enter VARRIUS.

                            How now, Varrius!
VARRIUS: This is most certain that I shall deliver:
    Mark Antony is every hour in Rome
    Expected; since he went from Egypt 'tis
    A space for farther travel.
POMPEY: I could have given less matter
    A better ear. Menas, I did not think
    This amorous surfeiter would have donn'd his helm
    For such a petty war. His soldiership
    Is twice the other twain; but let us rear
    The higher our opinion, that our stirring
    Can from the lap of Egypt's widow pluck
    The ne'er lust-wearied Antony.
MENAS: I cannot hope
    Caesar and Antony shall well greet together.
    His wife that's dead did trespasses to Caesar;
    His brother warr'd upon him, although, I think,
    Not mov'd by Antony.
POMPEY: I know not, Menas,
    How lesser enmities may give way to greater.
    Were't not that we stand up against them all,
    'Twere pregnant they should square between themselves;
    For they have entertained cause enough
    To draw their swords; but how the fear of us
    May cement their divisions and bind up
    The petty difference, we yet not know.
    Be't as our gods will have't! It only stands
    Our lives upon to use our strongest hands.
    Come, Menas.   *Exeunt.*

---

[5] [*prorogue:* suspend.]

SCENE TWO—*Rome. The house of* LEPIDUS.

Enter ENOBARBUS *and* LEPIDUS.

LEPIDUS: Good Enobarbus, 'tis a worthy deed,
　　And shall become you well, to entreat your captain
　　To soft and gentle speech.
ENOBARBUS:　　　　　　　I shall entreat him
　　To answer like himself. If Caesar move him,
　　Let Antony look over Caesar's head
　　And speak as loud as Mars. By Jupiter,
　　Were I the wearer of Antonius' beard,
　　I would not shave't to-day.
LEPIDUS:　　　　　　　'Tis not a time
　　For private stomaching.
ENOBARBUS:　　　　Every time
　　Serves for the matter that is then born in't.
LEPIDUS: But small to greater matters must give way.
ENOBARBUS: Not if the small come first.
LEPIDUS:　　　　　　　　　Your speech is passion;
　　But, pray you, stir no embers up. Here comes
　　The noble Antony.

Enter ANTONY *and* VENTIDIUS.

ENOBARBUS:　　　　And yonder, Caesar.

Enter CAESAR, MAECENAS, *and* AGRIPPA.

ANTONY: If we compose well here, to Parthia!
　　Hark, Ventidius.
CAESAR:　　　　I do not know,
　　Maecenas; ask Agrippa.
LEPIDUS:　　　　　　Noble friends,
　　That which combin'd us was most great, and let not
　　A leaner action rend us. What's amiss,
　　May it be gently heard; when we debate
　　Our trivial difference loud, we do commit
　　Murder in healing wounds; then, noble partners,

The rather, for I earnestly beseech,
 Touch you the sourest points with sweetest terms,
 Nor curstness grow to the matter.
ANTONY: 'Tis spoken well.
 Were we before our armies, and to fight,
 I should do thus.   *Flourish.*
CAESAR: Welcome to Rome.
ANTONY: Thank you.
CAESAR: Sit.
ANTONY: Sit, sir.
CAESAR: Nay, then.
ANTONY: I learn you take things ill which are not so,
 Or being, concern you not.
CAESAR: I must be laugh'd at,
 If, or for nothing or a little, I
 Should say myself offended, and with you
 Chiefly i' the world; more laugh'd at, that I should
 Once name you derogately, when to sound your name
 It not concern'd me.
ANTONY: My being in Egypt, Caesar,
 What was 't to you?
CAESAR: No more than my residing here at Rome
 Might be to you in Egypt; yet, if you there
 Did practise on my state, your being in Egypt
 Might be my question.
ANTONY: How intend you, practis'd?
CAESAR: You may be pleas'd to catch at mine intent
 By what did here befall me. Your wife and brother
 Made wars upon me; and their contestation
 Was theme for you, you were the word of war.
ANTONY: You do mistake your business; my brother never
 Did urge me in his act. I did inquire it,
 And have my learning from some true reports
 That drew their swords with you. Did he not rather
 Discredit my authority with yours,
 And make the wars alike against my stomach,

Having alike your cause? Of this my letters
Before did satisfy you. If you'll patch a quarrel,
As matter whole you have not to make it with,
It must not be with this.

CAESAR: You praise yourself
By laying defects of judgement to me; but
You patch'd up your excuses.

ANTONY: Not so, not so.
I know you could not lack, I am certain on't,
Very necessity of this thought, that I,
Your partner in the cause 'gainst which he fought,
Could not with graceful eyes attend those wars
Which fronted mine own peace. As for my wife,
I would you had her spirit in such another.
The third o' the world is yours, which with a snaffle
You may pace easy, but not such a wife.

ENOBARBUS: Would we had all such wives, that the men might
      go to wars with the women!

ANTONY: So much uncurbable her garboils, Caesar,
  Made out of her impatience, which not wanted
Shrewdness of policy too, I grieving grant
Did you too much disquiet. For that you must
But say, I could not help it.

CAESAR: I wrote to you
When rioting in Alexandria; you
Did pocket up my letters, and with taunts
Did gibe my missive out of audience.

ANTONY: Sir,
He fell upon me ere admitted. Then
Three kings I had newly feasted, and did want
Of what I was i' the morning; but next day
I told him of myself, which was as much
As to have ask'd him pardon. Let this fellow
Be nothing of our strife; if we contend,
Out of our question wipe him.

CAESAR: You have broken
  The article of your oath; which you shall never
  Have tongue to charge me with.
LEPIDUS: Soft, Caesar!
ANTONY: No,
  Lepidus, let him speak.
  The honour is sacred which he talks on now
  Supposing that I lack'd it. But, on, Caesar:
  The article of my oath.
CAESAR: To lend me arms and aid when I requir'd them;
  The which you both denied.
ANTONY: Neglected, rather;
  And then when poisoned hours had bound me up
  From mine own knowledge. As nearly as I may,
  I'll play the penitent to you; but mine honesty
  Shall not make poor my greatness, nor my power
  Work without it. Truth is, that Fulvia,
  To have me out of Egypt, made wars here;
  For which myself, the ignorant motive, do
  So far ask pardon as befits mine honour
  To stoop in such a case.
LEPIDUS: 'Tis noble spoken.
MAECENAS: If it might please you, to enforce no further
  The griefs between ye. To forget them quite
  Were to remember that the present need
  Speaks to atone you.
LEPIDUS: Worthily spoken, Maecenas.
ENOBARBUS: Or, if you borrow one another's love for the in-
    stant, you may, when you hear no more words of Pompey,
    return it again. You shall have time to wrangle in when
    you have nothing else to do.
ANTONY: Thou art a soldier only; speak no more.
ENOBARBUS: That truth should be silent I had almost forgot.
ANTONY: You wrong this presence; therefore speak no more.

ENOBARBUS: Go to, then; your considerate stone.

CAESAR: I do not much dislike the matter, but
    The manner of his speech; for't cannot be
    We shall remain in friendship, our conditions
    So diff'ring in their acts. Yet, if I knew
    What hoop should hold us stanch, from edge to edge
    O' the world I would pursue it.

AGRIPPA: Give me leave, Caesar,—

CAESAR: Speak, Agrippa.

AGRIPPA: Thou hast a sister by the mother's side,
    Admir'd Octavia. Great Mark Antony
    Is now a widower.

CAESAR: Say not so, Agrippa.
    If Cleopatra heard you, your reproof
    Were well deserv'd of rashness.

ANTONY: I am not married, Caesar; let me hear
    Agrippa further speak.

AGRIPPA: To hold you in perpetual amity,
    To make you brothers, and to knit your hearts
    With an unslipping knot, take Antony
    Octavia to his wife; whose beauty claims
    No worse a husband than the best of men;
    Whose virtue and whose general graces speak
    That which none else can utter. By this marriage,
    All little jealousies, which now seem great,
    And all great fears, which now import their dangers,
    Would then be nothing. Truths would be tales,
    Where now half-tales be truths; her love to both
    Would each to other and all loves to both
    Draw after her. Pardon what I have spoke;
    For 'tis a studied, not a present thought,
    By duty ruminated.

ANTONY: Will Caesar speak?

CAESAR: Not till he hears how Antony is touch'd
    With what is spoke already.

ANTONY: What power is in Agrippa,
    If I would say, "Agrippa, be it so,"
    To make this good?
CAESAR: The power of Caesar, and
    His power unto Octavia.
ANTONY: May I never
    To this good purpose, that so fairly shows,
    Dream of impediment! Let me have thy hand.
    Further this act of grace; and from this hour
    The heart of brothers govern in our loves
    And sway our great designs!
CAESAR: There's my hand.
    A sister I bequeath you, whom no brother
    Did ever love so dearly. Let her live
    To join our kingdoms and our hearts; and never
    Fly off our loves again!
LEPIDUS: Happily, amen!
ANTONY: I did not think to draw my sword 'gainst Pompey;
    For he hath laid strange courtesies and great
    Of late upon me. I must thank him only,
    Lest my remembrance suffer ill report;
    At heel of that, defy him.
LEPIDUS: Time calls upon's.
    Of us must Pompey presently be sought,
    Or else he seeks out us.
ANTONY: Where lies he?
CAESAR: About the mount Misenum.
ANTONY: What is his strength by land?
CAESAR: Great and increasing; but by sea
    He is an absolute master.
ANTONY: So is the fame.
    Would we had spoke together! Haste we for it;
    Yet, ere we put ourselves in arms, dispatch we
    The business we have talk'd of.
CAESAR: With most gladness;
    And do invite you to my sister's view,

Whither straight I'll lead you.

ANTONY: Let us, Lepidus,

Not lack your company.

LEPIDUS: Noble Antony,

Not sickness should detain me.

> *Flourish. Exeunt* CAESAR, ANTONY, LEPIDUS,
> *and* VENTIDIUS.

MAECENAS: Welcome from Egypt, sir.

ENOBARBUS: Half the heart of Caesar, worthy Maecenas!
My honourable friend, Agrippa!

AGRIPPA: Good Enobarbus!

MAECENAS: We have cause to be glad that matters are so well
digested. You stay'd well by't in Egypt.

ENOBARBUS: Ay, sir; we did sleep day out of countenance, and
made the night light with drinking.

MAECENAS: Eight wild boars roasted whole at a breakfast, and
but twelve persons there; is this true?

ENOBARBUS: This was but as a fly by an eagle. We had much
more monstrous matter of feast, which worthily deserved
noting.

MAECENAS: She's a most triumphant lady, if report be square
to her.

ENOBARBUS: When she first met Mark Antony, she purs'd up
his heart, upon the river of Cydnus.

AGRIPPA: There she appear'd indeed, or my reporter devis'd
well for her.

ENOBARBUS: I will tell you.

The barge she sat in, like a burnish'd throne,
Burn'd on the water. The poop was beaten gold;
Purple the sails, and so perfumed that
The winds were love-sick with them. The oars were silver,
Which to the tune of flutes kept stroke, and made
The water which they beat to follow faster,
As amorous of their strokes. For her own person,
It beggar'd all description: she did lie

In her pavilion—cloth-of-gold of tissue—
O'er-picturing that Venus where we see
The fancy outwork nature. On each side her
Stood pretty dimpled boys, like smiling Cupids,
With divers-colour'd fans, whose wind did seem
To glow the delicate cheeks which they did cool,
And what they undid did.

AGRIPPA: O, rare for Antony!

ENOBARBUS: Her gentlewomen, like the Nereides,
So many mermaids, tended her i' the eyes,
And made their bends adornings. At the helm
A seeming mermaid steers; the silken tackle
Swell with the touches of those flower-soft hands,
That yarely frame[6] the office. From the barge
A strange invisible perfume hits the sense
Of the adjacent wharfs. The city cast
Her people out upon her; and Antony
Enthron'd i' the market-place, did sit alone,
Whistling to the air, which, but for vacancy,
Had gone to gaze on Cleopatra too
And made a gap in nature.

AGRIPPA: Rare Egyptian!

ENOBARBUS: Upon her landing, Antony sent to her,
Invited her to supper. She replied,
It should be better he became her guest;
Which she entreated. Our courteous Antony,
Whom ne'er the word of "No" woman heard speak,
Being barber'd ten times o'er, goes to the feast,
And for his ordinary[7] pays his heart
For what his eyes eat only.

AGRIPPA: Royal wench!
She made great Caesar lay his sword to bed.
He plough'd her, and she cropp'd.

---

[6] [*yarely frame:* briskly perform.]

[7] [*ordinary:* meal.]

ENOBARBUS: I saw her once
  Hop forty paces through the public street;
  And having lost her breath, she spoke, and panted,
  That she did make defect perfection,
  And, breathless, power breathe forth.
MAECENAS: Now Antony must leave her utterly.
ENOBARBUS: Never; he will not.
  Age cannot wither her, nor custom stale
  Her infinite variety. Other women cloy
  The appetites they feed, but she makes hungry
  Where most she satisfies, for vilest things
  Become themselves in her, that the holy priests
  Bless her when she is riggish.[8]
MAECENAS: If beauty, wisdom, modesty, can settle
  The heart of Antony, Octavia is
  A blessed lottery to him.
AGRIPPA: Let us go.
  Good Enobarbus, make yourself my guest
  Whilst you abide here.
ENOBARBUS: Humbly, sir, I thank you.

                                       Exeunt.

SCENE THREE — *The same.* CAESAR's *house.*

Enter ANTONY, CAESAR, OCTAVIA *between them* [*and Attendants*].

ANTONY: The world and my great office will sometimes
  Divide me from your bosom.
OCTAVIA: All which time
  Before the gods my knee shall bow my prayers
  To them for you.
ANTONY: Good-night, sir. My Octavia,
  Read not my blemishes in the world's report.

---

[8] [*riggish:* wanton.]

I have not kept my square; but that to come
Shall all be done by the rule. Good-night, dear lady.
Good-night, sir.
CAESAR: Good-night.   *Exeunt* [CAESAR *and* OCTAVIA].

Enter SOOTHSAYER.

ANTONY: Now, sirrah; you do wish yourself in Egypt?
SOOTHSAYER: Would I had never come from thence, nor you
   Thither!
ANTONY: If you can, your reason?
SOOTHSAYER: I see it in
   My motion, have it not in my tongue; but yet
   Hie you to Egypt again.
ANTONY: Say to me,
   Whose fortunes shall rise higher, Caesar's or mine?
SOOTHSAYER: Caesar's.
   Therefore, O Antony, stay not by his side.
   Thy demon, that thy spirit which keeps thee, is
   Noble, courageous, high, unmatchable,
   Where Caesar's is not; but, near him, thy angel
   Becomes a fear, as being o'erpower'd: therefore
   Make space between you.
ANTONY: Speak this no more.
SOOTHSAYER: To none but thee; no more, but when to thee.
   If thou dost play with him at any game,
   Thou art sure to lose; and, of that natural luck,
   He beats thee 'gainst the odds. Thy lustre thickens
   When he shines by. I say again, thy spirit
   Is all afraid to govern thee near him;
   But, he away, 'tis noble.
ANTONY: Get thee gone. —
   Say to Ventidius I would speak with him;
                         Exit [SOOTHSAYER].
   He shall to Parthia. — Be it art or hap,
   He hath spoken true. The very dice obey him;
   And in our sports my better cunning faints

Under his chance. If we draw lots, he speeds;
His cocks do win the battle still of mine,
When it is all to nought; and his quails ever
Beat mine, inhoop'd, at odds. I will to Egypt;
And though I make this marriage for my peace,
I' the East my pleasure lies.

Enter VENTIDIUS.

                    O, come, Ventidius,
You must to Parthia. Your commission's ready;
Follow me, and receive't.   *Exeunt.*

SCENE FOUR—*The same. A street.*

Enter LEPIDUS, MAECENAS, *and* AGRIPPA.

LEPIDUS: Trouble yourselves no further; pray you, hasten
   Your generals after.
AGRIPPA: Sir, Mark Antony
   Will e'en but kiss Octavia, and we'll follow.
LEPIDUS: Till I shall see in your soldier's dress,
   Which will become you both, farewell.
MAECENAS: We shall,
   As I conceive the journey, be at the Mount
   Before you, Lepidus.
LEPIDUS: Your way is shorter;
   My purposes do draw me much about.
   You'll win two days upon me.
MAECENAS, AGRIPPA: Sir, good success!
LEPIDUS: Farewell.   *Exeunt.*

SCENE FIVE—*Alexandria.* CLEOPATRA's *palace.*

Enter CLEOPATRA, CHARMIAN, IRAS, *and* ALEXAS.

CLEOPATRA: Give me some music; music, moody food
   Of us that trade in love.

ALL: The music, ho!

Enter MARDIAN *the Eunuch.*

CLEOPATRA: Let it alone; let's to billiards. Come, Charmian.
CHARMIAN: My arm is sore; best play with Mardian.
CLEOPATRA: As well a woman with an eunuch play'd
  As with a woman. Come, you'll play with me, sir?
MARDIAN: As well as I can, madam.
CLEOPATRA: And when good will is show'd, though 't come
    too short,
  The actor may plead pardon. I'll none now.
  Give me mine angle, we'll to the river; there,
  My music playing far off, I will betray
  Tawny-finn'd fishes; my bended hook shall pierce
  Their slimy jaws; and, as I draw them up,
  I'll think them every one an Antony,
  And say, "Ah, ha! you're caught."
CHARMIAN: 'Twas merry when
  You wager'd on your angling; when your diver
  Did hang a salt-fish on his hook, which he
  With fervency drew up.
CLEOPATRA: That time,—O times!—
  I laugh'd him out of patience; and that night
  I laugh'd him into patience; and next morn,
  Ere the ninth hour, I drunk him to his bed;
  Then put my tires and mantles on him, whilst
  I wore his sword Philippan.

Enter a MESSENGER.

                              O, from Italy!
  Ram thou thy fruitful tidings in mine ears,
  That long time have been barren.
MESSENGER: Madam, madam,—
CLEOPATRA: Antonio's dead!—If thou say so, villain,
  Thou kill'st thy mistress; but well and free,
  If thou so yield him, there is gold, and here

My bluest veins to kiss; a hand that kings
Have lipp'd, and trembled kissing.

MESSENGER: First, madam, he is well.

CLEOPATRA: Why, there's more gold.
But, sirrah, mark, we use
To say the dead are well. Bring it to that,
The gold I give thee will I melt and pour
Down thy ill-uttering throat.

MESSENGER: Good madam, hear me.

CLEOPATRA: Well, go to, I will.
But there's no goodness in thy face; if Antony
Be free and healthful,—so tart a favour
To trumpet such good tidings! If not well,
Thou shouldst come like a Fury crown'd with snakes,
Not like a formal man.

MESSENGER: Will't please you hear me?

CLEOPATRA: I have a mind to strike thee ere thou speak'st;
Yet, if thou say Antony lives, 'tis well,
Or friends with Caesar, or not captive to him,
I'll set thee in a shower of gold, and hail
Rich pearls upon thee.

MESSENGER: Madam, he's well.

CLEOPATRA: Well said.

MESSENGER: And friends with Caesar.

CLEOPATRA: Thou'rt an honest man.

MESSENGER: Caesar and he are greater friends than ever.

CLEOPATRA: Make thee a fortune from me.

MESSENGER: But yet, madam,—

CLEOPATRA: I do not like "But yet," it does allay
The good precedence; fie upon "But yet"!
"But yet" is as a gaoler to bring forth
Some monstrous malefactor. Prithee, friend,
Pour out the pack of matter to mine ear,
The good and bad together. He's friends with Caesar;
In state of health thou say'st; and thou say'st free.

MESSENGER: Free, madam! no; I made no such report.
He's bound unto Octavia.
CLEOPATRA: For what good turn?
MESSENGER: For the best turn i' the bed.
CLEOPATRA: I am pale, Charmian.
MESSENGER: Madam, he's married to Octavia.
CLEOPATRA: The most infectious pestilence upon thee!
                                        Strikes him down.
MESSENGER: Good madam, patience.
CLEOPATRA: What say you? Hence,
                                        Strikes him again.
Horrible villain! or I'll spurn thine eyes
Like balls before me; I'll unhair thy head.
                                   She hales him up and down.
Thou shalt be whipp'd with wire, and stew'd in brine,
Smarting in ling'ring pickle.
MESSENGER: Gracious madam,
I that do bring the news made not the match.
CLEOPATRA: Say 'tis not so, a province I will give thee,
And make thy fortunes proud; the blow thou hadst
Shall make thy peace for moving me to rage;
And I will boot thee with what gift beside
Thy modesty can beg.
MESSENGER: He's married, madam.
CLEOPATRA: Rogue, thou hast liv'd too long. *Draws a knife.*
MESSENGER: Nay, then I'll run.
What mean you, madam? I have made no fault.   *Exit.*
CHARMIAN: Good madam, keep yourself within yourself:
The man is innocent.
CLEOPATRA: Some innocents scape not the thunderbolt.
Melt Egypt into Nile! and kindly creatures
Turn all to serpents! Call the slave again.
Though I am mad, I will not bite him; call.
CHARMIAN: He is afeard to come.
CLEOPATRA: I will not hurt him.
                                   [*Exit* CHARMIAN.]

These hands do lack nobility that they strike
A meaner than myself, since I myself
Have given myself the cause.

Re-enter [CHARMIAN *and*] MESSENGER.

                          Come hither, sir.
Though it be honest, it is never good
To bring bad news. Give to a gracious message
An host of tongues; but let ill tidings tell
Themselves when they be felt.

MESSENGER: I have done my duty.

CLEOPATRA: Is he married?
I cannot hate thee worser than I do,
If thou again say yes.

MESSENGER: He's married, madam.

CLEOPATRA: The gods confound thee! dost thou hold there still?

MESSENGER: Should I lie, madam?

CLEOPATRA: O, I would thou didst,
So half my Egypt were submerg'd and made
A cistern for scal'd snakes! Go, get thee hence!
Hadst thou Narcissus in thy face, to me
Thou wouldst appear most ugly. He is married?

MESSENGER: I crave your Highness' pardon.

CLEOPATRA: He is married?

MESSENGER: Take no offence that I would not offend you.
To punish me for what you make me do
Seems much unequal. He's married to Octavia.

CLEOPATRA: O, that his fault should make a knave of thee,
That art not what thou'rt sure of. Get thee hence;
The merchandise which thou hast brought from Rome
Are all too dear for me. Lie they upon thy hand,
And be undone by 'em!   [*Exit* MESSENGER.]

CHARMIAN: Good your Highness, patience.

CLEOPATRA: In praising Antony, I have disprais'd Caesar.

CHARMIAN: Many times, madam.
CLEOPATRA: I am paid for't now.
    Lead me from hence;
    I faint, O Iras, Charmian! 'Tis no matter.
    Go to the fellow, good Alexas; bid him
    Report the feature of Octavia, her years,
    Her inclination; let him not leave out
    The colour of her hair. Bring me word quickly.
                                    [*Exit* ALEXAS.]
    Let him for ever go;—let him not—Charmian,
    Though he be painted one way like a Gorgon,
    The other way's a Mars. Bid you Alexas   [*To* MARDIAN.]
    Bring me word how tall she is. Pity me, Charmian,
    But do not speak to me. Lead me to my chamber. *Exeunt.*

SCENE SIX—*Near Misenum.*

Flourish. Enter POMPEY *and* MENAS *at one door, with drum and trumpet: at another,* CAESAR, ANTONY, LEPIDUS, ENOBARBUS, MAECENAS, AGRIPPA, *with Soldiers marching.*

POMPEY: Your hostages I have, so have you mine;
    And we shall talk before we fight.
CAESAR: Most meet
    That first we come to words, and therefore have we
    Our written purposes before us sent;
    Which, if thou hast considered, let us know
    If 'twill tie up thy discontented sword,
    And carry back to Sicily much tall youth
    That else must perish here.
POMPEY: To you all three,
    The senators alone of this great world,
    Chief factors for the gods, I do not know
    Wherefore my father should revengers want,
    Having a son and friends; since Julius Caesar,

Who at Philippi the good Brutus ghosted,
There saw you labouring for him. What was't
That mov'd pale Cassius to conspire; and what
Made the all-honour'd, honest Roman, Brutus,
With the arm'd rest, courtiers of beauteous freedom,
To drench the Capitol, but that they would
Have one man but a man? And that is it
Hath made me rig my navy, at whose burden
The anger'd ocean foams; with which I meant
To scourge the ingratitude that despiteful Rome
Cast on my noble father.

CAESAR:　　　　　　　　Take your time.

ANTONY: Thou canst not fear us, Pompey, with thy sails;
We'll speak with thee at sea. At land, thou know'st
How much we do o'er-count thee.

POMPEY:　　　　　　　　At land, indeed,
Thou dost o'er-count me of my father's house;
But, since the cuckoo builds not for himself,
Remain in't as thou mayst.

LEPIDUS:　　　　　　　　Be pleas'd to tell us—
For this is from the present—how you take
The offers we have sent you.

CAESAR:　　　　　　　　There's the point.

ANTONY: Which do not be entreated to, but weigh
What it is worth embrac'd.

CAESAR:　　　　　　　　And what may follow.
To try a larger fortune.

POMPEY:　　　　　　　You have made me offer
Of Sicily, Sardinia; and I must
Rid all the sea of pirates; then, to send
Measures of wheat to Rome. This 'greed upon,
To part with unhack'd edges, and bear back
Our targes[9] undinted.

———————

[9] [*targes:* shields.]

CAESAR, ANTONY, LEPIDUS: That's our offer.
POMPEY: Know, then,
    I came before you here a man prepar'd
    To take this offer; but Mark Antony
    Put me to some impatience.—Though I lose
    The praise of it by telling, you must know,
    When Caesar and your brother were at blows,
    Your mother came to Sicily and did find
    Her welcome friendly.
ANTONY: I have heard it, Pompey;
    And am well studied for a liberal thanks
    Which I do owe you.
POMPEY: Let me have your hand.
    I did not think, sir, to have met you here.
ANTONY: The beds i' the East are soft; and thanks to you,
    That call'd me timelier than my purpose hither,
    For I have gain'd by't.
CAESAR: Since I saw you last,
    There is a change upon you.
POMPEY: Well, I know not
    What counts harsh Fortune casts upon my face;
    But in my bosom shall she never come,
    To make my heart her vassal.
LEPIDUS: Well met here.
POMPEY: I hope so, Lepidus. Thus we are agreed.
    I crave our composition may be written,
    And seal'd between us.
CAESAR: That's the next to do.
POMPEY: We'll feast each other ere we part; and let's
    Draw lots who shall begin.
ANTONY: That will I, Pompey.
POMPEY: No, Antony, take the lot; but, first
    Or last, your fine Egyptian cookery
    Shall have the fame. I have heard that Julius Caesar
    Grew fat with feasting there.
ANTONY: You have heard much.

POMPEY: I have fair meanings, sir.

ANTONY: And fair words to them.

POMPEY: Then so much have I heard;

And I have heard, Apollodorus carried—

ENOBARBUS: No more of that; he did so.

POMPEY: What, I pray you?

ENOBARBUS: A certain queen to Caesar in a mattress.

POMPEY: I know thee now. How far'st thou, soldier?

ENOBARBUS: Well;

And well am like to do; for, I perceive,

Four feasts are toward.[10]

POMPEY: Let me shake thy hand;

I never hated thee. I have seen thee fight,

When I have envied thy behaviour.

ENOBARBUS: Sir,

I never lov'd you much; but I ha' prais'd ye,

When you have well deserv'd ten times as much

As I have said you did.

POMPEY: Enjoy thy plainness,

It nothing ill becomes thee.

Aboard my galley I invite you all:

Will you lead, lords?

CAESAR, ANTONY, LEPIDUS: Show us the way, sir.

POMPEY: Come.

Exeunt all but MENAS *and* ENOBARBUS.

MENAS [*aside*]: Thy father, Pompey, would ne'er have made
    this treaty.—You and I have known, sir.

ENOBARBUS: At sea, I think.

MENAS: We have, sir.

ENOBARBUS: You have done well by water.

MENAS: And you by land.

ENOBARBUS: I will praise any man that will praise me; though
    it cannot be denied what I have done by land.

---

[10] [*toward:* in preparation.]

MENAS: Nor what I have done by water.

ENOBARBUS: Yes, something you can deny for your own safety. You have been a great thief by sea.

MENAS: And you by land.

ENOBARBUS: There I deny my land service. But give me your hand, Menas. If our eyes had authority, here they might take two thieves kissing.

MENAS: All men's faces are true, whatsoe'er their hands are.

ENOBARBUS: But there is never a fair woman has a true face.

MENAS: No slander; they steal hearts.

ENOBARBUS: We came hither to fight with you.

MENAS: For my part, I am sorry it is turn'd to a drinking. Pompey doth this day laugh away his fortune.

ENOBARBUS: If he do, sure, he cannot weep't back again.

MENAS: You've said, sir. We look'd not for Mark Antony here. Pray you, is he married to Cleopatra?

ENOBARBUS: Caesar's sister is called Octavia.

MENAS: True, sir; she was the wife of Caius Marcellus.

ENOBARBUS: But she is now the wife of Marcus Antonius.

MENAS: Pray ye, sir?

ENOBARBUS: 'Tis true.

MENAS: Then is Caesar and he for ever knit together.

ENOBARBUS: If I were bound to divine of this unity, I would not prophesy so.

MENAS: I think the policy of that purpose made more in the marriage than the love of the parties.

ENOBARBUS: I think so too. But you shall find the band that seems to tie their friendship together will be the very strangler of their amity. Octavia is of a holy, cold, and still conversation.

MENAS: Who would not have his wife so?

ENOBARBUS: Not he that himself is not so; which is Mark Antony. He will to his Egyptian dish again. Then shall the sighs of Octavia blow the fire up in Caesar; and, as I said before, that which is the strength of their amity shall prove the immediate author of their variance. Antony will use his affection where it is; he married but his occasion here.

MENAS: And thus it may be. Come, sir, will you aboard? I have a health for you.

ENOBARBUS: I shall take it, sir; we have us'd our throats in Egypt.

MENAS: Come, let's away.   *Exeunt.*

SCENE SEVEN — *On board* POMPEY's *galley, off Misenum.*

Music plays. Enter two or three Servants with a banquet.

FIRST SERVANT: Here they'll be, man. Some o' their plants are ill-rooted already; the least wind i' the world will blow them down.

SECOND SERVANT: Lepidus is high-colour'd.

FIRST SERVANT: They have made him drink alms-drink.

SECOND SERVANT: As they pinch one another by the disposition, he cries out, "No more"; reconciles them to his entreaty, and himself to the drink.

FIRST SERVANT: But it raises the greater war between him and his discretion.

SECOND SERVANT: Why, this it is to have a name in great men's fellowship. I had as lief have a reed that will do me no service as a partisan I could not heave.

FIRST SERVANT: To be called into a huge sphere, and not to be seen to move in't, are the holes where eyes should be, which pitifully disaster the cheeks.

A sennet sounded. Enter CAESAR, ANTONY, LEPIDUS, POMPEY, AGRIPPA, MAECENAS, ENOBARBUS, MENAS, *with other captains.*

ANTONY [*to* CAESAR]: Thus do they, sir: they take the flow o' the Nile
By certain scales i' the pyramid; they know,
By the height, the lowness, or the mean, if dearth

Or foison follow. The higher Nilus swells,
The more it promises; as it ebbs, the seedsman
Upon the slime and ooze scatters his grain,
And shortly comes to harvest.

LEPIDUS: You've strange serpents there?

ANTONY: Ay, Lepidus.

LEPIDUS: Your serpent of Egypt is bred now of your mud by the operation of your sun. So is your crocodile.

ANTONY: They are so.

POMPEY: Sit,—and some wine! A health to Lepidus!

LEPIDUS: I am not so well as I should be, but I'll ne'er out.

ENOBARBUS: Not till you have slept; I fear me you'll be in till then.

LEPIDUS: Nay, certainly, I have heard the Ptolemies' pyramises are very goodly things; without contradiction, I have heard that.

MENAS [aside to POMPEY]: Pompey, a word.

POMPEY [aside to MENAS]: Say in mine ear: what is't?

MENAS [aside to POMPEY]: Forsake thy seat, I do beseech thee, captain,
And hear me speak a word.

POMPEY [whispers in 's ear]: Forbear me till anon.—
This wine for Lepidus!

LEPIDUS: What manner o' thing is your crocodile?

ANTONY: It is shap'd, sir, like itself; and it is as broad as it hath breadth. It is just so high as it is, and moves with it own organs. It lives by that which nourisheth it; and the elements once out of it, it transmigrates.

LEPIDUS: What colour is it of?

ANTONY: Of it own colour too.

LEPIDUS: 'Tis a strange serpent.

ANTONY: 'Tis so. And the tears of it are wet.

CAESAR: Will this description satisfy him?

ANTONY: With the health that Pompey gives him, else he is a very epicure.

POMPEY [*aside to* MENAS]: Go hang, sir, hang! Tell me of that?
    Away!
Do as I bid you.—Where's this cup I call'd for?
MENAS [*aside to* POMPEY]: If for the sake of merit thou wilt
    hear me,
Rise from thy stool.
POMPEY [*aside to* MENAS]: I think thou'rt mad. The matter?
                        [*Rises, and walks aside.*]

MENAS: I have ever held my cap off to thy fortunes.
POMPEY: Thou hast serv'd me with much faith. What's else
    to say?
Be jolly, lords.
ANTONY: These quick-sands, Lepidus,
Keep off them, for you sink.
MENAS: Wilt thou be lord of all the world?
POMPEY: What say'st thou?
MENAS: Wilt thou be lord of the whole world? That's twice.
POMPEY: How should that be?
MENAS: But entertain it,
And, though thou think me poor, I am the man
Will give thee all the world.
POMPEY: Hast thou drunk well?
MENAS: No, Pompey, I have kept me from the cup.
Thou art, if thou dar'st be, the earthly Jove.
Whate'er the ocean pales, or sky inclips,
Is thine, if thou wilt ha't.
POMPEY: Show me which way.
MENAS: These three world-sharers, these competitors,
Are in thy vessel: let me cut the cable;
And, when we are put off, fall to their throats.
All there is thine.
POMPEY: Ah, this thou shouldst have done,
And not have spoke on't! In me 'tis villany;
 In thee't had been good service. Thou must know,
'Tis not my profit that does lead mine honour;

Mine honour, it. Repent that e'er thy tongue
Hath so betray'd thine act. Being done unknown,
I should have found it afterwards well done;
But must condemn it now. Desist, and drink.

MENAS [aside]: For this,
I'll never follow thy pall'd fortunes more.
Who seeks, and will not take when once 'tis offer'd,
Shall never find it more.

POMPEY: This health to Lepidus!

ANTONY: Bear him ashore. I'll pledge it for him, Pompey.

ENOBARBUS: Here's to thee, Menas!

MENAS: Enobarbus, welcome!

POMPEY: Fill till the cup be hid.

ENOBARBUS: There's a strong fellow, Menas.
        [Pointing to the Attendant who carries off LEPIDUS.]

MENAS: Why?

ENOBARBUS: 'A bears the third part of the world, man; see'st
    not?

MENAS: The third part, then, is drunk. Would it were all,
    That it might go on wheels!

ENOBARBUS: Drink thou; increase the reels.

MENAS: Come.

POMPEY: This is not yet an Alexandrian feast.

ANTONY: It ripens towards it. Strike the vessels, ho!
    Here's to Caesar!

CAESAR: I could well forbear't.
    It's monstrous labour when I wash my brain
    And it grows fouler.

ANTONY: Be a child o' the time.

CAESAR: Possess it, I'll make answer.
    But I had rather fast from all, four days,
    Than drink so much in one.

ENOBARBUS: Ha, my brave emperor!   [To ANTONY.]
    Shall we dance now the Egyptian Bacchanals,
    And celebrate our drink?

POMPEY: Let's ha't, good soldier.
ANTONY: Come, let's all take hands,
    Till that the conquering wine hath steep'd our sense
    In soft and delicate Lethe.
ENOBARBUS: All take hands.
    Make battery to our ears with the loud music;
    The while I'll place you; then the boy shall sing.
    The holding every man shall bear as loud
    As his strong sides can volley.
            Music plays. ENOBARBUS *places them hand in hand.*

THE SONG

        Come, thou monarch of the vine,
        Plumpy Bacchus with pink eyne!
        In thy vats our cares be drown'd,
        With thy grapes our hairs be crown'd!
        Cup us, till the world go round,
        Cup us, till the world go round!

CAESAR: What would you more? Pompey, good-night. Good
    brother,
    Let me request you off; our graver business
    Frowns at this levity. Gentle lords, let's part;
    You see we have burnt our cheeks. Strong Enobarb
    Is weaker than the wine, and mine own tongue
    Splits what it speaks; the wild disguise hath almost
    Antick'd us all. What needs more words? Good-night.
    Good Antony, your hand.
POMPEY: I'll try you on the shore.
ANTONY: And shall, sir; give's your hand.
POMPEY: O Antony,
    You have my father's house,—But, what? we are friends.
    Come, down into the boat.
ENOBARBUS: Take heed you fall not.
            [*Exeunt all but* ENOBARBUS *and* MENAS.]
    Menas, I'll not on shore.

MENAS: No, to my cabin.
These drums! these trumpets, flutes! what!
Let Neptune hear we bid a loud farewell
To these great fellows. Sound and be hang'd, sound out!
                              Sound a flourish, with drums.

ENOBARBUS: Ho! says 'a. There's my cap.
MENAS: Ho! Noble captain, come.   *Exeunt.*

ACT III

Scene One—*A plain in Syria.*

Enter VENTIDIUS *as it were in triumph [with* SILIUS, *and other Romans, Officers, and Soldiers;] the dead body of Pacorus borne before him.*

VENTIDIUS: Now, darting Parthia, art thou struck; and now
    Pleas'd Fortune does of Marcus Crassus' death
    Make me revenger. Bear the King's son's body
    Before our army. Thy Pacorus, Orodes,
    Pays this for Marcus Crassus.
SILIUS: Noble Ventidius,
    Whilst yet with Parthian blood thy sword is warm,
    The fugitive Parthians follow. Spur through Media,
    Mesopotamia, and the shelters whither
    The routed fly; so thy grand captain Antony
    Shall set thee on triumphant chariots and
    Put garlands on thy head.
VENTIDIUS: O Silius, Silius,
    I have done enough; a lower place, note well,
    May make too great an act. For learn this, Silius;

Better to leave undone, than by our deed
Acquire too high a fame when him we serve's away.
Caesar and Antony have ever won
More in their officer than person. Sossius,
One of my place in Syria, his lieutenant,
For quick accumulation of renown,
Which he achiev'd by the minute, lost his favour.
Who does i' the wars more than his captain can
Becomes his captain's captain; and ambition,
The soldier's virtue, rather makes choice of loss,
Than gain which darkens him.
I could do more to do Antonius good,
But 'twould offend him; and in his offence
Should my performance perish.

SILIUS: Thou hast, Ventidius, that
Without the which a soldier and his sword
Grants scarce distinction. Thou wilt write to Antony?

VENTIDIUS: I'll humbly signify what in his name,
That magical word of war, we have effected;
How, with his banners and his well-paid ranks,
The ne'er-yet-beaten horse of Parthia
We have jaded out o' the field.

SILIUS: Where is he now?

VENTIDIUS: He purposeth to Athens; whither, with what haste
The weight we must convey with 's will permit,
We shall appear before him. On, there; pass along!

                                  Exeunt.

SCENE TWO—*Rome. An ante-chamber in* CAESAR'*s house.*

Enter AGRIPPA *at one door,* ENOBARBUS *at another.*

AGRIPPA: What, are the brothers parted?

ENOBARBUS: They have dispatch'd with Pompey, he is gone;
The other three are sealing. Octavia weeps
To part from Rome; Caesar is sad; and Lepidus,

Since Pompey's feast, as Menas says, is troubled
With the green sickness.

AGRIPPA: 'Tis a noble Lepidus.

ENOBARBUS: A very fine one. O, how he loves Caesar!

AGRIPPA: Nay, but how dearly he adores Mark Antony!

ENOBARBUS: Caesar? Why, he's the Jupiter of men.

AGRIPPA: What's Antony? The god of Jupiter.

ENOBARBUS: Spake you of Caesar? How! the nonpareil!

AGRIPPA: O Antony! O thou Arabian bird!

ENOBARBUS: Would you praise Caesar, say "Caesar"; go no
    further.

AGRIPPA: Indeed, he plied them both with excellent praises.

ENOBARBUS: But he loves Caesar best; yet he loves Antony.
    Ho! hearts, tongues, figures, scribes, bards, poets, cannot
    Think, speak, cast, write, sing, number, ho
    His love to Antony. But as for Caesar,
    Kneel down, kneel down, and wonder.

AGRIPPA: Both he loves.

ENOBARBUS: They are his shards, and he their beetle. [*Trumpets
    within.*] So;
    This is to horse. Adieu, noble Agrippa.

AGRIPPA: Good fortune, worthy soldier; and farewell.

Enter CAESAR, ANTONY, LEPIDUS, *and* OCTAVIA.

ANTONY: No further, sir.

CAESAR: You take from me a great part of myself;
    Use me well in't. Sister, prove such a wife
    As my thoughts make thee, and as my farthest band
    Shall pass on thy approof. Most noble Antony,
    Let not the piece of virtue which is set
    Betwixt us as the cement of our love,
    To keep it builded, be the ram to batter
    The fortress of it; for better might we
    Have lov'd without this mean, if on both parts
    This be not cherish'd.

ANTONY: Make me not offended

In your distrust.

CAESAR: I have said.

ANTONY: You shall not find,
  Though you be therein curious, the least cause
  For what you seem to fear. So, the gods keep you,
  And make the hearts of Romans serve your ends!
  We will here part.

CAESAR: Farewell, my dearest sister, fare thee well!
  The elements be kind to thee, and make
  Thy spirits all of comfort! Fare thee well!

OCTAVIA: My noble brother!

ANTONY: The April's in her eyes; it is love's spring,
  And these the showers to bring it on. Be cheerful.

OCTAVIA: Sir, look well to my husband's house; and—

CAESAR: What, Octavia?

OCTAVIA: I'll tell you in your ear.

ANTONY: Her tongue will not obey her heart, nor can
  Her heart inform her tongue,—the swan's down-feather,
  That stands upon the swell at full of tide,
  And neither way inclines.

ENOBARBUS [*aside to* AGRIPPA]:   Will Caesar weep?

AGRIPPA [*aside to* ENOBARBUS]: He has a cloud in's face.

ENOBARBUS [*aside to* AGRIPPA]: He were the worse for that,
    were he a horse;
  So is he, being a man.

AGRIPPA [*aside to* ENOBARBUS]:   Why, Enobarbus,
  When Antony found Julius Caesar dead,
  He cried almost to roaring; and he wept
  When at Philippi he found Brutus slain.

ENOBARBUS [*aside to* AGRIPPA]: That year, indeed, he was trou-
    bled with a rheum;
  What willingly he did confound he wail'd,
  Believe't, till I wept too.

CAESAR: No, sweet Octavia,
  You shall hear from me still; the time shall not
  Out-go my thinking on you.

ANTONY: Come, sir, come;
  I'll wrestle with you in my strength of love.
  Look, here I have you; thus I let you go,
  And give you to the gods.
CAESAR: Adieu; be happy!
LEPIDUS: Let all the number of the stars give light
  To thy fair way!
CAESAR: Farewell, farewell!   *Kisses* OCTAVIA.
ANTONY: Farewell!
                        Trumpets sound. Exeunt.

SCENE THREE—*Alexandria.* CLEOPATRA's *palace.*

Enter CLEOPATRA, CHARMIAN, IRAS, *and* ALEXAS.

CLEOPATRA: Where is the fellow?
ALEXAS: Half afeard to come.
CLEOPATRA: Go to, go to. Come hither, sir.

Enter the MESSENGER *as before.*

ALEXAS: Good Majesty,
  Herod of Jewry dare not look upon you
  But when you are well pleas'd.
CLEOPATRA: That Herod's head
  I'll have; but how, when Antony is gone
  Through whom I might command it? Come thou near.
MESSENGER: Most gracious Majesty,—
CLEOPATRA: Didst thou behold Octavia?
MESSENGER: Ay, dread queen.
CLEOPATRA: Where?
MESSENGER: Madam, in Rome;
  I look'd her in the face, and saw her led
  Between her brother and Mark Antony.
CLEOPATRA: Is she as tall as me?
MESSENGER: She is not, madam.

CLEOPATRA: Didst hear her speak? Is she shrill-tongu'd or low?
MESSENGER: Madam, I heard her speak; she is low-voic'd.
CLEOPATRA: That's not so good. He cannot like her long?
CHARMIAN: Like her! O Isis! 'tis impossible.
CLEOPATRA: I think so, Charmian. Dull of tongue, and dwarf-
    ish!
  What majesty is in her gait? Remember,
  If e'er thou look'dst on majesty.
MESSENGER: She creeps;
  Her motion and her station are as one;
  She shows a body rather than a life,
  A statue than a breather.
CLEOPATRA: Is this certain?
MESSENGER: Or I have no observance.
CHARMIAN: Three in Egypt
  Cannot make better note.
CLEOPATRA: He's very knowing;
  I do perceive't. There's nothing in her yet.
  The fellow has good judgement.
CHARMIAN: Excellent.
CLEOPATRA: Guess at her years, I prithee.
MESSENGER: Madam,
  She was a widow,—
CLEOPATRA: Widow! Charmian, hark.
MESSENGER: And I do think she's thirty.
CLEOPATRA: Bear'st thou her face in mind? Is't long or round?
MESSENGER: Round even to faultiness.
CLEOPATRA: For the most part, too, they are foolish that are
    so.
  Her hair, what colour?
MESSENGER: Brown, madam; and her forehead
  As low as she would wish it.
CLEOPATRA: There's gold for thee.
  Thou must not take my former sharpness ill.
  I will employ thee back again; I find thee
  Most fit for business. Go make thee ready;

Our letters are prepar'd.   [*Exit* MESSENGER.]

CHARMIAN: A proper man.

CLEOPATRA: Indeed, he is so; I repent me much
That so I harried him. Why, methinks, by him,
This creature's no such thing.

CHARMIAN: Nothing, madam.

CLEOPATRA: The man hath seen some majesty, and should know.

CHARMIAN: Hath he seen majesty? Isis else defend,
And serving you so long!

CLEOPATRA: I have one thing more to ask him yet, good Char-
mian:
But 'tis no matter; thou shalt bring him to me
Where I will write. All may be well enough.

CHARMIAN: I warrant you, madam.   *Exeunt.*

SCENE FOUR — *Athens. A room in* ANTONY'*s house.*

Enter ANTONY *and* OCTAVIA.

ANTONY: Nay, nay, Octavia, not only that, —
That were excusable, that, and thousands more
Of semblable import, — but he hath wag'd
New wars 'gainst Pompey; made his will, and read it
To public ear;
Spoke scantly of me; when perforce he could not
But pay me terms of honour, cold and sickly
He vented them; most narrow measure lent me:
When the best hint was given him, he not took't,
Or did it from his teeth.

OCTAVIA: O my good lord,
Believe not all; or, if you must believe,
Stomach not all. A more unhappy lady,
If this division chance, ne'er stood between,
Praying for both parts.
The good gods will mock me presently,
When I shall pray, "O, bless my lord and husband!"

Undo that prayer, by crying out as loud,
"O, bless my brother!" Husband win, win brother,
Prays, and destroys the prayer; no midway
'Twixt these extremes at all.

ANTONY: Gentle Octavia,
Let your best love draw to that point which seeks
Best to preserve it. If I lose mine honour,
I lose myself; better I were not yours
Than yours so branchless. But, as you requested,
Yourself shall go between 's. The meantime, lady,
I'll raise the preparation of a war
Shall stain your brother. Make your soonest haste;
So your desires are yours.

OCTAVIA: Thanks to my lord.
The Jove of power make me most weak, most weak,
Your reconciler! Wars 'twixt you twain would be
As if the world should cleave, and that slain men
Should solder up the rift.

ANTONY: When it appears to you where this begins,
Turn your displeasure that way; for our faults
Can never be so equal, that your love
Can equally move with them. Provide your going;
Choose your own company, and command what cost
Your heart has mind to.   *Exeunt.*

SCENE FIVE—*The same. Another room.*

Enter ENOBARBUS *and* EROS [*meeting*].

ENOBARBUS: How now, friend Eros!
EROS: There's strange news come, sir.
ENOBARBUS: What, man?
EROS: Caesar and Lepidus have made wars upon Pompey.
ENOBARBUS: This is old; what is the success?

EROS: Caesar, having made use of him in the wars 'gainst Pompey, presently denied him rivality, would not let him partake in the glory of the action; and not resting here, accuses him of letters he had formerly wrote to Pompey; upon his own appeal, seizes him. So the poor third is up, till death enlarge his confine.

ENOBARBUS: Then, world, thou hast a pair of chaps, no more;
And throw between them all the food thou hast,
They'll grind the one the other. Where's Antony?

EROS: He's walking in the garden—thus; and spurns
The rush that lies before him; cries, "Fool Lepidus!"
And threats the throat of that his officer
That murder'd Pompey.

ENOBARBUS: Our great navy's rigg'd.

EROS: For Italy and Caesar. More, Domitius;
My lord desires you presently; my news
I might have told hereafter.

ENOBARBUS: 'Twill be nought;
But let it be. Bring me to Antony.

EROS: Come, sir.   *Exeunt.*

SCENE SIX—*Rome.* CAESAR'*s house.*

Enter CAESAR, AGRIPPA, *and* MAECENAS.

CAESAR: Contemning Rome, he has done all this, and more,
In Alexandria. Here's the manner of 't:
I' the market-place, on a tribunal silver'd,
Cleopatra and himself in chairs of gold
Were publicly enthron'd. At the feet sat
Caesarion, whom they call my father's son,
And all the unlawful issue that their lust
Since then hath made between them. Unto her
He gave the stablishment of Egypt; made her
Of lower Syria, Cyprus, Lydia,
Absolute queen.

MAECENAS: This in the public eye?

CAESAR: I' the common show-place, where they exercise.
   His sons he there proclaim'd the kings of kings:
   Great Media, Parthia, and Armenia,
   He gave to Alexander; to Ptolemy he assign'd
   Syria, Cilicia, and Phoenicia. She
   In the habiliments of the goddess Isis
   That day appear'd; and oft before gave audience,
   As 'tis reported, so.

MAECENAS: Let Rome be thus
   Inform'd.

AGRIPPA: Who, queasy with his insolence
   Already, will their good thoughts call from him.

CAESAR: The people knows it; and have now receiv'd
   His accusations.

AGRIPPA: Who does he accuse?

CAESAR: Caesar; and that, having in Sicily
   Sextus Pompeius spoil'd, we had not rated him
   His part o' the isle. Then does he say, he lent me
   Some shipping unrestor'd. Lastly, he frets
   That Lepidus of the triumvirate
   Should be depos'd; and, being, that we detain
   All his revenue.

AGRIPPA: Sir, this should be answer'd.

CAESAR: 'Tis done already, and the messenger gone.
   I have told him Lepidus was grown too cruel;
   That he his high authority abus'd,
   And did deserve his change. For what I have conquer'd,
   I grant him part; but then, in his Armenia
   And other of his conquer'd kingdoms, I
   Demand the like.

MAECENAS: He'll never yield to that.

CAESAR: Nor must not then be yielded to in this.

Enter OCTAVIA *with her train.*

OCTAVIA: Hail, Caesar, and my lord! Hail, most dear Caesar!
CAESAR: That ever I should call thee castaway!
OCTAVIA: You have not call'd me so, nor have you cause.
CAESAR: Why have you stolen upon us thus? You come not
    Like Caesar's sister. The wife of Antony
    Should have an army for an usher, and
    The neighs of horse to tell of her approach
    Long ere she did appear; the trees by the way
    Should have borne men, and expectation fainted,
    Longing for what it had not; nay, the dust
    Should have ascended to the roof of heaven,
    Rais'd by your populous troops. But you are come
    A market-maid to Rome, and have prevented
    The ostentation of our love, which, left unshown,
    Is often left unlov'd. We should have met you
    By sea and land; supplying every stage
    With an augmented greeting.
OCTAVIA: Good my lord,
    To come thus was I not constrain'd, but did
    On my free will. My lord, Mark Antony,
    Hearing that you prepar'd for war, acquainted
    My grieved ear withal; whereon, I begg'd
    His pardon for return.
CAESAR: Which soon he granted,
    Being an obstruct 'tween his lust and him.
OCTAVIA: Do not say so, my lord.
CAESAR: I have eyes upon him,
    And his affairs come to me on the wind.
    Where is he now?
OCTAVIA: My lord, in Athens.
CAESAR: No, my most wronged sister; Cleopatra
    Hath nodded him to her. He hath given his empire
    Up to a whore; who now are levying
    The kings o' the earth for war. He hath assembled
    Bocchus, the King of Libya; Archelaus,
    Of Cappadocia; Philadelphos, King

Of Paphlagonia; the Thracian king, Adallas;
King Malchus of Arabia; King of Pont;
Herod of Jewry; Mithridates, King
Of Comagene; Polemon and Amyntas,
The Kings of Mede and Lycaonia,
With a more larger list of sceptres.

OCTAVIA: Ay me, most wretched,
That have my heart parted betwixt two friends
That do afflict each other!

CAESAR: Welcome hither!
Your letters did withhold our breaking forth,
Till we perceiv'd both how you were wrong led
And we in negligent danger. Cheer your heart.
Be you not troubled with the time, which drives
O'er your content these strong necessities;
But let determin'd things to destiny
Hold unbewail'd their way. Welcome to Rome;
Nothing more dear to me. You are abus'd
Beyond the mark of thought; and the high gods,
To do you justice, make them ministers
Of us and those that love you. Best of comfort,
And ever welcome to us.

AGRIPPA: Welcome, lady.

MAECENAS: Welcome, dear madam.
Each heart in Rome does love and pity you;
Only the adulterous Antony, most large
In his abominations, turns you off,
And gives his potent regiment to a trull,
That noises it against us.

OCTAVIA: Is it so, sir?

CAESAR: Most certain. Sister, welcome. Pray you,
Be ever known to patience. My dear'st sister!   *Exeunt.*

SCENE SEVEN — *Near Actium.* ANTONY's *camp.*

Enter CLEOPATRA *and* ENOBARBUS.

CLEOPATRA: I will be even with thee, doubt it not.

ENOBARBUS: But why, why, why?

CLEOPATRA: Thou hast forspoke my being in these wars,
And say'st it is not fit.

ENOBARBUS: Well, is it, is it?

CLEOPATRA: If not denounc'd against us, why should not we
Be there in person?

ENOBARBUS: Well, I could reply:
If we should serve with horse and mares together,
The horse were merely lost; the mares would bear
A soldier and his horse.

CLEOPATRA: What is't you say?

ENOBARBUS: Your presence needs must puzzle Antony;
Take from his heart, take from his brain, from 's time,
What should not then be spar'd. He is already
Traduc'd for levity; and 'tis said in Rome
That Photinus an eunuch and your maids
Manage this war.

CLEOPATRA: Sink Rome, and their tongues rot
That speak against us! A charge we bear i' the war,
And, as the president of my kingdom, will
Appear there for a man. Speak not against it;
I will not stay behind.

Enter ANTONY *and* CANIDIUS.

ENOBARBUS: Nay, I have done.
Here comes the Emperor.

ANTONY: Is it not strange, Canidius,
That from Tarentum and Brundusium
He could so quickly cut the Ionian Sea,
And take in Toryne? You have heard on't, sweet?

CLEOPATRA: Celerity is never more admir'd
Than by the negligent.

ANTONY: A good rebuke,
Which might have well becom'd the best of men,
To taunt at slackness. Canidius, we
Will fight with him by sea.

CLEOPATRA: By sea! what else?
CANIDIUS: Why will my lord do so?
ANTONY: For what he dares us to't.
ENOBARBUS: So hath my lord dar'd him to single fight.
CANIDIUS: Ay, and to wage this battle at Pharsalia,
   Where Caesar fought with Pompey; but these offers,
   Which serve not for his vantage, he shakes off;
   And so should you.
ENOBARBUS: Your ships are not well mann'd;
   Your mariners are muleters, reapers, people
   Ingross'd by swift impress. In Caesar's fleet
   Are those that often have 'gainst Pompey fought.
   Their ships are yare; yours, heavy: no disgrace
   Shall fall you for refusing him at sea,
   Being prepar'd for land.
ANTONY: By sea, by sea.
ENOBARBUS: Most worthy sir, you therein throw away
   The absolute soldiership you have by land;
   Distract your army, which doth most consist
   Of war-mark'd footmen; leave unexecuted
   Your own renowned knowledge; quite forego
   The way which promises assurance; and
   Give up yourself merely to chance and hazard,
   From firm security.
ANTONY: I'll fight at sea.
CLEOPATRA: I have sixty sails, Caesar none better.
ANTONY: Our overplus of shipping will we burn;
   And, with the rest full-mann'd, from the head of Actium
   Beat the approaching Caesar. But if we fail,
   We then can do't at land.

Enter a MESSENGER.

                         Thy business?
MESSENGER: The news is true, my lord; he is descried;
   Caesar has taken Toryne.

ANTONY: Can he be there in person? 'Tis impossible;
  Strange that his power should be. Canidius,
  Our nineteen legions thou shalt hold by land,
  And our twelve thousand horse. We'll to our ship;
  Away, my Thetis!

Enter a SOLDIER.

                    How now, worthy soldier!
SOLDIER: O noble emperor, do not fight by sea;
  Trust not to rotten planks! Do you misdoubt
  This sword and these my wounds? Let the Egyptians
  And the Phoenicians go a-ducking; we
  Have us'd to conquer, standing on the earth,
  And fighting foot to foot.
ANTONY: Well, well: away!
          Exeunt ANTONY, CLEOPATRA, *and* ENOBARBUS.

SOLDIER: By Hercules, I think I am i' the right.
CANIDIUS: Soldier, thou art; but his whole action grows
  Not in the power on't. So our leader's led,
  And we are women's men.
SOLDIER: You keep by land
  The legions and the horse whole, do you not?
CANIDIUS: Marcus Octavius, Marcus Justeius,
  Publicola, and Caelius, are for sea;
  But we keep whole by land. This speed of Caesar's
  Carries beyond belief.
SOLDIER: While he was yet in Rome,
  His power went out in such distractions as
  Beguil'd all spies.
CANIDIUS: Who's his lieutenant, hear you?
SOLDIER: They say, one Taurus.
CANIDIUS: Well I know the man.

Enter a MESSENGER.

MESSENGER: The Emperor calls Canidius.

CANIDIUS: With news the time's with labour, and throes forth,
Each minute, some.   *Exeunt.*

SCENE EIGHT—*A plain near Actium.*

Enter CAESAR [*and* TAURUS], *with his army, marching.*

CAESAR: Taurus!

TAURUS: My lord?

CAESAR: Strike not by land; keep whole; provoke not battle
Till we have done at sea. Do not exceed
The prescript of this scroll. Our fortune lies
Upon this jump.   *Exeunt.*

SCENE NINE—*Another part of the plain.*

Enter ANTONY *and* ENOBARBUS.

ANTONY: Set we our squadrons on yond side o' the hill,
In eye of Caesar's battle; from which place
We may the number of the ships behold,
And so proceed accordingly.   *Exeunt.*

SCENE TEN—*Another part of the plain.*

CANIDIUS *marcheth with his land army one way over the stage;
and* TAURUS, *the lieutenant of* CAESAR, *the other way. After their
going in, is heard the noise of a sea-fight.*
Alarum. Enter ENOBARBUS.

ENOBARBUS: Nought, nought, all nought! I can behold no
longer.
The Antoniad, the Egyptian admiral,
With all their sixty, fly and turn the rudder.
To see't mine eyes are blasted.

Enter SCARUS.

SCARUS: Gods and goddesses,
  All the whole synod of them!
ENOBARBUS: What's thy passion?
SCARUS: The greater cantle[11] of the world is lost
  With very ignorance; we have kiss'd away
  Kingdoms and provinces.
ENOBARBUS: How appears the fight?
SCARUS: On our side like the token'd pestilence,
  Where death is sure. Yon ribaudred nag of Egypt,—
  Whom leprosy o'ertake!—i' the midst o' the fight,
  When vantage like a pair of twins appear'd,
  Both as the same, or rather ours the elder,
  The breese upon her, like a cow in June,
  Hoists sails and flies.
ENOBARBUS: That I beheld.
  Mine eyes did sicken at the sight, and could not
  Endure a further view.
SCARUS: She once being loof'd,
  The noble ruin of her magic, Antony,
  Claps on his sea-wing, and, like a doting mallard,
  Leaving the fight in height, flies after her.
  I never saw an action of such shame;
  Experience, manhood, honour, ne'er before
  Did violate so itself.
ENOBARBUS: Alack, alack!

Enter CANIDIUS.

CANIDIUS: Our fortune on the sea is out of breath,
  And sinks most lamentably. Had our general
  Been what he knew himself, it had gone well.
  O, he has given example for our flight,
  Most grossly, by his own!

---

[11] [*cantle:* piece.]

ENOBARBUS: Ay, are you thereabouts?
  Why, then, good-night indeed.
CANIDIUS: Toward Peloponnesus are they fled.
SCARUS: 'Tis easy to't; and there I will attend
  What further comes.
CANIDIUS: To Caesar will I render
  My legions and my horse. Six kings already
  Show me the way of yielding.
ENOBARBUS: I'll yet follow
  The wounded chance of Antony, though my reason
  Sits in the wind against me.   [*Exeunt.*]

SCENE ELEVEN—*Alexandria.* CLEOPATRA's *palace.*

Enter ANTONY *with Attendants.*

ANTONY: Hark! the land bids me tread no more upon't;
  It is asham'd to bear me! Friends, come hither.
  I am so lated in the world, that I
  Have lost my way for ever. I have a ship
  Laden with gold; take that, divide it; fly,
  And make your peace with Caesar.
ALL: Fly! not we.
ANTONY: I have fled myself; and have instructed cowards
  To run and show their shoulders. Friends, be gone;
  I have myself resolv'd upon a course
  Which has no need of you; be gone.
  My treasure's in the harbour, take it. O,
  I follow'd that I blush to look upon.
  My very hairs do mutiny; for the white
  Reprove the brown for rashness, and they them
  For fear and doting. Friends, be gone; you shall
  Have letters from me to some friends that will
  Sweep your way for you. Pray you, look not sad,
  Nor make replies of loathness. Take the hint
  Which my despair proclaims; let that be left

Which leaves itself. To the sea-side straight-way;
I will possess you of that ship and treasure.
Leave me, I pray, a little; pray you now.
Nay, do so; for, indeed, I have lost command,
Therefore I pray you. I'll see you by and by.   *Sits down.*

Enter CLEOPATRA, *led by* CHARMIAN *and* [IRAS;] EROS
[*following*].

EROS: Nay, gentle madam, to him, comfort him.
IRAS: Do, most dear queen.
CHARMIAN: Do! Why, what else?
CLEOPATRA: Let me sit down. O Juno!
ANTONY: No, no, no, no, no.
EROS: See you here, sir?
ANTONY: O fie, fie, fie!
CHARMIAN: Madam!
IRAS: Madam, O good empress!
EROS: Sir, sir,—
ANTONY: Yes, my lord, yes; he at Philippi kept
  His sword e'en like a dancer, while I struck
  The lean and wrinkled Cassius; and 'twas I
  That the mad Brutus ended. He alone
  Dealt on lieutenantry, and no practice had
  In the brave squares of war; yet now—No matter.
CLEOPATRA: Ah, stand by.
EROS: The Queen, my lord, the Queen.
IRAS: Go to him, madam, speak to him;
  He is unqualitied with very shame.
CLEOPATRA: Well then, sustain me. Oh!
EROS: Most noble sir, arise; the Queen approaches.
  Her head's declin'd, and death will seize her, but
  Your comfort makes the rescue.
ANTONY: I have offended reputation,
  A most unnoble swerving.
EROS: Sir, the Queen.

ANTONY: O, whither hast thou led me, Egypt? See,
How I convey my shame out of thine eyes
By looking back what I have left behind
'Stroy'd in dishonour.

CLEOPATRA: O my lord, my lord,
Forgive my fearful sails! I little thought
You would have follow'd.

ANTONY: Egypt, thou knew'st too well
My heart was to thy rudder tied by the strings,
And thou shouldst tow me after. O'er my spirit
Thy full supremacy thou knew'st, and that
Thy beck might from the bidding of the gods
Command me.

CLEOPATRA: O, my pardon!

ANTONY: Now I must
To the young man send humble treaties, dodge
And palter in the shifts of lowness; who
With half the bulk o' the world play'd as I pleas'd,
Making and marring fortunes. You did know
How much you were my conqueror; and that
My sword, made weak by my affection, would
Obey it on all cause.

CLEOPATRA: Pardon, pardon!

ANTONY: Fall not a tear, I say; one of them rates
All that is won and lost. Give me a kiss.
Even this repays me. We sent our schoolmaster;
Is 'a come back? Love, I am full of lead.
Some wine, within there, and our viands! Fortune knows
We scorn her most when most she offers blows.   *Exeunt.*

SCENE TWELVE—*Egypt.* CAESAR's *camp.*

Enter CAESAR, AGRIPPA, DOLABELLA, THYREUS, *with others.*

CAESAR: Let him appear that's come from Antony.
Know you him?

DOLABELLA: Caesar, 'tis his schoolmaster:
An argument that he is pluck'd, when hither
He sends so poor a pinion of his wing,
Which had superfluous kings for messengers
Not many moons gone by.

Enter EUPHRONIUS, *ambassador from* ANTONY.

CAESAR: Approach, and speak.
EUPHRONIUS: Such as I am, I come from Antony.
I was of late as petty to his ends
As is the morn-dew on the myrtle-leaf
To his grand sea.
CAESAR: Be't so: declare thine office.
EUPHRONIUS: Lord of his fortunes he salutes thee, and
Requires to live in Egypt; which not granted,
He lessens his requests, and to thee sues
To let him breathe between the heavens and earth,
A private man in Athens. This for him.
Next, Cleopatra does confess thy greatness;
Submits her to thy might; and of thee craves
The circle of the Ptolemies for her heirs,
Now hazarded to thy grace.
CAESAR: For Antony,
I have no ears to his request. The Queen
Of audience nor desire shall fail, so she
From Egypt drive her all-disgraced friend,
Or take his life there. This if she perform,
She shall not sue unheard. So to them both.
EUPHRONIUS: Fortune pursue thee!
CAESAR: Bring him through the bands.
                                   [*Exit* EUPHRONIUS.]
[*To* THYREUS.] To try thy eloquence, now 'tis time; dispatch.
From Antony win Cleopatra; promise,
And in our name, what she requires; add more,
From thine invention, offers. Women are not
In their best fortunes strong; but want will perjure

The ne'er-touch'd vestal. Try thy cunning, Thyreus;
Make thine own edict for thy pains, which we
Will answer as a law.
THYREUS: Caesar, I go.
CAESAR: Observe how Antony becomes his flaw,
And what thou think'st his very action speaks
In every power that moves.
THYREUS: Caesar, I shall.   *Exeunt.*

SCENE THIRTEEN — *Alexandria.* CLEOPATRA'*s palace.*

Enter CLEOPATRA, ENOBARBUS, CHARMIAN, *and* IRAS.

CLEOPATRA: What shall we do, Enobarbus?
ENOBARBUS: Think, and die.
CLEOPATRA: Is Antony or we in fault for this?
ENOBARBUS: Antony only, that would make his will
Lord of his reason. What though you fled
From that great face of war, whose several ranges
Frighted each other? Why should he follow?
The itch of his affection should not then
Have nick'd his captainship, at such a point,
When half to half the world oppos'd, he being
The mered question. 'Twas a shame no less
Than was his loss, to course your flying flags,
And leave his navy gazing.
CLEOPATRA: Prithee, peace.

Enter ANTONY *with* [EUPHRONIUS,] *the Ambassador.*

ANTONY: Is that his answer?
EUPHRONIUS: Ay, my lord.
ANTONY: The Queen shall then have courtesy, so she
Will yield us up.
EUPHRONIUS: He says so.
ANTONY: Let her know't.
To the boy Caesar send this grizzled head,

And he will fill thy wishes to the brim
With principalities.

CLEOPATRA: That head, my lord?

ANTONY: To him again. Tell him he wears the rose
Of youth upon him, from which the world should note
Something particular. His coin, ships, legions,
May be a coward's; whose ministers would prevail
Under the service of a child as soon
As i' the command of Caesar. I dare him therefore
To lay his gay comparisons apart,
And answer me declin'd, sword against sword,
Ourselves alone. I'll write it. Follow me.

                    [*Exeunt* ANTONY *and* EUPHRONIUS.]

ENOBARBUS [*aside*]: Yes, like enough high-battl'd Caesar will
Unstate his happiness, and be stag'd to the show,
Against a sworder! I see men's judgements are
A parcel of their fortunes; and things outward
Do draw the inward quality after them,
To suffer all alike. That he should dream,
Knowing all measures, the full Caesar will
Answer his emptiness! Caesar, thou hast subdu'd
His judgement too.

Enter a Servant.

SERVANT: A messenger from Caesar.

CLEOPATRA: What, no more ceremony? See, my women!
Against the blown rose may they stop their nose
That kneel'd unto the buds. Admit him, sir.

                    [*Exit* Servant.]

ENOBARBUS [*aside*]: Mine honesty and I begin to square.
The loyalty well held to fools does make
Our faith mere folly; yet he that can endure
To follow with allegiance a fallen lord
Does conquer him that did his master conquer,
And earns a place i' the story.

Enter THYREUS.

CLEOPATRA: Caesar's will?

THYREUS: Hear it apart.

CLEOPATRA: None but friends: say boldly.

THYREUS: So, haply, are they friends to Antony.

ENOBARBUS: He needs as many, sir, as Caesar has;
   Or needs not us. If Caesar please, our master
   Will leap to be his friend; for us, you know
   Whose he is we are, and that is, Caesar's.

THYREUS: So.
   Thus then, thou most renown'd: Caesar entreats
   Not to consider in what case thou stand'st
   Further than he is Caesar.

CLEOPATRA: Go on: right royal.

THYREUS: He knows that you embrace not Antony
   As you did love, but as you feared him.

CLEOPATRA: Oh!

THYREUS: The scars upon your honour, therefore, he   .
   Does pity, as constrained blemishes,
   Not as deserved.

CLEOPATRA: He is a god, and knows
   What is most right. Mine honour was not yielded,
   But conquer'd merely.

ENOBARBUS [*aside*]:   To be sure of that,
   I will ask Antony. Sir, sir, thou art so leaky,
   That we must leave thee to thy sinking, for
   Thy dearest quit thee.   *Exit.*

THYREUS: Shall I say to Caesar
   What you require of him? for he partly begs
   To be desir'd to give. It much would please him,
   That of his fortunes you should make a staff
   To lean upon; but it would warm his spirits
   To hear from me you had left Antony,
   And put yourself under his shroud,
   The universal landlord.

CLEOPATRA: What's your name?
THYREUS: My name is Thyreus.
CLEOPATRA: Most kind messenger,
    Say to great Caesar this: in deputation
    I kiss his conqu'ring hand. Tell him, I am prompt
    To lay my crown at 's feet, and there to kneel.
    Tell him, from his all-obeying breath I hear
    The doom of Egypt.
THYREUS: 'Tis your noblest course.
    Wisdom and fortune combating together,
    If that the former dare but what it can,
    No chance may shake it. Give me grace to lay
    My duty on your hand.
CLEOPATRA: Your Caesar's father oft,
    When he hath mus'd of taking kingdoms in,
    Bestow'd his lips on that unworthy place,
    As it rain'd kisses.

Re-enter ANTONY *and* ENOBARBUS.

ANTONY: Favours, by Jove that thunders!
    What art thou, fellow?
THYREUS: One that but performs
    The bidding of the fullest man, and worthiest
    To have command obey'd.
ENOBARBUS [*aside*]:   You will be whipp'd.
ANTONY: Approach there! Ah, you kite! Now, gods and devils!
    Authority melts from me. Of late, when I cried "Ho!"
    Like boys unto a muss, kings would start forth,
    And cry, "Your will?" Have you no ears? I am
    Antony yet.

Enter a Servant.

      Take hence this Jack, and whip him.
ENOBARBUS [*aside*]: 'Tis better playing with a lion's whelp
    Than with an old one dying.

ANTONY: Moon and stars!
Whip him! Were't twenty of the greatest tributaries
That do acknowledge Caesar, should I find them
So saucy with the hand of she here,—what's her name,
Since she was Cleopatra? Whip him, fellows,
Till, like a boy, you see him cringe his face,
And whine aloud for mercy. Take him hence.

THYREUS: Mark Antony,—

ANTONY: Tug him away. Being whipp'd,
Bring him again; this Jack of Caesar's shall
Bear us an errand to him. *Exit* SERVANT *with* THYREUS.
You were half blasted ere I knew you; ha!
Have I my pillow left unpress'd in Rome,
Forborne the getting of a lawful race,
And by a gem of women, to be abus'd
By one that looks on feeders?[12]

CLEOPATRA: Good my lord,—

ANTONY: You have been a boggler[13] ever:
And when we in our viciousness grow hard—
O misery on't!—the wise gods seel our eyes;
In our own filth drop our clear judgements; make us
Adore our errors; laugh at 's, while we strut
To our confusion.

CLEOPATRA: O, is't come to this?

ANTONY: I found you as a morsel cold upon
Dead Caesar's trencher; nay, you were a fragment
Of Cneius Pompey's; besides what hotter hours,
Unregister'd in vulgar fame, you have
Luxuriously pick'd out; for, I am sure,
Though you can guess what temperance should be,
You know not what it is.

CLEOPATRA: Wherefore is this?

---

[12] [*feeders:* servants.]

[13] [*boggler:* shifty person.]

ANTONY: To let a fellow that will take rewards
     And say, "God quit you!" be familiar with
     My playfellow, your hand; this kingly seal
     And plighter of high hearts! O, that I were
     Upon the hill of Basan, to outroar
     The horned herd! For I have savage cause;
     And to proclaim it civilly, were like
     A halter'd neck which does the hangman thank
     For being yare about him.

Re-enter SERVANT *with* THYREUS.

                         Is he whipp'd?
SERVANT: Soundly, my lord.
ANTONY: Cried he? and begg'd a pardon?
SERVANT: He did ask favour.
ANTONY: If that thy father live, let him repent
     Thou wast not made his daughter; and be thou sorry
     To follow Caesar in his triumph, since
     Thou hast been whipp'd for following him. Henceforth
     The white hand of a lady fever thee,
     Shake thou to look on't. Get thee back to Caesar,
     Tell him thy entertainment. Look thou say
     He makes me angry with him; for he seems
     Proud and disdainful, harping on what I am,
     Not what he knew I was. He makes me angry;
     And at this time most easy 'tis to do't,
     When my good stars, that were my former guides,
     Have empty left their orbs, and shot their fires
     Into the abysm of hell. If he mislike
     My speech and what is done, tell him he has
     Hipparchus, my enfranched bondman, whom
     He may at pleasure whip, or hang, or torture,
     As he shall like, to quit me. Urge it thou.
     Hence with thy stripes, begone!   *Exit* THYREUS.

CLEOPATRA: Have you done yet?

ANTONY: .   Alack, our terrene moon
  Is now eclips'd; and it protends alone
  The fall of Antony!

CLEOPATRA: I must stay his time.

ANTONY: To flatter Caesar, would you mingle eyes
  With one that ties his points?[14]

CLEOPATRA: Not know me yet?

ANTONY: Cold-hearted toward me?

CLEOPATRA: Ah, dear, if I be so,
  From my cold heart let heaven engender hail
  And poison it in the source, and the first stone
  Drop in my neck; as it determines, so
  Dissolve my life! The next Caesarion smite!
  Till by degrees the memory of my womb,
  Together with my brave Egyptians all,
  By the discandying[15] of this pelleted storm,
  Lie graveless, till the flies and gnats of Nile
  Have buried them for prey!

ANTONY: I am satisfied.
  Caesar sits down in Alexandria; where
  I will oppose his fate. Our force by land
  Hath nobly held; our sever'd navy too
  Have knit again, and fleet, threat'ning most sea-like.
  Where hast thou been, my heart? Dost thou hear, lady?
  If from the field I shall return once more
  To kiss these lips, I will appear in blood;
  I and my sword will earn our chronicle.
  There's hope in't yet.

CLEOPATRA: That's my brave lord!

ANTONY: I will be treble-sinewed, hearted, breath'd,
  And fight maliciously; for when mine hours

---

[14] [*one that ties his points:* his valet.]

[15] [*discandying:* melting, dissolving.]

Were nice and lucky, men did ransom lives
Of me for jests; but now I'll set my teeth,
And send to darkness all that stop me. Come,
Let's have one other gaudy night. Call to me
All my sad captains; fill our bowls once more;
Let's mock the midnight bell.
CLEOPATRA: It is my birthday.
    I had thought to have held it poor; but, since my lord
    Is Antony again, I will be Cleopatra.
ANTONY: We will yet do well.
CLEOPATRA: Call all his noble captains to my lord.
ANTONY: Do so, we'll speak to them; and to-night I'll force
    The wine peep through their scars. Come on, my queen;
    There's sap in't yet. The next time I do fight,
    I'll make Death love me; for I will contend
    Even with his pestilent scythe.

                                    Exeunt [*all but* ENOBARBUS].

ENOBARBUS: Now he'll outstare the lightning. To be furious,
    Is to be frighted out of fear; and in that mood
    The dove will peck the estridge; and I see still,
    A diminution in our captain's brain
    Restores his heart. When valour preys on reason,
    It eats the sword it fights with. I will seek
    Some way to leave him.   *Exit.*

ACT IV

SCENE ONE—*Before Alexandria.* CAESAR'*s camp.*

Enter CAESAR, AGRIPPA, *and* MAECENAS, *with his Army;* CAESAR
reading a letter.

CAESAR: He calls me boy; and chides as he had power
    To beat me out of Egypt. My messenger
    He hath whipp'd with rods; dares me to personal combat,
    Caesar to Antony. Let the old ruffian know
    I have many other ways to die; meantime
    Laugh at his challenge.
MAECENAS: Caesar must think,
    When one so great begins to rage, he's hunted
    Even to falling. Give him no breath, but now
    Make boot of his distraction. Never anger
    Made good guard for itself.
CAESAR: Let our best heads
    Know that to-morrow the last of many battles
    We mean to fight. Within our files there are,
    Of those that serv'd Mark Antony but late,
    Enough to fetch him in. See it done,
    And feast the army; we have store to do't,
    And they have earn'd the waste. Poor Antony!   *Exeunt.*

SCENE TWO—*Alexandria.* CLEOPATRA'*s palace.*

Enter ANTONY, CLEOPATRA, ENOBARBUS, CHARMIAN, IRAS,
ALEXAS, *with others.*

ANTONY: He will not fight with me, Domitius.
ENOBARBUS: No?
ANTONY: Why should he not?
ENOBARBUS: He thinks, being twenty times of better fortune,
    He is twenty men to one.
ANTONY: To-morrow, soldier,

By sea and land I'll fight; or I will live,
Or bathe my dying honour in the blood
Shall make it live again. Woo't thou fight well?
ENOBARBUS: I'll strike, and cry, "Take all!"
ANTONY: Well said; come on.
Call forth my household servants; let's to-night
Be bounteous at our meal.

Enter three or four Servitors.

                                    Give me thy hand,
Thou hast been rightly honest;—so hast thou;—
Thou,—and thou,—and thou. You have serv'd me well,
And kings have been your fellows.
CLEOPATRA [*aside to* ENOBARBUS]:   What means this?
ENOBARBUS [*aside to* CLEOPATRA]:   'Tis one of those odd tricks
    which sorrow shoots
Out of the mind.
ANTONY: And thou art honest too.
I wish I could be made so many men,
And all of you clapp'd up together in
An Antony, that I might do you service
So good as you have done.
ALL: The gods forbid!
ANTONY: Well, my good fellows, wait on me to-night.
Scant not my cups; and make as much of me
As when mine empire was your fellow too,
And suffer'd my command.
CLEOPATRA [*aside to* ENOBARBUS]: What does he mean?
ENOBARBUS [*aside to* CLEOPATRA]: To make his followers weep.
ANTONY: Tend me to-night;
May be it is the period of your duty:
Haply you shall not see me more; or if,
A mangled shadow. Perchance to-morrow
You'll serve another master. I look on you
As one that takes his leave. Mine honest friends,
I turn you not away; but, like a master

Married to your good service, stay till death.
Tend me to-night two hours, I ask no more,
And the gods yield you for't!
ENOBARBUS: What mean you, sir,
To give them this discomfort? Look, they weep;
And I, an ass, am onion-ey'd. For shame,
Transform us not to women.
ANTONY: Ho, ho, ho!
Now the witch take me, if I meant it thus!
Grace grow where those drops fall! My hearty friends,
You take me in too dolorous a sense;
For I spake to you for your comfort, did desire you
To burn this night with torches. Know, my hearts,
I hope well of to-morrow; and will lead you
Where rather I'll expect victorious life
Than death and honour. Let's to supper, come,
And drown consideration.   *Exeunt.*

SCENE THREE—*The same. Before the palace.*

Enter [*two*] SOLDIERS [*to their guard*].

FIRST SOLDIER: Brother, good-night; to-morrow is the day.
SECOND SOLDIER: It will determine one way; fare you well.
Heard you of nothing strange about the streets?
FIRST SOLDIER: Nothing. What news?
SECOND SOLDIER: Belike 'tis but a rumour. Good-night to you.
FIRST SOLDIER: Well, sir, good-night.
                    They meet other SOLDIERS.
SECOND SOLDIER: Soldiers, have careful watch.
THIRD SOLDIER: And you. Good-night, good-night.
          They place themselves in every corner of the stage.

FOURTH SOLDIER: Here we. And if to-morrow
Our navy thrive, I have an absolute hope
Our landmen will stand up.

THIRD SOLDIER: 'Tis a brave army,
  And full of purpose.
                        Music of the hautboys as under the stage.

SECOND SOLDIER: Peace! what noise?
FIRST SOLDIER: List, list!
SECOND SOLDIER: Hark!
FIRST SOLDIER: Music i' the air!
THIRD SOLDIER: Under the earth.
FOURTH SOLDIER: It signs well, does it not?
THIRD SOLDIER: No.
FIRST SOLDIER: Peace, I say!
  What should this mean?
SECOND SOLDIER: 'Tis the god Hercules, whom Antony loved,
  Now leaves him.
FIRST SOLDIER: Walk; let's see if other watchmen
  Do hear what we do.   [*They advance to another post.*]
SECOND SOLDIER: How now, masters!   *Speak together.*
ALL: How now!
  How now! do you hear this?
FIRST SOLDIER: Ay; is't not strange?
THIRD SOLDIER: Do you hear, masters? Do you hear?
FIRST SOLDIER: Follow the noise so far as we have quarter;
  Let's see how it will give off.
ALL: Content. 'Tis strange.   *Exeunt.*

SCENE FOUR — *The same. A room in the palace.*

Enter ANTONY *and* CLEOPATRA, [CHARMIAN,] *and others*
[*attending*].

ANTONY: Eros! mine amour, Eros!
CLEOPATRA: Sleep a little.
ANTONY: No, my chuck. Eros, come; mine armour, Eros!

Enter EROS [*with armour*].

Come, good fellow, put mine iron on.

If Fortune be not ours to-day, it is
Because we brave her. Come.
CLEOPATRA: Nay, I'll help too.
  What's this for?
[ANTONY]:   Ah, let be, let be! thou art
  The armourer of my heart. False, false; this, this.
CLEOPATRA: Sooth, la. I'll help. Thus it must be.
ANTONY: Well, well;
  We shall thrive now. Seest thou, my good fellow?
  Go put on thy defences.
EROS: Briefly, sir.
CLEOPATRA: Is not this buckled well?
ANTONY: Rarely, rarely:
  He that unbuckles this, till we do please
  To daff 't for our repose, shall hear a storm.
  Thou fumblest, Eros; and my queen's a squire
  More tight at this than thou. Dispatch. O love,
  That thou couldst see my wars to-day, and knew'st
  The royal occupation! Thou shouldst see
  A workman in't.

Enter an armed SOLDIER.

                      Good-morrow to thee; welcome.
  Thou look'st like him that knows a warlike charge.
  To business that we love we rise betime
  And go to't with delight.
SOLDIER: A thousand, sir,
  Early though't be, have on their riveted trim,
  And at the port expect you.   *Shout. Trumpets flourish.*

Enter CAPTAINS *and* SOLDIERS.

CAPTAIN: The morn is fair. Good-morrow, general.
ALL: Good-morrow, general.
ANTONY: 'Tis well blown, lads.
  This morning, like the spirit of a youth
  That means to be of note, begins betimes.

So, so; come, give me that. This way; well said.
Fare thee well, dame, whate'er becomes of me.
This is a soldier's kiss; rebukeable [*Kisses her.*]
And worthy shameful check it were, to stand
On more mechanic compliment. I'll leave thee
Now, like a man of steel. You that will fight,
Follow me close; I'll bring you to't. Adieu.
        Exeunt [ANTONY, EROS, CAPTAINS, *and* SOLDIERS].

CHARMIAN: Please you, retire to your chamber.
CLEOPATRA: Lead me.
    He goes forth gallantly. That he and Caesar might
    Determine this great war in single fight!
    Then, Antony,—but now—Well, on.   *Exeunt.*

SCENE FIVE—*Alexandria.* ANTONY'*s camp.*

Trumpets sound. Enter ANTONY *and* EROS. [*A* SOLDIER *meets them.*]

[SOLDIER]: The gods make this a happy day to Antony!
ANTONY: Would thou and those thy scars had once prevail'd
    To make me fight at land!
[SOLDIER]:   Hadst thou done so,
    The kings that have revolted, and the soldier
    That has this morning left thee, would have still
    Followed thy heels.
ANTONY: Who's gone this morning?
[SOLDIER]:   Who!
    One ever near thee. Call for Enobarbus,
    He shall not hear thee; or from Caesar's camp
    Say, "I am none of thine."
ANTONY: What sayest thou?
SOLDIER: Sir,
    He is with Caesar.
EROS: Sir, his chests and treasure

He has not with him.

ANTONY: Is he gone?

SOLDIER: Most certain.

ANTONY: Go, Eros, send his treasure after; do it;
Detain no jot, I charge thee. Write to him—
I will subscribe—gentle adieus and greetings;
Say that I wish he never find more cause
To change a master. O, my fortunes have
Corrupted honest men! Dispatch.—Enobarbus! *Exeunt.*

SCENE SIX—*Alexandria.* CAESAR's *camp.*

Flourish. Enter CAESAR, AGRIPPA, *with* ENOBARBUS, *and*
DOLABELLA.

CAESAR: Go forth, Agrippa, and begin the fight.
Our will is Antony be took alive;
Make it so known.

AGRIPPA: Caesar, I shall. *Exit.*

CAESAR: The time of universal peace is near.
Prove this a prosperous day, the three-nook'd world
Shall bear the olive freely.

Enter a MESSENGER.

MESSENGER: Antony
Is come into the field.

CAESAR: Go charge Agrippa
Plant those that have revolted in the van,
That Antony may seem to spend his fury
Upon himself. *Exeunt [all but* ENOBARBUS].

ENOBARBUS: Alexas did revolt; and went to Jewry on
Affairs of Antony; there did persuade
Great Herod to incline himself to Caesar,
And leave his master Antony: for this pains
Caesar hath hang'd him. Canidius and the rest
That fell away have entertainment, but

No honourable trust. I have done ill;
Of which I do accuse myself so sorely
That I will joy no more.

Enter a SOLDIER *of* CAESAR's.

SOLDIER: Enobarbus, Antony
  Hath after thee sent all thy treasure, with
  His bounty overplus. The messenger
  Came on my guard; and at thy tent is now
  Unloading of his mules.
ENOBARBUS: I give it you.
SOLDIER: Mock not, Enobarbus;
  I tell you true. Best you saf'd the bringer
  Out of the host; I must attend mine office,
  Or would have done't myself. Your emperor
  Continues still a Jove.   *Exit.*
ENOBARBUS: I am alone the villain of the earth,
  And feel I am so most. O Antony,
  Thou mine of bounty, how wouldst thou have paid
  My better service, when my turpitude
  Thou dost so crown with gold! This blows my heart.
  If swift thought break it not, a swifter mean
  Shall outstrike thought; but thought will do't, I feel.
  I fight against thee! No! I will go seek
  Some ditch wherein to die; the foul'st best fits
  My latter part of life.   *Exit.*

SCENE SEVEN — *Field of battle between the camps.*

Alarum. Drums and trumpets. Enter AGRIPPA [*and others*].

AGRIPPA: Retire, we have engag'd ourselves too far.
  Caesar himself has work, and our oppression
  Exceeds what we expected.   *Exeunt.*

Alarums. Enter ANTONY, *and* SCARUS *wounded.*

SCARUS: O my brave emperor, this is fought indeed!
   Had we done so at first, we had droven them home
   With clouts about their heads.
ANTONY: Thou bleed'st apace.
SCARUS: I had a wound here that was like a T,
   But now 'tis made an H.
ANTONY: They do retire.
SCARUS: We'll beat 'em into bench-holes. I have yet
   Room for six scotches more.

Enter EROS.

EROS: They are beaten, sir; and our advantage serves
   For a fair victory.
SCARUS: Let us score their backs,
   And snatch 'em up, as we take hares, behind.
   'Tis sport to maul a runner.
ANTONY: I will reward thee
   Once for thy sprightly comfort, and tenfold
   For thy good valour. Come thee on.
SCARUS: I'll halt after.   *Exeunt.*

SCENE EIGHT—*Under the walls of Alexandria.*

Alarum. Enter ANTONY, *in a march;* SCARUS, *with others.*

ANTONY: We have beat him to his camp. Run one before,
   And let the Queen know of our gests.[16] To-morrow,
   Before the sun shall see 's, we'll spill the blood
   That has to-day escap'd. I thank you all;
   For doughty-handed are you, and have fought
   Not as you serv'd the cause, but as't had been
   Each man's like mine; you have shown all Hectors.
   Enter the city, clip your wives, your friends,
   Tell them your feats; whilst they with joyful tears

---

[16] [*gests:* exploits.]

Wash the congealment from your wounds, and kiss
The honour'd gashes whole.

Enter CLEOPATRA [*attended*].

[*To* SCARUS.]   Give me thy hand;
To this great fairy I'll commend thy acts,
Make her thanks bless thee. [*To* CLEOPATRA.] O thou day
    o' the world,
Chain mine arm'd neck; leap thou, attire and all,
Through proof of harness to my heart, and there
Ride on the pants triumphing!
CLEOPATRA: Lord of lords!
O infinite virtue, com'st thou smiling from
The world's great snare uncaught?
ANTONY: My nightingale,
We have beat them to their beds. What, girl! though grey
Do something mingle with our younger brown, yet ha' we
A brain that nourishes our nerves, and can
Get goal for goal of youth. Behold this man;
Commend unto his lips thy favouring hand.
Kiss it, my warrior; he hath fought to-day
As if a god, in hate of mankind, had
Destroyed in such a shape.
CLEOPATRA: I'll give thee, friend,
An armour all of gold; it was a king's.
ANTONY: He has deserv'd it, were it carbuncled
Like holy Phoebus' car. Give me thy hand.
Through Alexandria make a jolly march;
Bear our hack'd targets like the men that owe them.
Had our great palace the capacity
To camp this host, we all would sup together
And drink carouses to the next day's fate,
Which promises royal peril. Trumpeters,
With brazen din blast you the city's ear,
Make mingle with our rattling tabourines,

That heaven and earth may strike their sounds together,
Applauding our approach.   *Exeunt.*

SCENE NINE—CAESAR'*s camp.*

Enter a SENTRY, *and his Company.* ENOBARBUS *follows.*

SENTRY: If we be not reliev'd within this hour,
    We must return to the court of guard. The night
    Is shiny; and they say we shall embattle
    By the second hour i' the morn.
FIRST SOLDIER: This last day was
    A shrewd one to's.
ENOBARBUS: O, bear me witness, night,—
SECOND SOLDIER: What man is this?
FIRST SOLDIER: Stand close, and list him.
ENOBARBUS: Be witness to me, O thou blessed moon,
    When men revolted shall upon record
    Bear hateful memory, poor Enobarbus did
    Before thy face repent!
SENTRY: Enobarbus!
SECOND SOLDIER: Peace!
    Hark further.
ENOBARBUS: O sovereign mistress of true melancholy,
    The poisonous damp of night disponge upon me,
    That life, a very rebel to my will,
    May hang no longer on me. Throw my heart
    Against the flint and hardness of my fault;
    Which, being dried with grief, will break to powder,
    And finish all foul thoughts. O Antony,
    Nobler than my revolt is infamous,
    Forgive me in thine own particular;
    But let the world rank me in register
    A master-leaver and a fugitive.
    O Antony! O Antony!   [*Dies.*]
FIRST SOLDIER: Let's speak

To him.

SENTRY: Let's hear him, for the things he speaks
  May concern Caesar.

SECOND SOLDIER: Let's do so. But he sleeps.

SENTRY: Swoons rather; for so bad a prayer as his
  Was never yet for sleep.

FIRST SOLDIER: Go we to him.

SECOND SOLDIER: Awake, sir, awake; speak to us.

FIRST SOLDIER: Hear   you,
  sir?

SENTRY: The hand of death hath raught him. [*Drums afar off.*]
    Hark! the drums
  Demurely wake the sleepers. Let us bear him
  To the court of guard; he is of note. Our hour
  Is fully out.

SECOND SOLDIER: Come on, then;
  He may recover yet.   *Exeunt* [*with the body*].

SCENE TEN — *Between the two camps.*

Enter ANTONY *and* SCARUS, *with their Army.*

ANTONY: Their preparation is to-day by sea;
  We please them not by land.

SCARUS: For both, my lord.

ANTONY: I would they'd fight i' the fire or i' the air;
  We'd fight there too. But this it is: our foot
  Upon the hills adjoining to the city
  Shall stay with us — order for sea is given;
  They have put forth the haven,
  Where their appointment we may best discover
  And look on their endeavour.   *Exeunt.*

SCENE ELEVEN — *Another part of the same.*

Enter CAESAR, *and his Army.*

CAESAR: But being charg'd, we will be still by land,
   Which, as I take't, we shall; for his best force
   Is forth to man his galleys. To the vales,
   And hold our best advantage.   *Exeunt.*

SCENE TWELVE — *Another part of the same.*

Enter ANTONY *and* SCARUS.

ANTONY: Yet they are not join'd. Where yond pine does stand,
   I .shall discover all; I'll bring thee word
   Straight, how 'tis like to go.   *Exit.*
SCARUS: Swallows have built
   In Cleopatra's sails their nests. The augurers
   Say they know not, they cannot tell; look grimly,
   And dare not speak their knowledge. Antony
   Is valiant, and dejected; and, by starts,
   His fretted fortunes give him hope and fear,
   Of what he has and has not.
                    Alarum afar off, as at a sea-fight.

Re-enter ANTONY.

ANTONY: All is lost!
   This foul Egyptian hath betrayed me.
   My fleet hath yielded to the foe, and yonder
   They cast their caps up and carouse together
   Like friends long lost. Triple-turn'd whore! 'tis thou
   Hast sold me to this novice; and my heart
   Makes only wars on thee. Bid them all fly;
   For when I am reveng'd upon my charm,
   I have done all. Bid them all fly; begone.   [*Exit* SCARUS.]
   O sun, thy uprise shall I see no more:
   Fortune and Antony part here; even here

Do we shake hands. All come to this? The hearts
That spaniel'd me at heels, to whom I gave
Their wishes, do discandy, melt their sweets
On blossoming Caesar; and this pine is bark'd,
That overtopp'd them all. Betray'd I am.
O this false soul of Egypt! this grave charm,—
Whose eye beck'd forth my wars, and call'd them home;
Whose bosom was my crownet, my chief end,—
Like a right gipsy, hath, at fast and loose,
Beguil'd me to the very heart of loss.
What, Eros, Eros!

Enter CLEOPATRA.

      Ah, thou spell! Avaunt!
CLEOPATRA: Why is my lord enrag'd against his love?
ANTONY: Vanish, or I shall give thee thy deserving,
 And blemish Caesar's triumph. Let him take thee,
 And hoist thee up to the shouting plebeians!
 Follow his chariot, like the greatest spot
 Of all thy sex; most monster-like, be shown
 For poor'st diminutives, for dolts; and let
 Patient Octavia plough thy visage up
 With her prepared nails.   *Exit* CLEOPATRA.
      'Tis well thou'rt gone,
 If it be well to live; but better 'twere
 Thou fell'st into my fury, for one death
 Might have prevented many. Eros, ho!
 The shirt of Nessus is upon me. Teach me,
 Alcides, thou mine ancestor, thy rage.
 Let me lodge Lichas on the horns o' the moon;
 And with those hands, that grasp'd the heaviest club,
 Subdue my worthiest self. The witch shall die.
 To the young Roman boy she hath sold me, and I fall
 Under this plot. She dies for't. Eros, ho! *Exit.*

SCENE THIRTEEN—*Alexandria.* CLEOPATRA'*s palace.*

Enter CLEOPATRA, CHARMIAN, IRAS, *and* MARDIAN.

CLEOPATRA: Help me, my women! O, he is more mad
   Than Telamon for his shield; the boar of Thessaly
   Was never so emboss'd.[17]
CHARMIAN: To the monument!
   There lock yourself, and send him word you are dead.
   The soul and body rive not more in parting
   Than greatness going off.
CLEOPATRA: To the monument!
   Mardian, go tell him I have slain myself;
   Say, that the last I spoke was "Antony,"
   And word it, prithee, piteously. Hence, Mardian,
   And bring me how he takes my death. To the monument!
                                  Exeunt.

SCENE FOURTEEN—*The same. Another room.*

Enter ANTONY *and* EROS.

ANTONY: Eros, thou yet behold'st me?
EROS: Ay, noble lord.
ANTONY: Sometime we see a cloud that's dragonish;
   A vapour sometime like a bear or lion,
   A tower'd citadel, a pendent rock,
   A forked mountain, or blue promontory
   With trees upon't, that nod unto the world,
   And mock our eyes with air. Thou hast seen these signs;
   They are black vesper's pageants.
EROS: Ay, my lord.
ANTONY: That which is now a horse, even with a thought

---

[17] [*emboss'd:* enraged.]

The rack dislimns,[18] and makes it indistinct,
As water is in water.

EROS: It does, my lord.

ANTONY: My good knave Eros, now thy captain is
Even such a body. Here I am Antony;
Yet cannot hold this visible shape, my knave.
I made these walls for Egypt; and the Queen, —
Whose heart I thought I had, for she had mine,
Which whilst it was mine had annex'd unto't
A million more, now lost, — she, Eros, has
Pack'd cards with Caesar, and false-play'd my glory
Unto an enemy's triumph.
Nay, weep not, gentle Eros; there is left us
Ourselves to end ourselves.

Enter MARDIAN.

                              O, thy vile lady!
She has robb'd me of my sword.

MARDIAN: No, Antony;
My mistress lov'd thee, and her fortunes mingled
With thine entirely.

ANTONY: Hence, saucy eunuch; peace!
She hath betray'd me and shall die the death.

MARDIAN: Death of one person can be paid but once,
And that she has discharg'd. What thou wouldst do
Is done unto thy hand; the last she spake
Was "Antony! most noble Antony!"
Then in the midst a tearing groan did break
The name of Antony; it was divided
Between her heart and lips. She render'd life,
Thy name so buried in her.

ANTONY: Dead, then?

MARDIAN: Dead.

---

[18] [*rack:* cloud; *dislimns:* unshapes.]

ANTONY: Unarm, Eros; the long day's task is done,
And we must sleep. [*To* MARDIAN.] That thou depart'st hence safe,
Does pay thy labour richly; go.   *Exit* MARDIAN.
                              Off, pluck off!
The seven-fold shield of Ajax cannot keep
The battery from my heart. O, cleave, my sides!
Heart, once be stronger than thy continent,
Crack thy frail case! Apace, Eros, apace.
No more a soldier. Bruised pieces, go;
You have been nobly borne.—From me a while.
                                        Exit EROS.

I will o'ertake thee, Cleopatra, and
Weep for my pardon. So it must be, for now
All length is torture; since the torch is out,
Lie down, and stray no farther. Now all labour
Mars what it does; yea, very force entangles
Itself with strength. Seal then, and all is done.
Eros!—I come, my queen!—Eros!—Stay for me!
Where souls do couch on flowers, we'll hand in hand,
And with our sprightly port make the ghosts gaze.
Dido and her Aeneas shall want troops,
And all the haunt be ours. Come, Eros, Eros!

Re-enter EROS.

EROS: What would my lord?
ANTONY: Since Cleopatra died,
I have liv'd in such dishonour, that the gods
Detest my baseness. I, that with my sword
Quarter'd the world, and o'er green Neptune's back
With ships made cities, condemn myself to lack
The courage of a woman; less noble mind
Than she which by her death our Caesar tells,
"I am conqueror of myself." Thou art sworn, Eros,
That, when the exigent should come, which now
Is come indeed, when I should see behind me

The inevitable prosecution of
Disgrace and horror, that, on my command,
Thou then wouldst kill me. Do't; the time is come.
Thou strik'st not me, 'tis Caesar thou defeat'st.
Put colour in thy cheek.

EROS: The gods withhold me!
Shall I do that which all the Parthian darts,
Though enemy, lost aim, and could not?

ANTONY: Eros,
Wouldst thou be window'd in great Rome and see
Thy master thus with pleach'd arms, bending down
His corrigible neck, his face subdu'd
To penetrative shame, whilst the wheel'd seat
Of fortunate Caesar, drawn before him, branded
His baseness that ensued?

EROS: I would not see't.

ANTONY: Come, then; for with a wound I must be cur'd.
Draw that thy honest sword, which thou hast worn
Most useful for thy country.

EROS: O, sir, pardon me!

ANTONY: When I did make thee free, swor'st thou not then
To do this when I bade thee? Do it at once;
Or thy precedent services are all
But accidents unpurpos'd. Draw, and come.

EROS: Turn from me, then, that noble countenance,
Wherein the worship of the whole world lies.

ANTONY: Lo thee! [*Turning from him.*]

EROS: My sword is drawn.

ANTONY: Then let it do at once
The thing why thou hast drawn it.

EROS: My dear master,
My captain, and my emperor, let me say,
Before I strike this bloody stroke, farewell.

ANTONY: 'Tis said, man; and farewell.

EROS: Farewell, great chief. Shall I strike now?

ANTONY: Now, Eros.

EROS: Why, there then. [*Kills himself.*] Thus I do escape the
    sorrow
Of Antony's death.

ANTONY: Thrice-nobler than myself!
    Thou teachest me, O valiant Eros, what
    I should, and thou couldst not. My queen and Eros
    Have by their brave instruction got upon me
    A nobleness in record; but I will be
    A bridegroom in my death, and run into't
    As to a lover's bed. Come, then; and, Eros,
    Thy master dies thy scholar: to do thus
                       [*Falling on his sword.*]
    I learn'd of thee. How! not dead? not dead?
    The guard, ho! O, dispatch me!

Enter [DERCETAS *and*] GUARD.

FIRST GUARD: What's the noise?

ANTONY: I have done my work ill, friends. O, make an end
    Of what I have begun.

SECOND GUARD: The star is fallen.

FIRST GUARD: And time is at his period.

ALL: Alas, and woe!

ANTONY: Let him that loves me strike me dead.

FIRST GUARD: Not I.

SECOND GUARD: Nor I.

THIRD GUARD: Nor any one.   *Exeunt* GUARD.

DERCETAS: Thy death and fortunes bid thy followers fly.
    This sword but shown to Caesar, with this tidings,
    Shall enter me with him.

Enter DIOMEDES.

DIOMEDES: Where's Antony?

DERCETAS: There, Diomed, there.

DIOMEDES: Lives he?
  Wilt thou not answer, man?   [*Exit* DERCETAS.]
ANTONY: Art thou there, Diomed? Draw thy sword, and give
    me
  Sufficing strokes for death.
DIOMEDES: Most absolute lord,
  My mistress Cleopatra sent me to thee.
ANTONY: When did she send thee?
DIOMEDES: Now, my lord.
ANTONY: Where is she?
DIOMEDES: Lock'd in her monument. She had a prophesying
    fear
  Of what hath come to pass; for when she saw—
  Which never shall be found—you did suspect
  She had dispos'd with Caesar, and that your rage
  Would not be purg'd, she sent you word she was dead;
  But, fearing since how it might work, hath sent
  Me to proclaim the truth; and I am come,
  I dread, too late.
ANTONY: Too late, good Diomed. Call my guard, I prithee.
DIOMEDES: What, ho, the Emperor's guard! The guard, what,
    ho!
  Come, your lord calls!

Enter four or five of the Guard *of* ANTONY.

ANTONY: Bear me, good friends, where Cleopatra bides;
  'Tis the last service that I shall command you.
FIRST GUARD: Woe, woe are we, sir, you may not live to wear
  All your true followers out.
ALL: Most heavy day!
ANTONY: Nay, good my fellows, do not please sharp fate
  To grave it with your sorrows; bid that welcome
  Which comes to punish us, and we punish it
  Seeming to bear it lightly. Take me up.
  I have led you oft; carry me now, good friends,
  And have my thanks for all.   *Exeunt, bearing* ANTONY.

SCENE FIFTEEN — *The same. A monument.*

Enter CLEOPATRA, *and her maids aloft, with* CHARMIAN *and* IRAS.

CLEOPATRA: O Charmian, I will never go from hence.
CHARMIAN: Be comforted, dear madam.
CLEOPATRA: No, I will not.
All strange and terrible events are welcome,
But comforts we despise; our size of sorrow,
Proportion'd to our cause, must be as great
As that which makes it.

Enter [below] DIOMEDES.

                              How now! is he dead?
DIOMEDES: His death's upon him, but not dead.
Look out o' the other side your monument;
His guard have brought him thither.

Enter [below] ANTONY, *borne by the* Guard.

CLEOPATRA: O sun,
Burn the great sphere thou mov'st in! Darkling stand
The varying shore o' the world. O Antony,
Antony, Antony! Help, Charmian, help, Iras, help;
Help, friends below; let's draw him hither.
ANTONY: Peace!
Not Caesar's valour hath o'erthrown Antony,
But Antony's hath triumph'd on itself.
CLEOPATRA: So it should be, that none but Antony
Should conquer Antony; but woe 'tis so!
ANTONY: I am dying, Egypt, dying; only
I here importune death a while, until
Of many thousand kisses the poor last
I lay upon thy lips.
CLEOPATRA: I dare not, dear, —
Dear my lord, pardon, — I dare not,
Lest I be taken. Not the imperious show

Of the full-fortun'd Caesar ever shall
Be brooch'd with me; if knife, drugs, serpents, have
Edge, sting, or operation, I am safe.
Your wife Octavia, with her modest eyes
And still conclusion, shall acquire no honour
Demuring upon me. But come, come, Antony,—
Help me, my women,—we must draw thee up.
Assist, good friends.

ANTONY: O, quick, or I am gone.

CLEOPATRA: Here's sport indeed! How heavy weighs my lord!
Our strength is all gone into heaviness,
That makes the weight. Had I great Juno's power,
The strong-wing'd Mercury should fetch thee up
And set thee by Jove's side. Yet come a little,—
Wishers were ever fools,—O, come, come, come;

They heave ANTONY *aloft to* CLEOPATRA.

And welcome, welcome! Die where thou hast liv'd;
Quicken with kissing. Had my lips that power,
Thus would I wear them out.

ALL: A heavy sight!

ANTONY: I am dying, Egypt, dying.
Give me some wine, and let me speak a little.

CLEOPATRA: No, let me speak; and let me rail so high,
That the false housewife Fortune break her wheel,
Provok'd by my offence.

ANTONY: One word, sweet queen:
Of Caesar seek your honour, with your safety. O!

CLEOPATRA: They do not go together.

ANTONY: Gentle, hear me:
None about Caesar trust but Proculeius.

CLEOPATRA: My resolution and my hands I'll trust;
None about Caesar.

ANTONY: The miserable change now at my end
Lament nor sorrow at; but please your thoughts
In feeding them with those my former fortunes
Wherein I liv'd, the greatest prince o' the world,

The noblest; and do now not basely die,
Not cowardly put off my helmet to
My countryman,—a Roman by a Roman
Valiantly vanquish'd. Now my spirit is going;
I can no more.

CLEOPATRA: Noblest of men, woo't die?
Hast thou no care of me? Shall I abide
In this dull world, which in thy absence is
No better than a sty? O, see, my women,   [*Antony dies.*]
The crown o' the earth doth melt. My lord!
O, wither'd is the garland of the war,
The soldier's pole is fall'n! Young boys and girls
Are level now with men; the odds is gone,
And there is nothing left remarkable
Beneath the visiting moon.   [*Faints.*]

CHARMIAN: O, quietness, lady!

IRAS: She is dead too, our sovereign.

CHARMIAN: Lady!

IRAS: Madam!

CHARMIAN: O madam, madam, madam!

IRAS: Royal Egypt,
Empress!

CHARMIAN: Peace, peace, Iras!

CLEOPATRA: No more but e'en a woman, and commanded
By such poor passion as the maid that milks
And does the meanest chares. It were for me
To throw my sceptre at the injurious gods;
To tell them that this world did equal theirs
Till they had stolen our jewel. All's but nought;
Patience is sottish, and impatience does
Become a dog that's mad: then is it sin
To rush into the secret house of death,
Ere death dare come to us? How do you, women?
What, what! good cheer! Why, how now, Charmian!
My noble girls! Ah, women, women, look,
Our lamp is spent, it's out! Good sirs, take heart.

We'll bury him; and then, what's brave, what's noble,
Let's do it after the high Roman fashion,
And make Death proud to take us. Come, away;
This case of that huge spirit now is cold.
Ah, women, women! come; we have no friend
But resolution and the briefest end.

           Exeunt; [*those above*] *bearing off* ANTONY's *body.*

ACT V·

SCENE ONE—*Alexandria.* CAESAR's *camp.*

Enter CAESAR, AGRIPPA, DOLABELLA, [MAECENAS, GALLUS, PROCULEIUS, *and others,*] *his council of war.*

CAESAR: Go to him, Dolabella, bid him yield;
    Being so frustrate, tell him he mocks
    The pauses that he makes.

DOLABELLA: Caesar, I shall.   [*Exit.*]

Enter DERCETAS *with the sword of* ANTONY.

CAESAR: Wherefore is that? and what art thou that dar'st
    Appear thus to us?

DERCETAS: I am call'd Dercetas;
    Mark Antony I serv'd, who best was worthy
    Best to be serv'd. Whilst he stood up and spoke,
    He was my master; and I wore my life
    To spend upon his haters. If thou please
    To take me to thee, as I was to him
    I'll be to Caesar; if thou pleasest not,
    I yield thee up my life.

CAESAR: What is't thou say'st?

DERCETAS: I say, O Caesar, Antony is dead.

CAESAR: The breaking of so great a thing should make
A greater crack. The round world
Should have shook lions into civil streets,
And citizens to their dens. The death of Antony
Is not a single doom; in the name lay
A moiety of the world.

DERCETAS: He is dead, Caesar;
Not by a public minister of justice,
Nor by a hired knife; but that self hand
Which writ his honour in the acts it did
Hath, with the courage which the heart did lend it,
Splitted the heart. This is his sword;
I robb'd his wound of it; behold it stain'd
With his most noble blood.

CAESAR: Look you sad, friends?
The gods rebuke me, but it is tidings
To wash the eyes of kings.

AGRIPPA: And strange it is
That nature must compel us to lament
Our most persisted deeds.

MAECENAS: His taints and honours
Wag'd equal with him.

AGRIPPA: A rarer spirit never
Did steer humanity; but you, gods, will give us
Some faults to make us men. Caesar is touch'd.

MAECENAS: When such a spacious mirror's set before him,
He needs must see himself.

CAESAR: O Antony!
I have followed thee to this; but we do lance
Diseases in our bodies. I must perforce
Have shown to thee such a declining day,
Or look on thine; we could not stall together
In the whole world: but yet let me lament,
With tears as sovereign as the blood of hearts,
That thou, my brother, my competitor

In top of all design, my mate in empire,
Friend and companion in the front of war,
The arm of mine own body, and the heart
Where mine his thoughts did kindle,—that our stars,
Unreconciliable, should divide
Our equalness to this. Hear me, good friends,—
But I will tell you at some meeter season.

Enter an EGYPTIAN.

The business of this man looks out of him;
We'll hear him what he says.—Whence are you?
EGYPTIAN: A poor Egyptian yet. The Queen my mistress,
Confin'd in all she has, her monument,
Of thy intents desires instruction,
That she preparedly may frame herself
To the way she's forc'd to.
CAESAR: Bid her have good heart.
She soon shall know of us, by some of ours,
How honourable and how kindly we
Determine for her; for Caesar cannot live
To be ungentle.
EGYPTIAN: So the gods preserve thee!   *Exit.*
CAESAR: Come hither, Proculeius. Go and say,
We purpose her no shame. Give her what comforts
The quality of her passion shall require,
Lest, in her greatness, by some mortal stroke
She do defeat us; for her life in Rome
Would be eternal in our triumph. Go,
And with your speediest bring us what she says,
And how you find of her.
PROCULEIUS: Caesar, I shall.   *Exit.*
CAESAR: Gallus, go you along. [*Exit* GALLUS.] Where's
     Dolabella,
To second Proculeius?
ALL: Dolabella!

CAESAR: Let him alone, for I remember now
  How he's employ'd; he shall in time be ready.
  Go with me to my tent, where you shall see
  How hardly I was drawn into this war,
  How calm and gentle I proceeded still
  In all my writings. Go with me, and see
  What I can show in this.   *Exeunt.*

SCENE TWO — *Alexandria. A room in the monument.*

Enter CLEOPATRA, CHARMIAN, IRAS, *and* MARDIAN.

CLEOPATRA: My desolation does begin to make
  A better life. 'Tis paltry to be Caesar;
  Not being Fortune, he's but Fortune's knave,
  A minister of her will: and it is great
  To do that thing that ends all other deeds;
  Which shackles accidents and bolts up change;
  Which sleeps, and never palates more the dung,
  The beggar's nurse and Caesar's.

Enter [to the gates of the monument] PROCULEIUS *[and*
Soldiers].

PROCULEIUS: Caesar sends greetings to the Queen of Egypt;
  And bids thee study on what fair demands
  Thou mean'st to have him grant thee.
CLEOPATRA: What's thy name?
PROCULEIUS: My name is Proculeius.
CLEOPATRA: Antony
  Did tell me of you, bade me trust you; but
  I do not greatly care to be deceiv'd,
  That have no use for trusting. If your master
  Would have a queen his beggar, you must tell him
  That majesty, to keep decorum, must
  No less beg than a kingdom. If he please
  To give me conquer'd Egypt for my son,

He gives me so much of mine own as I
Will kneel to him with thanks.
PROCULEIUS: Be of good cheer;
You're fallen into a princely hand; fear nothing.
Make your full reference freely to my lord,
Who is so full of grace that it flows over
On all that need. Let me report to him
Your sweet dependency, and you shall find
A conqueror that will pray in aid for kindness
Where he for grace is kneel'd to.
CLEOPATRA: Pray you, tell him
I am his fortune's vassal, and I send him
The greatness he has got. I hourly learn
A doctrine of obedience, and would gladly
Look him i' the face.
PROCULEIUS: This I'll report, dear lady.
Have comfort, for I know your plight is pitied
Of him that caus'd it.

> [*Here* PROCULEIUS *and two of the* Guard *go out*
> *below and reappear beind* CLEOPATRA.]

—You see how easily she may be surpris'd.
Guard her till Caesar come.
IRAS: Royal queen!
CHARMIAN: O Cleopatra! thou art taken, queen.
CLEOPATRA: Quick, quick, good hands. [*Drawing a dagger.*]
PROCULEIUS: Hold, worthy lady, hold!

> [*Seizes and disarms her.*]

Do not yourself such wrong, who are in this
Reliev'd, but not betray'd.
CLEOPATRA: What, of death too,
That rids our dogs of languish?
PROCULEIUS: Cleopatra,
Do not abuse my master's bounty by
The undoing of yourself. Let the world see
His nobleness well acted, which your death
Will never let come forth.

CLEOPATRA: Where art thou, Death?
  Come hither, come! Come, come, and take a queen
  Worth many babes and beggars!
PROCULEIUS: O, temperance, lady!
CLEOPATRA: Sir, I will eat no meat, I'll not drink, sir;
  If idle talk will once be necessary,
  I'll not sleep neither; this mortal house I'll ruin,
  Do Caesar what he can. Know, sir, that I
  Will not wait pinion'd at your master's court;
  Nor once be chastis'd with the sober eye
  Of dull Octavia. Shall they hoist me up
  And show me to the shouting varletry
  Of censuring Rome? Rather a ditch in Egypt
  Be gentle grave unto me! Rather on Nilus' mud
  Lay me stark nak'd, and let the water-flies
  Blow me into abhorring! Rather make
  My country's high pyramides my gibbet,
  And hang me up in chains!
PROCULEIUS: You do extend
  These thoughts of horror further than you shall
  Find cause in Caesar.

Enter DOLABELLA.

DOLABELLA: Proculeius,
  What thou hast done thy master Caesar knows,
  And he hath sent for thee. For the Queen,
  I'll take her to my guard.
PROCULEIUS: So, Dolabella,
  It shall content me best. Be gentle to her.
  [*To* CLEOPATRA.] To Caesar I will speak what you shall please,
  If you'll employ me to him.
CLEOPATRA: Say, I would die.
                    Exeunt PROCULEIUS [*and* Soldiers].

DOLABELLA: Most noble empress, you have heard of me?

CLEOPATRA: I cannot tell.

DOLABELLA: Assuredly you know me.

CLEOPATRA: No matter, sir, what I have heard or known.
You laugh when boys or women tell their dreams;
Is't not your trick?

DOLABELLA: I understand not, madam.

CLEOPATRA: I dream'd there was an Emperor Antony.
O, such another sleep, that I might see
But such another man!

DOLABELLA: If it might please ye,—

CLEOPATRA: His face was as the heavens; and therein stuck
A sun and moon, which kept their course and lighted
The little O, the earth.

DOLABELLA: Most sovereign creature,—

CLEOPATRA: His legs bestrid the ocean; his rear'd arm
Crested the world; his voice was propertied
As all the tuned spheres, and that to friends;
But when he meant to quail and shake the orb,
He was as rattling thunder. For his bounty,
There was no winter in't; an autumn 'twas
That grew the more by reaping. His delights
Were dolphin-like, they show'd his back above
The element they liv'd in. In his livery
Walk'd crowns and crownets; realms and islands were
As plates dropp'd from his pocket.

DOLABELLA: Cleopatra!

CLEOPATRA: Think you there was or might be such a man
As this I dream'd of?

DOLABELLA: Gentle madam, no.

CLEOPATRA: You lie, up to the hearing of the gods!
But, if there be or ever were one such,
It's past the size of dreaming. Nature wants stuff
To vie strange forms with fancy; yet, to imagine
An Antony, were nature's piece 'gainst fancy,
Condemning shadows quite.

DOLABELLA: Hear me, good madam.

Your loss is as yourself, great; and you bear it
As answering to the weight. Would I might never
O'ertake pursu'd success, but I do feel,
By the rebound of yours, a grief that smites
My very heart at root.
CLEOPATRA: I thank you, sir.
Know you what Caesar means to do with me?
DOLABELLA: I am loath to tell you what I would you knew.
CLEOPATRA: Nay, pray you, sir,—
DOLABELLA: Though he be honourable,—
CLEOPATRA: He'll lead me, then, in triumph?
DOLABELLA: Madam, he will; I know't.   *Flourish.*

Enter CAESAR, GALLUS, PROCULEIUS, MAECENAS, [SELEUCUS,]
and others of his train.

ALL: Make way there! Caesar!
CAESAR: Which is the Queen of Egypt?
DOLABELLA: It is the Emperor, madam.   CLEOPATRA *kneels.*
CAESAR: Arise, you shall not kneel.
     I pray you, rise; rise, Egypt.
CLEOPATRA: Sir, the gods
     Will have it thus; my master and my lord
     I must obey.
CAESAR: Take to you no hard thoughts.
     The record of what injuries you did us,
     Though written in our flesh, we shall remember
     As things but done by chance.
CLEOPATRA: Sole sir o' the world,
     I cannot project mine own cause so well
     To make it clear; but do confess I have
     Been laden with like frailties which before
     Have often sham'd our sex.
CAESAR: Cleopatra, know
     We will extenuate rather than enforce.
     If you apply yourself to our intents,
     Which towards you are most gentle, you shall find

A benefit in this change; but if you seek
To lay on me a cruelty, by taking
Antony's course, you shall bereave yourself
Of my good purposes, and put your children
To that destruction which I'll guard them from,
If thereon you rely. I'll take my leave.

CLEOPATRA: And may, through all the world; 'tis yours; and
    we,
  Your scutcheons and your signs of conquest, shall
  Hang in what place you please. Here, my good lord.

CAESAR: You shall advise me in all for Cleopatra.

CLEOPATRA: This is the brief of money, plate, and jewels,
  I am possess'd of. 'Tis exactly valued,
  Not petty things admitted. Where's Seleucus?

SELEUCUS: Here, madam.

CLEOPATRA: This is my treasurer; let him speak, my lord,
  Upon his peril, that I have reserv'd
  To myself nothing. Speak the truth, Seleucus.

SELEUCUS: Madam,
  I had rather seal my lips, than, to my peril,
  Speak that which is not.

CLEOPATRA: What have I kept back?

SELEUCUS: Enough to purchase what you have made known.

CAESAR: Nay, blush not, Cleopatra; I approve
  Your wisdom in the deed.

CLEOPATRA: See, Caesar! O, behold,
  How pomp is followed! Mine will now be yours;
  And, should we shift estates, yours would be mine,
  Th' ingratitude of this Seleucus does
  Even make me wild. O slave, of no more trust
  Than love that's hir'd! What, goest thou back? Thou shalt
  Go back, I warrant thee; but I'll catch thine eyes,
  Though they had wings. Slave, soulless villain, dog!
  O rarely base!

CAESAR: Good queen, let us entreat you.

CLEOPATRA: O Caesar, what a wounding shame is this,
That thou, vouchsafing here to visit me,
Doing the honour of thy lordliness
To one so meek, that mine own servant should
Parcel the sum of my disgraces by
Addition of his envy! Say, good Caesar,
That I some lady trifles have reserv'd,
Immoment toys, things of such dignity
As we greet modern friends withal; and say,
Some nobler token I have kept apart
For Livia and Octavia, to induce
Their mediation; must I be unfolded
With one that I have bred? The gods! it smites me
Beneath the fall I have. [*To* SELEUCUS.] Prithee, go hence;
Or I shall show the cinders of my spirits
Through the ashes of my chance. Wert thou a man,
Thou wouldst have mercy on me.

CAESAR: Forbear, Seleucus.
                                   [*Exit* SELEUCUS.]

CLEOPATRA: Be it known, that we, the greatest, are misthought
For things that others do; and, when we fall,
We answer others' merits in our name,
Are therefore to be pitied.

CAESAR: Cleopatra,
Not what you have reserv'd, nor what acknowledg'd,
Put we i' the roll of conquest. Still be't yours,
Bestow it at your pleasure; and believe,
Caesar's no merchant, to make prize with you
Of things that merchants sold. Therefore be cheer'd,
Make not your thoughts your prisons; no, dear queen;
For we intend to dispose you as
Yourself shall give us counsel. Feed, and sleep.
Our care and pity is so much upon you,
That we remain your friend; and so, adieu.

CLEOPATRA: My master, and my lord!
CAESAR: Not so. Adieu.
                    Flourish. Exeunt CAESAR *and his train.*

CLEOPATRA: He words me, girls, he words me, that I should
    not
    Be noble to myself; but, hark thee, Charmian.
                                        [*Whispers* CHARMIAN.]

IRAS: Finish, good lady; the bright day is done,
    And we are for the dark.
CLEOPATRA: Hie thee again.
    I have spoke already, and it is provided;
    Go put it to the haste.
CHARMIAN: Madam, I will.

Re-enter DOLABELLA.

DOLABELLA: Where is the Queen?
CHARMIAN: Behold, sir.   [*Exit.*]
CLEOPATRA: Dolabella!
DOLABELLA: Madam, as thereto sworn by your command,
    Which my love makes religion to obey,
    I tell you this: Caesar through Syria
    Intends his journey; and within three days
    You with your children will he send before.
    Make your best use of this. I have perform'd
    Your pleasure and my promise.
CLEOPATRA: Dolabella,
    I shall remain your debtor.
DOLABELLA: I your servant.
    Adieu, good queen; I must attend on Caesar.   *Exit.*
CLEOPATRA: Farewell, and thanks! Now, Iras, what think'st
    thou?
    Thou, an Egyptian puppet, shall be shown
    In Rome, as well as I. Mechanic slaves
    With greasy aprons, rules, and hammers, shall
    Uplift us to the view; in their thick breaths,

Rank of gross diet, shall we be enclouded,
And forc'd to drink their vapour.

IRAS: The gods forbid!

CLEOPATRA: Nay, 'tis most certain, Iras. Saucy lictors
Will catch at us, like strumpets; and scald rimers
Ballad us out o' tune. The quick comedians
Extemporally will stage us, and present
Our Alexandrian revels; Antony
Shall be brought drunken forth, and I shall see
Some squeaking Cleopatra boy my greatness
I' the posture of a whore.

IRAS: O the good gods!

CLEOPATRA: Nay, that's certain.

IRAS: I'll never see't; for, I am sure, my nails
Are stronger than mine eyes.

CLEOPATRA: Why, that's the way
To fool their preparation, and to conquer
Their most absurd intents.

Re-enter CHARMIAN.

Now, Charmian!
Show me, my women, like a queen. Go fetch
My best attires; I am again for Cydnus
To meet Mark Antony. Sirrah, Iras, go.
Now, noble Charmian, we'll dispatch indeed;
And, when thou hast done this chare, I'll give thee leave
To play till doomsday. Bring our crown and all.
Wherefore's this noise? [*Exit* IRAS.] *A noise within.*

Enter a GUARDSMAN.

GUARDSMAN: Here is a rural fellow
That will not be deni'd your Highness' presence.
He brings you figs.

CLEOPATRA: Let him in. *Exit* GUARDSMAN.
What poor an instrument
May do a noble deed! He brings me liberty.

My resolution's plac'd, and I have nothing
Of woman in me; now from head to foot
I am marble-constant; now the fleeting moon
No planet is of mine.

Re-enter GUARDSMAN, *with* CLOWN [*bringing in a basket*].

GUARDSMAN: This is the man.
CLEOPATRA: Avoid, and leave him.   *Exit* GUARDSMAN.
    Hast thou the pretty worm of Nilus there,
    That kills and pains not?
CLOWN: Truly, I have him; but I would not be the party that
    should desire you to touch him, for his biting is immortal;
    those that do die of it do seldom or never recover.
CLEOPATRA: Remember'st thou any that have died on't?
CLOWN: Very many, men and women too. I heard of one of
    them no longer than yesterday; a very honest woman, but
    something given to lie, as a woman should not do, but in
    the way of honesty; how she died of the biting of it, what
    pain she felt; truly, she makes a very good report o' the
    worm. But he that will believe all that they say, shall never
    be saved by half that they do. But this is most fallible,
    the worm's an odd worm.
CLEOPATRA: Get thee hence; farewell.
CLOWN: I wish you all joy of the worm.
                                    [*Setting down his basket.*]

CLEOPATRA: Farewell.
CLOWN: You must think this, look you, that the worm will
    do his kind.
CLEOPATRA: Ay, ay; farewell.
CLOWN: Look you, the worm is not to be trusted but in the
    keeping of wise people; for, indeed, there is no goodness
    in the worm.
CLEOPATRA: Take thou no care; it shall be heeded.
CLOWN: Very good. Give it nothing, I pray you, for it is not
    worth the feeding.

CLEOPATRA: Will it eat me?

CLOWN: You must not think I am so simple but I know the devil himself will not eat a woman. I know that a woman is a dish for the gods, if the devil dress her not. But, truly, these same whoreson devils do the gods great harm in their women; for in every ten that they make, the devils mar five.

CLEOPATRA: Well, get thee gone; farewell.

CLOWN: Yes, forsooth; I wish you joy o' the worm.   *Exit.*

[*Re-enter* IRAS *with a robe, crown, etc.*]

CLEOPATRA: Give me my robe, put on my crown; I have
　　Immortal longings in me. Now no more
　　The juice of Egypt's grape shall moist this lip.
　　Yare, yare, good Iras; quick. Methinks I hear
　　Antony call; I see him rouse himself
　　To praise my noble act; I hear him mock
　　The luck of Caesar, which the gods give men
　　To excuse their after wrath. Husband, I come!
　　Now to that name my courage prove my title!
　　I am fire and air; my other elements
　　I give to baser life. So; have you done?
　　Come then, and take the last warmth of my lips
　　Farewell, kind Charmian; Iras, long farewell.
　　　　　　　　　　　[*Kisses them.* IRAS *falls and dies.*]
　　Have I the aspic in my lips? Dost fall?
　　If thou and nature can so gently part,
　　The stroke of death is as a lover's pinch,
　　Which hurts, and is desir'd. Dost thou lie still?
　　If thus thou vanishest, thou tell'st the world
　　It is not worth leave-taking.

CHARMIAN: Dissolve, thick cloud, and rain; that I may say
　　The gods themselves do weep!

CLEOPATRA:　　　　　　　　　This proves me base.
　　If she first meet the curled Antony,
　　He'll make demand of her, and spend that kiss

Which is my heaven to have. Come, thou mortal wretch,
> [*To an asp, which she applies to her breast.*]

With thy sharp teeth this knot intrinsicate
Of life at once untie. Poor venomous fool,
Be angry, and dispatch. O, couldst thou speak,
That I might hear thee call great Caesar ass
Unpolicied!

CHARMIAN: O eastern star!

CLEOPATRA: Peace, peace!
Dost thou not see my baby at my breast,
That sucks the nurse asleep?

CHARMIAN: O, break! O, break!

CLEOPATRA: As sweet as balm, as soft as air, as gentle,—
O Antony!—Nay, I will take thee too:
> [*Applying another asp to her arm.*]

What should I stay—   *Dies.*

CHARMIAN: In this vile world? So, fare thee well!
Now boast thee, death, in thy possession lies
A lass unparallel'd. Downy windows, close;
And golden Phoebus never be beheld
Of eyes again so royal! Your crown's awry;
I'll mend it, and then play—

Enter the GUARD, *rushing in.*

FIRST GUARD: Where's the Queen?

CHARMIAN: Speak softly, wake her not.

FIRST GUARD: Caesar hath sent—

CHARMIAN: Too slow a messenger.
> [*Applies an asp.*]

O, come apace, dispatch! I partly feel thee.

FIRST GUARD: Approach, ho! All's not well; Caesar's beguil'd.

SECOND GUARD: There's Dolabella sent from Caesar; call him.

FIRST GUARD: What work is here! Charmian, is this well done?

CHARMIAN: It is well done, and fitting for a princess
Descended of so many royal kings.
Ah, soldier!   *Dies.*

Re-enter DOLABELLA.

DOLABELLA: How goes it here?
SECOND GUARD: All dead.
DOLABELLA: Caesar, thy thoughts
    Touch their effects in this; thyself art coming
    To see perform'd the dreaded act which thou
    So sought'st to hinder.

Re-enter CAESAR *and all his train, marching.*

ALL: A way there, a way for Caesar!
DOLABELLA: O sir, you are too sure an augurer;
    That you did fear is done.
CAESAR: Bravest at the last,
    She levell'd at our purposes, and, being royal,
    Took her own way. The manner of their deaths?
    I do not see them bleed.
DOLABELLA: Who was last with them?
FIRST GUARD: A simple countryman, that brought her figs.
    This was his basket.
CAESAR: Poison'd, then.
FIRST GUARD: O Caesar,
    This Charmian liv'd but now; she stood and spake.
    I found her trimming up the diadem
    On her dead mistress. Tremblingly she stood
    And on the sudden dropp'd.
CAESAR: O noble weakness!
    If they had swallow'd poison, 'twould appear
    By external swelling; but she looks like sleep,
    As she would catch another Antony
    In her strong toil of grace.
DOLABELLA: Here, on her breast,
    There is a vent of blood and something blown.
    The like is on her arm.
FIRST GUARD: This is an aspic's trail; and these fig-leaves
    Have slime upon them, such as the aspic leaves

Upon the caves of Nile.

CAESAR: Most probable
That so she died; for her physician tells me
She hath pursu'd conclusions infinite
Of easy ways to die. Take up her bed;
And bear her women from the monument.
She shall be buried by her Antony;
No grave upon the earth shall clip in it
A pair so famous. High events as these
Strike those that make them; and their story is
No less in pity than his glory which
Brought them to be lamented. Our army shall
In solemn show attend this funeral;
And then to Rome. Come, Dolabella, see
High order in this great solemnity.   *Exeunt omnes.*

SØREN AABYE KIERKEGAARD was born in Copenhagen, Denmark, in 1813. His father made a fortune
as a merchant in Copenhagen, rising above his humble
origins as a shepherd and farmhand and providing
Kierkegaard with an independent income, but the
"melancholy" of the man left its mark on his son.
"With the help of the thorn in my foot I spring higher
than anyone with sound feet," insisted Kierkegaard,
despite the "despair, lusts, and excesses" to which he
confessed himself prone. He studied philosophy and
theology at the University of Copenhagen and the
University of Berlin, then returned to Copenhagen to
live. He wrote feverishly and under various pseudonyms
works of a "poet-philosopher": *Either/Or: A Fragment
of Life* (1843), *Fear and Trembling* (1843), and *The
Sickness Unto Death* (1849), among others. Engaged
once, Kierkegaard broke it off and remained a bachelor.
He wrote: "Women or ideas are what beckon men out
into existence. Naturally there is the great difference
that for the thousands who run after a skirt there is not
always one who is moved by ideas." Kierkegaard's
lifelong dissatisfaction with established religion culmi-
nated in his refusal of the last sacraments at his death
in 1855.

From *Fear and Trembling; Repetition,* edited and translated by Howard V. Hong and Edna H. Hong. Publisher: Princeton University Press, 1983. Pages 9–14
and 35–53.

The Knight of Faith *

EXORDIUM

Once upon a time there was a man who as a child had heard that beautiful story of how God tempted Abraham and of how Abraham withstood the temptation, kept the faith, and, contrary to expectation, got a son a second time. When he grew older, he read the same story with even greater admiration, for life had fractured what had been united in the pious simplicity of the child. The older he became, the more often his thoughts turned to that story; his enthusiasm for it became greater and greater, and yet he could understand the story less and less. Finally, he forgot everything else because of it; his soul had but one wish, to see Abraham, but one longing, to have witnessed that event. His craving was not to see the beautiful regions of the East, not the earthly glory of the promised land, not that God-fearing couple whose old age God had blessed, not the venerable figure of the aged patriarch, not the vigorous adolescence God bestowed upon Isaac—the same thing could just as well have occurred on a barren heath. His craving was to go along on the three-day journey when Abraham rode with sorrow before him and Isaac beside him. His wish was to be present in that hour when Abraham raised his eyes and saw Mount

---

* [From *Fear and Trembling,* which was published under the pseudonym Johannes de Silentio (John of Silence), a character created by Kierkegaard. It is Johannes who is the narrator of this selection.]

291

Moriah in the distance, the hour when he left the asses behind and went up the mountain alone with Isaac—for what occupied him was not the beautiful tapestry of imagination but the shudder of the idea.

That man was not a thinker. He did not feel any need to go beyond faith; he thought that it must be supremely glorious to be remembered as its father, an enviable destiny to possess it, even if no one knew it.

That man was not an exegetical scholar. He did not know Hebrew; if he had known Hebrew, he perhaps would easily have understood the story and Abraham.

1

And God tempted Abraham and said to him, take Isaac, your only son, whom you love, and go to the land of Moriah and offer him there as a burnt offering on a mountain that I shall show you.

It was early in the morning when Abraham arose, had the asses saddled, and left his tent, taking Isaac with him, but Sarah watched them from the window as they went down the valley—until she could see them no longer. They rode in silence for three days. On the morning of the fourth day, Abraham said not a word but raised his eyes and saw Mount Moriah in the distance. He left the young servants behind and, taking Isaac's hand, went up the mountain alone. But Abraham said to himself, "I will not hide from Isaac where this walk is taking him." He stood still, he laid his hand on Isaac's head in blessing, and Isaac kneeled to receive it. And Abraham's face epitomized fatherliness; his gaze was gentle, his words admonishing. But Isaac could not understand him, his soul could not be uplifted; he clasped Abraham's knees, he pleaded at his feet, he begged for his young life, for his beautiful hopes; he called to mind the joy in Abraham's house, he called to mind the sorrow and the solitude. Then Abraham lifted the boy up and walked on, holding his hand, and his words were full of comfort and admonition. But Isaac could not understand him. Abraham climbed Mount Moriah, but Isaac did not understand him. Then Abraham turned away from him for a moment, but when Isaac saw Abraham's face again, it had changed: his gaze was wild, his whole being was sheer terror. He seized Isaac by the chest, threw him to the ground, and said, "Stupid boy, do you think I am your father? I am an idolater. Do you think it is God's command? No, it is my desire." Then Isaac trembled and cried out in his anguish: "God in heaven, have mercy on me, God of Abraham, have mercy on me; if I have no father on earth, then you be my father!" But Abraham said softly to himself, "Lord God in heaven, I thank you; it is better that he believes me a monster than that he should lose faith in you."

When the child is to be weaned, the mother blackens her breast. It would be hard to have the breast look inviting when the child must not have it. So the child believes that the breast has changed, but the mother—she is still the same, her gaze is tender and loving as ever. How fortunate the one who did not need more terrible means to wean the child!

2

It was early in the morning when Abraham arose: he embraced Sarah, the bride of his old age, and Sarah kissed Isaac, who took away her disgrace, Isaac her pride, her hope for all the generations to come. They rode along the road in silence, and Abraham stared continuously and fixedly at the ground until the fourth day, when he looked up and saw Mount Moriah far away, but once again he turned his eyes toward the ground. Silently he arranged the firewood and bound Isaac; silently he drew the knife—then he saw the ram that God had selected. This he sacrificed and went home. . . . From that day henceforth, Abraham was old; he could not forget that God had ordered him to do this. Isaac flourished as before, but Abraham's eyes were darkened, and he saw joy no more.

When the child has grown big and is to be weaned, the mother virginally conceals her breast, and then the child no longer has a mother. How fortunate the child who has not lost his mother in some other way!

3

It was early in the morning when Abraham arose: he kissed Sarah, the young mother, and Sarah kissed Isaac, her delight, her joy forever. And Abraham rode thoughtfully down the road; he thought of Hagar and the son, whom he drove out into the desert. He climbed Mount Moriah, he drew the knife.

It was a quiet evening when Abraham rode out alone, and he rode to Mount Moriah; he threw himself down on his face, he prayed God to forgive him his sin, that he had been willing to sacrifice Isaac, that the father had forgotten his duty to his son. He often rode his lonesome road, but he found no peace. He could not comprehend that it was a sin that he had been willing to sacrifice to God the best that he had, the possession for which he himself would have gladly died many times; and if it was a sin, if he had not loved Isaac in this manner, he could not understand that it could be forgiven, for what more terrible sin was there?

When the child is to be weaned, the mother, too, is not without sorrow, because she and the child are more and more to be separated, because the child who first lay under her heart and later rested upon her breast will never again be so close. So they grieve together the brief sorrow. How fortunate the one who kept the child so close and did not need to grieve any more!

4

It was early in the morning, and everything in Abraham's house was ready for the journey. He took leave of Sarah, and Eliezer, the faithful servant, accompanied him along the road until he turned back again. They rode along in harmony, Abraham and Isaac, until they came to Mount Moriah. Abraham made everything ready for the sacrifice, calmly and gently, but when he turned away and drew the knife, Isaac saw that Abraham's left hand was clenched in despair, that a shudder went through his whole body—but Abraham drew the knife.

Then they returned home again, and Sarah hurried to meet them, but Isaac had lost the faith. Not a word is ever said of this in the world, and Isaac never talked to anyone about what he had seen, and Abraham did not suspect that anyone had seen it.

When the child is to be weaned, the mother has stronger sustenance at hand so that the child does not perish. How fortunate the one who has this stronger sustenance at hand!

Thus and in many similar ways did the man of whom we speak ponder this event. Every time he returned from a pilgrimage to Mount Moriah, he sank down wearily, folded his hands, and said, "No one was as great as Abraham. Who is able to understand him?"

EULOGY ON ABRAHAM

. . . Abraham I cannot understand; in a certain sense I can learn nothing from him except to be amazed. If someone deludes himself into thinking he may be moved to have faith by pondering the outcome of that story, he cheats himself and cheats God out of the first movement of faith—he wants to suck worldly wisdom out of the paradox. Someone might succeed, for our generation does not stop with faith, does not stop with the miracle of faith, turning water into wine—it goes further and turns wine into water.

Would it not be best to stop with faith, and is it not shocking that everyone wants to go further? Where will it all end when in our age, as declared in so many ways, one does not want to stop with love? In worldly shrewdness, in petty calculation, in paltriness and meanness, in everything that can make man's divine origin doubtful. Would it not be best to remain standing at faith and for him who stands to see to it that he does not fall, for the movement of faith must continually be made by virtue of the absurd, but yet in such a way, please note, that one does not lose the finite but gains it whole and intact. For my part, I presumably can describe the movements of faith, but I cannot make them. In learning to go through the motions of swimming, one can be suspended from the ceiling in a harness and then presumably describe the movements, but one is not swimming. In the same way I can describe the movements of faith. If I am thrown out into the water, I presumably do swim (for I do not belong to the waders), but I make different movements, the movements of infinity, whereas faith makes the opposite movements: after having made the movements of infinity, it makes the movements of finitude. Fortunate is the person who can make these movements! He does the marvelous, and I shall never weary of admiring him; it makes no difference to me whether it is Abraham or a slave in Abraham's house, whether it is a professor of philosophy or a poor servant girl— I pay attention only to the movements. But I do pay attention to them, and I do not let myself be fooled, either by myself or by anyone else. The knights of the infinite resignation are easily recognizable—their walk is light and bold. But they who carry the treasure of faith are likely to disappoint, for externally they have a striking resemblance to bourgeois philistinism, which infinite resignation, like faith, deeply disdains.

I honestly confess that in my experience I have not found a single authentic instance, although I do not therefore deny that every second person may be such an instance. Meanwhile, I have been looking for it for many years, but in vain. Generally, people travel around the world to see rivers and mountains, new stars, colorful birds, freakish fish, preposterous races of mankind; they indulge in the brutish stupor that gawks at life and thinks it has seen something. That does not occupy me. But if I knew where a knight of faith lived, I would travel on foot to him, for this marvel occupies me absolutely. I would not leave him for a second, I would watch him every minute to see how he made the movements; I would consider myself taken care of for life and would divide my time between watching him and practicing myself, and thus spend all my time in admiring him. As I said before, I have not found anyone like that; meanwhile, I may very well imagine him. Here he is. The acquaintance is made, I am introduced to him. The instant I first lay eyes on him, I set him apart at once; I jump back, clap my hands, and say half aloud, "Good Lord, is this the man, is this really the one—he looks just like a tax collector!" But this is indeed the one. I move a little closer to him, watch his slightest movement to see if it reveals a bit of heterogeneous optical telegraphy from the infinite, a glance, a facial expression, a gesture, a sadness, a smile that would betray the infinite in its heterogeneity with the finite. No! I examine his figure from top to toe to see if there may not be a crack through which the infinite would peek. No! He is solid all the way through. His stance? It is vigorous, belongs entirely to finitude; no spruced-up burgher walking out to Fresberg on a Sunday afternoon treads the earth more solidly. He belongs entirely to the world; no bourgeois philistine could belong to it more. Nothing is detectable of that distant and aristocratic nature by which the knight of the infinite is recognized. He finds pleasure in everything, takes part in everything, and every time one sees him participating in something particular, he does it with an assiduousness that marks the worldly man who is attached to such things. He attends to his job. To see him makes one think of him as a pen-pusher who has lost his soul to Italian bookkeeping, so punctilious is he. Sunday is for him a holiday. He goes to church. No heavenly gaze or any sign of the incommensurable betrays him; if one did not know him, it would be impossible to distinguish him from the rest of the crowd, for at most his hearty and powerful singing of the hymns proves that he has good lungs. In the afternoon, he takes a walk to the woods. He enjoys everything he sees, the swarms of people, the new omnibuses, the Sound. Encountering him on Strandveien, one would take him for a mercantile soul enjoying himself. He finds pleasure in this way, for he is not a poet, and I have tried in vain to lure the poetic incommensurability out of him. Toward evening, he goes home, and his gait is as steady as a postman's. On the way, he thinks that his wife surely will have a special hot meal for him when he comes home—for example, roast lamb's head with vegetables. If he meets a kindred soul, he would go on talking all the way to Østerport about this delicacy with a passion befitting a restaurant operator. It so happens that he does not have four shillings to his name, and yet he firmly believes that his wife has this delectable meal waiting for him. If she has, to see him eat would be the envy of the elite and an inspiration to the common man, for his appetite is keener than Esau's. His wife does not have it—curiously enough, he is just the same. On the way he passes a building site and meets another man. They converse for a moment; in an instant he erects a building, and he himself has at his disposition everything required. The stranger leaves him thinking that he surely is a capitalist, while my admired knight thinks: Well, if it came right down to it, I could easily get it. He sits at an open window and surveys the neighborhood where he lives: everything that happens—a rat scurrying under a plank across the gutter, children playing—engages him with an equanimity akin to that of a sixteen-year-old girl. And yet he is no genius, for I have sought in vain to spy out the incommensurability of genius in him. In the evening, he smokes his pipe; seeing him, one would swear it was the butcher across the way vegetating in the gloaming. With the freedom from care of a reckless good-for-nothing, he lets things take care of themselves, and yet every moment of his life he buys the opportune time at the highest price, for he does not do even the slightest thing except by virtue of the absurd. And yet, yet— yes, I could be infuriated over it if for no other reason than envy—and yet this man has made and at every moment is making the movement of infinity. He drains the deep sadness of life in infinite resignation, he knows the blessedness of infinity, he has felt the pain of renouncing everything, the most precious thing in the world, and yet the finite tastes just as good to him as to one who never knew anything higher, because his remaining in finitude would have no trace of a timorous, anxious routine, and yet he has this security that makes him delight in it as if finitude were the surest thing of all. And yet, yet the whole earthly figure he presents is a new creation by virtue of the absurd. He resigned everything infinitely, and then he grasped everything again by virtue of the absurd. He is continually making the movement of infinity, but he does it with such precision and assurance that he continually gets finitude out of it, and no one ever suspects anything else. It is supposed to be the most difficult feat for a ballet dancer to leap into a specific posture in such a way that he never once strains for the posture but in the very leap assumes the posture. Perhaps there is no ballet dancer who can do it—but this knight does it. Most people live completely absorbed in worldly joys and sorrows; they are benchwarmers who do not take part in the dance. The knights of infinity are ballet dancers and have elevation. They make the upward movement and come down again, and this, too, is not an unhappy diversion and is not unlovely to see. But every time they come down, they are unable to assume the posture immediately, they waver for a moment, and this wavering shows that they are aliens in the world. It is more or less conspicuous according to their skill, but even the most skillful of these knights cannot hide this wavering. One does not need to see them in the air; one needs only to see them the instant they touch and have touched the earth—and then one recognizes them. But to be able to come down in such a way that instantaneously one seems to stand and to walk, to change the leap into life into walking, absolutely to express the sublime in the pedestrian—only that knight can do it, and this is the one and only marvel.

Nevertheless, this marvel can so easily deceive that I shall describe the movements in a specific case that can illuminate their relation to actuality, for this is the central issue. A young lad falls in love with a princess, and this love is the entire substance of his life, and yet the relation is such that it cannot possibly be realized, cannot possibly be translated from ideality into reality. Of course, the slaves of the finite, the frogs in the swamp of life, scream: That kind of love is foolishness; the rich brewer's widow is just as good and solid a match. Let them go on croaking in the swamp. The knight of infinite resignation does not do any such thing; he does not give up the love, not for all the glories of the world. He is no fool. First of all, he assures himself that it actually is the substance of his life, and his soul is too healthy and too proud to waste the least of it in an intoxication. He is not cowardly; he is not afraid to let it steal into his most secret, his most remote thoughts, to let it twist and entwine itself intricately around every ligament of his consciousness—if his love comes to grief, he will never be able to wrench himself out of it. He feels a blissful delight in letting love palpitate in every nerve, and yet his soul is as solemn as the soul of one who has drunk the poisoned cup and feels the juice penetrate every drop of blood—for this is the moment of crisis. Having totally absorbed this love and immersed himself in it, he does not lack the courage to attempt and to risk everything. He examines the conditions of his life, he convenes the swift thoughts that obey his every hint like well-trained doves; he flourishes his staff, and they scatter in all directions. But now when they all come back, all of them like messengers of grief, and explain that it is an impossibility, he becomes very quiet, he dismisses them, he becomes solitary, and then he undertakes the movement. If what I say here is to have any meaning, the point is that the movement is carried out normatively. In the first place, the knight will then have the power to concentrate the whole substance of his life and the meaning of actuality into one single desire. If a person lacks this concentration, this focus, his soul is dissipated in multiplicity from the beginning, and then he never manages to make the movement; he acts as shrewdly in life as the financiers who put their resources into widely diversified investments in order to gain on one if they lose on another—in short, he is not a knight. In the next place, the knight will have the power to concentrate the conclusion of all his thinking into one act of consciousness. If he lacks this focus, his soul is dissipated in multiplicity from the beginning, and he will never find the time to make the movement; he will continually be running errands in life and will never enter into eternity, for in the very moment he approaches it, he will suddenly discover that he has forgotten something and therefore must go back. In the next moment, he thinks, it will be possible, and this is quite true, but with such observations one will never come to make the movement but with their help will sink deeper and deeper into the mire.

The knight, then, makes the movements, but which one? Will he forget it all, for this, too, constitutes a kind of concentration? No, for the knight does not contradict himself, and it is a contradiction to forget the whole substance of his life and yet remain the same. He feels no inclination to become another person, by no means regards that as something great. Only the lower natures forget themselves and become something new. The butterfly, for example, completely forgets that it was a caterpillar, and may in turn so completely forget that it was a butterfly that it may become a fish. The deeper natures never forget themselves and never become anything other than what they were. The knight, then, will recollect everything, but this recollection is precisely the pain, and yet in infinite resignation he is reconciled with existence. His love for that princess would become for him the expression of an eternal love, would assume a religious character, would be transfigured into a love of the eternal being, which true enough denied the fulfillment but nevertheless did reconcile him once more in the eternal consciousness of its validity in an eternal form that no actuality can take away from him. Fools and young people say that everything is possible for a human being. But that is a gross error. Spiritually speaking, everything is possible, but in the finite world there is much that is not possible. The knight, however, makes this impossibility possible by expressing it spiritually, but he expresses it spiritually by renouncing it. The desire that would lead him out into actuality but has been stranded on impossibility is now turned inward, but it is not therefore lost, nor is it forgotten. Sometimes it is the vague emotions of desire in him that awaken recollection; sometimes he awakens it himself, for he is too proud to be willing to let the whole substance of his life turn out to have been an affair of the fleeting moment. He keeps this love young, and it grows along with him in years and in beauty. But he needs no finite occasion for its growth. From the moment he has made the movement, the princess is lost. He does not need the erotic titillation of seeing the beloved, etc., nor does he in the finite sense continually need to be bidding her farewell, because in the eternal sense he recollects her, and he knows very well that the lovers who are so bent on seeing each other for the last time in order to say farewell once again are justified in their eagerness, justified in thinking it to be the last time, for they forget each other very quickly. He has grasped the deep secret that even in loving another person one ought to be sufficient to oneself. He is no longer finitely concerned about what the princess does, and precisely this proves that he has made the movement infinitely. Here one has occasion to see whether the movement in an individual is authentic or feigned. There was one who also believed that he had made the movement; but look, time passed, the princess did something else—she married, for example, a prince—and his soul lost the resilience of resignation. He thereby demonstrated that he had not made the movement properly, for one who has resigned infinitely is sufficient to oneself. The knight does not cancel his resignation, he keeps his love just as young as it was in the first movement; he never loses it simply because he has made the movement infinitely. What the princess does cannot disturb him; it is only the lower natures who have the law for their actions in someone else, the premises for their actions outside themselves. If, however, the princess is similarly disposed, something beautiful will emerge. She will then introduce herself into the order of knighthood into which one is not taken by election but of which everyone is a member who has the courage to enroll oneself, the order of knighthood that proves its immortality by making no distinction between male and female. She, too, will keep her love young and sound; she, too, will have overcome her agony, even though she does not, as the ballad says, lie by her lord's side every night. These two will in all eternity be compatible, with such a rhythmical *harmonia praeastabilita* that if the moment ever came—a moment, however, that does not concern them finitely, for then they would grow old—if the moment ever came that allowed them to give love its expression in time, they would be capable of beginning right where they would have begun if they had been united in the beginning. The person who understands this, whether man or woman, can never be deceived, for it is only the baser natures that fancy that they are deceived. No girl who does not have this pride actually understands what it means to love, but if she does have this pride, the craftiness and cunning of the whole world cannot deceive her.

In infinite resignation there is peace and rest; every person who wills it, who has not debased himself by self-disdain—which is still more dreadful than being too proud—can discipline himself to make this movement, which in its pain reconciles one to existence. Infinite resignation is that shirt mentioned in an old legend. The thread is spun with tears, bleached with tears; the shirt is sewn in tears—but then it also gives protection better than iron or steel. The defect in the legend is that a third person can work up this linen. The secret in life is that each person must sew it himself, and the remarkable thing is that a man can sew it fully as well as a woman. In infinite resignation there is peace and rest and comfort in the pain, that is, when the movement is made normatively. I could easily write a whole book if I were to expound the various misunderstandings, the awkward positions, the botched up movements I have encountered in just my own little experience. There is little belief in spirit, and yet the essential thing in making this movement is spirit. It is essential that it not be a unilateral result of a *dira necessitas* [cruel constraint of necessity], and the more this is present, the more doubtful it always is that the movement is normal. Thus, if one believes that cold, barren necessity must necessarily be present, then one is declaring thereby that no one can experience death before one actually dies, which to me seems to be crass materialism. But in our age people are less concerned about making pure movements. If someone who wanted to learn to dance were to say: For centuries, one generation after the other has learned the positions, and it is high time that I take advantage of this and promptly begin with the quadrille—people would presumably laugh a little at him, but in the world of spirit this is very plausible. What, then, is education? I believe it is the course the individual goes through in order to catch up with himself, and the person who will not go through this course is not much helped by being born in the most enlightened age.

Infinite resignation is the last stage before faith, so that anyone who has not made this movement does not have faith, for only in infinite resignation do I become conscious of my eternal validity, and only then can one speak of grasping existence by virtue of faith.

Now let us meet the knight of faith on the occasion previously mentioned. He does exactly the same as the other knight did: he infinitely renounces the love that is the substance of his life, he is reconciled in pain. But then the marvel happens; he makes one more movement even more wonderful than all the others, for he says: Nevertheless I have faith that I will get her—that is, by virtue of the absurd, by virtue of the fact that for God all things are possible. The absurd does not belong to the differences that lie within the proper domain of the understanding. It is not identical with the improbable, the unexpected, the unforeseen. The moment the knight executed the act of resignation, he was convinced of the impossibility, humanly speaking; that was the conclusion of the understanding, and he had sufficient energy to think it. But in the infinite sense it was possible, that is, by relinquishing it, but this having, after all, is also a giving up. Nevertheless, to the understanding this having is no absurdity, for the understanding continues to be right in maintaining that in the finite world where it dominates this having was and continues to be an impossibility. The knight of faith realizes this just as clearly; consequently, he can be saved only by the absurd, and this he grasps by faith. Consequently, he acknowledges the impossibility, and in the very same moment he believes the absurd, for if he wants to imagine that he has faith without passionately acknowledging the impossibility with

his whole heart and soul, he is deceiving himself and his testimony is neither here nor there, since he has not even attained
infinite resignation.

Precisely because resignation is antecedent, faith is no esthetic
emotion but something far higher; it is not the spontaneous
inclination of the heart but the paradox of existence. If, for
example, in the face of every difficulty, a young girl still remains
convinced that her desire will be fulfilled, this assurance is by
no means the assurance of faith, even though she has been
brought up by Christian parents and perhaps has had confirmation instruction from the pastor for a whole year. She is
convinced in all her childlike naiveté and innocence, and this
assurance ennobles her nature and gives her a supranatural magnitude so that like a thaumaturge she can invoke the finite
powers of existence and bring the very stones to tears, while on
the other hand in her perplexity she can just as well run to
Herod as to Pilate and move the whole world with her pleas.
Her assurance is most captivating, and one can learn much from
her, but there is one thing that cannot be learned from her—
how to make movements—for her assurance does not dare, in
the pain of resignation, to look the impossibility in the eye.

So I can perceive that it takes strength and energy and spiritual
freedom to make the infinite movement of resignation; I can
also perceive that it can be done. The next [movement] amazes
me, my brain reels, for, after having made the movement of
resignation, then by virtue of the absurd to get everything, to
get one's desire totally and completely—that is over and beyond
human powers, that is a marvel. But this I can perceive: that
the young girl's assurance is nothing but rashness compared
with the unshakability of faith in the full recognition of the
impossibility. Every time I want to make this movement, I
almost faint; the very same moment I admire absolutely, I am
seized with great anxiety. For what is it to tempt God? And
yet this is the movement of faith and continues to be that, even

though philosophy, so as to confuse the concepts, wants to delude us into thinking it has faith, even though theology is willing to sell it off at a low price.

The act of resignation does not require faith, for what I gain in resignation is my eternal consciousness. This is a purely philosophical movement that I venture to make when it is demanded and can discipline myself to make, because every time some finitude will take power over me, I starve myself into submission until I make the movement, for my eternal consciousness is my love for God, and for me that is the highest of all. The act of resignation does not require faith, but to get the least little bit more than my eternal consciousness requires faith, for this is the paradox. The movements are often confused. It is said that faith is needed in order to renounce everything. Indeed, one hears what is even more curious: a person laments that he has lost his faith, and when a check is made to see where he is on the scale, curiously enough, he has only reached the point where he is to make the infinite movement of resignation. Through resignation I renounce everything. I make this movement all by myself, and if I do not make it, it is because I am too cowardly and soft and devoid of enthusiasm and do not feel the significance of the high dignity assigned to every human being, to be his own censor, which is far more exalted than to be the censor general of the whole Roman republic. This movement I make all by myself, and what I gain thereby is my eternal consciousness in blessed harmony with my love for the eternal being. By faith I do not renounce anything; on the contrary, by faith I receive everything exactly in the sense in which it is said that one who has faith like a mustard seed can move mountains. It takes a purely human courage to renounce the whole temporal realm in order to gain eternity, but this I do gain and in all eternity can never renounce—it is a self-contradiction. But it takes a paradoxical and humble courage to grasp the whole temporal realm now by virtue of the absurd, and this is the courage of faith. By faith Abraham did not renounce Isaac, but by faith Abraham received Isaac. By virtue of resignation, that rich young man should have given away everything, but if he had done so, then the knight of faith would have said to him: By virtue of the absurd, you will get every penny back again —believe it! And the formerly rich young man should by no means treat these words lightly, for if he were to give away his possessions because he is bored with them, then his resignation would not amount to much.

Temporality, finitude—that is what it is all about. I can resign everything by my own strength and find peace and rest in the pain; I can put up with everything—even if that dreadful demon, more horrifying than the skeletal one who terrifies men, even if madness held its fool's costume before my eyes and I understood from its face that it was I who should put it on— I can still save my soul as long as my concern that my love of God conquer within me is greater than my concern that I achieve earthly happiness. In his very last moment, a person can still concentrate his whole soul in one single look to heaven, from whence come all good gifts, and this look will be understood by himself and by him whom it seeks to mean that he has been true to his love. Then he will calmly put on the costume. He whose soul lacks this romanticism has sold his soul, whether he gets a kingdom or a wretched piece of silver for it. By my own strength I cannot get the least little thing that belongs to finitude, for I continually use my strength in resigning everything. By my own strength I can give up the princess, and I will not sulk about it but find joy and peace and rest in my pain, but by my own strength I cannot get her back again, for I use all my strength in resigning. On the other hand, by faith, says that marvelous knight, by faith you will get her by virtue of the absurd.

But this movement I cannot make. As soon as I want to begin, everything reverses itself, and I take refuge in the pain of resignation. I am able to swim in life, but I am too heavy for this mystical hovering. To exist in such a way that my contrast to existence constantly expresses itself as the most beautiful and secure harmony with it—this I cannot do. And yet, I repeatedly say, it must be wonderful to get the princess. The knight of resignation who does not say this is a deceiver; he has not had one single desire, and he has not kept his desire young in his pain. There may be someone who found it quite convenient that the desire was no longer alive and that the arrow of his pain had grown dull, but such a person is no knight. A free-born soul who caught himself doing this would despise himself and begin all over again, and above all would not allow his soul to be self-deceived. And yet it must be wonderful to get the princess, and the knight of faith is the only happy man, the heir to the finite, while the knight of resignation is a stranger and an alien. To get the princess this way, to live happily with her day after day (for it is also conceivable that the knight of resignation could get the princess, but his soul had full insight into the impossibility of their future happiness), to live happily every moment this way by virtue of the absurd, every moment to see the sword hanging over the beloved's head, and yet not to find rest in the pain of resignation but to find joy by virtue of the absurd—this is wonderful. The person who does this is great, the only great one; the thought of it stirs my soul, which never was stingy in admiring the great.

If everyone in my generation who does not wish to stop with faith is actually a person who has grasped the horror of life, has grasped the meaning of Daub's statement that a soldier standing alone with a loaded rifle at his post near a powder magazine on a stormy night thinks strange thoughts; if everyone who does not wish to stop with faith is actually a person who has the spiritual power to comprehend that the wish was an impossibility and then to take time to be alone with the thought; if everyone who does not wish to stop with faith is a person who in pain is reconciled and is reconciled through pain; if everyone who does not wish to stop with faith is a person who subsequently (and if he has not done all the foregoing, then he should not trouble himself when the issue is that of faith) performed the marvel and grasped existence in its totality by virtue of the absurd—then what I am writing is the loftiest eulogy upon the generation by its most inferior member, who could make only the movement of resignation. But why are they not willing to stop with faith? Why do we sometimes hear that people are ashamed to acknowledge that they have faith? I cannot comprehend it. If I ever manage to be able to make this movement, I will in the future drive with four horses.

Is it actually the case that all the bourgeois philistinism I see in life—which I do not permit myself to condemn with my words but with my deeds—is actually not what it seems, is the marvel? It is indeed conceivable, for that hero of faith did, after all, have a striking resemblance to it, for that hero of faith was not even an ironist and humorist but something much higher. There is a lot of talk these days about irony and humor, especially by people who have never been able to practice them but nevertheless know how to explain everything. I am not completely unfamiliar with these two passions; I know a little more about them than is found in German and German-Danish compendiums. Therefore I know that these two passions are essentially different from the passion of faith. Irony and humor are also self-reflective and thus belong to the sphere of infinite resignation; their elasticity is owing to the individual's incommensurability with actuality.

Be it a duty or whatever, I cannot make the final movement, the paradoxical movement of faith, although there is nothing I wish more. Whether a person has the right to say this must be his own decision; whether he can come to an amicable agreement in this respect is a matter between himself and the eternal being, who is the object of faith. Every person can make the movement of infinite resignation, and for my part I would not hesitate to call a coward anyone who imagines that he cannot do it. Faith is another matter, but no one has the right to lead others to believe that faith is something inferior or that it is an easy matter, since on the contrary it is the greatest and most difficult of all.

The story of Abraham is understood in another way. We praise God's mercy, that he gave him Isaac again and that the whole thing was only an ordeal. An ordeal, this word can say much and little, and yet the whole thing is over as soon as it is spoken. We mount a winged horse, and in the same instant we are on Mount Moriah, in the same instant we see the ram. We forget that Abraham only rode an ass, which trudges along the road, that he had a journey of three days, that he needed some time to chop the firewood, to bind Isaac, and to sharpen the knife.

And yet we pay tribute to Abraham. The speaker can just as well sleep until the last quarter hour before he has to speak; the listener can just as well go to sleep during the speech, for everything goes along splendidly without any trouble on either side. If someone were present who suffered from sleeplessness, he would perhaps go home, sit down in a corner, and think: The whole thing is over in a moment; all you have to do is wait for a minute and you will see the ram, and the ordeal will be over. If the speaker were to meet him in this situation, I think he would step up to him in all his dignity and say, "What a wretched man, to let your soul sink into such foolishness; no miracle takes place, and all life is an ordeal." As the speaker grew more effusive, he would become more and more emotional, more and more pleased with himself, and although he noticed no gorged blood vessels when he was talking about Abraham, he now would feel the veins on his forehead swell. Perhaps he would be dumbfounded if the sinner quietly and with dignity answered: After all, that was what you preached about last Sunday.

Let us then either cancel out Abraham or learn to be horrified by the prodigious paradox that is the meaning of his life, so that we may understand that our age, like every other age, can rejoice if it has faith. If Abraham is not a nobody, a phantom, a showpiece used for diversion, then the sinner can never err in wanting to do likewise, but the point is to perceive the greatness of what Abraham did so that the person can judge for himself whether he has the vocation and the courage to be tried in something like this. The comic contradiction in the speaker's behavior was that he made a nonentity of Abraham and yet wanted to forbid the other to conduct himself in the same way.

Should we, then, not dare to speak about Abraham? I surely think we can. If I were to speak about him, I would first of all describe the pain of the ordeal. To that end, I would, like a leech, suck all the anxiety and distress and torment out of a father's suffering in order to describe what Abraham suffered, although under it all he had faith. I would point out that the journey lasted three days and a good part of the fourth; indeed, these three and a half days could be infinitely longer than the few thousand years that separate me from Abraham. I would point out—and this is my view—that every person may still turn back before he begins such a thing and at any time may repentantly turn back. If one does this, I am not apprehensive; I do not fear arousing a desire in people to be tried as Abraham was. But to sell a cheap edition of Abraham and yet forbid everyone to do likewise is ludicrous.

. . . The prodigious paradox of faith, a paradox that makes a murder into a holy and God-pleasing act, a paradox that gives Isaac back to Abraham again, . . . no thought can grasp, because faith begins precisely where thought stops.